Super Easy Mediterranean Diet
Cookbook for Beginners

2000 Days Quick & Delicious Recipes Book for Living and Eating Well Every Day | No-Stress 30-Day Meal Plan

Dorothy D. Ingram

Table of Contents

Chapter 3 Beans and Grains

Chapter 4 Beef, Pork, and Lamb

Chapter 5 Fish and Seafood

Chapter 7 Vegetables and Sides   59

Chapter 8 Vegetarian Mains   68

Chapter 9 Desserts   76

Chapter 10 Salads   84

Chapter 11 Pizzas, Wraps, and Sandwiches 90

Chapter 12 Pasta 96

Chapter 13 Staples, Sauces, Dips, and Dressings 102

Appendix 1: Measurement Conversion Chart 106

Appendix 2: The Dirty Dozen and Clean Fifteen 107

INTRODUCTION

Calling all food enthusiasts and culinary adventurers! Are you ready to embark on a gastronomic voyage to the sun-drenched lands of the Mediterranean? If you crave bold flavors, vibrant colors, and wholesome ingredients that will transport your taste buds to a culinary paradise, then this cookbook is your ultimate ticket to Mediterranean bliss!

As a seasoned chef with a flair for the exotic and a passion for palate-pleasing creations, I am thrilled to unveil a treasure trove of Mediterranean recipes that will make your kitchen sizzle with excitement. From the tangy zest of citrus-infused marinades to the rich aroma of aromatic herbs and spices, each dish is a masterpiece that tells a story of centuries-old culinary traditions and Mediterranean heritage.

Imagine treating your taste buds to the succulent and juicy delights of Mediterranean-style grilled lamb chops, the velvety smoothness of creamy tzatziki sauce made with fresh cucumbers and tangy yogurt, or the burst of flavors in a zesty tabbouleh salad brimming with herbs and plump tomatoes. With this cookbook in your hands, you'll unlock the secrets to creating these culinary gems and more, right in the comfort of your own kitchen.

All About Mediterranean Diet

What is Mediterranean Diet?

The Mediterranean diet is a dietary pattern that is based on the traditional eating habits of the countries surrounding the Mediterranean Sea, such as Italy, Greece, Spain, and Turkey. It is characterized by a high consumption of fruits, vegetables, legumes, whole grains, nuts, seeds, and olive oil, along with moderate consumption of fish, dairy products, and red wine, and low consumption of red meat, processed foods, and sweets.

This dietary pattern has been associated with a range of health benefits, including reduced risk of heart disease, stroke, diabetes, and certain cancers, as well as improved cognitive function and longevity. The Mediterranean diet is not a rigid or prescriptive diet, but rather a flexible and adaptable way of eating that emphasizes whole, nutrient-dense foods and encourages moderation and balance.

In practical terms, the Mediterranean diet involves eating plenty of colorful fruits and vegetables, whole grains, legumes, and nuts, as well as incorporating healthy fats such as olive oil and fatty fish like salmon or sardines. It also encourages the use of herbs and spices to add flavor to dishes, and moderate consumption of dairy products, eggs, and lean meats like chicken and turkey. Red meat and processed foods are limited, and sugary drinks and sweets are avoided or consumed in moderation.

While the Mediterranean diet is not a magic bullet for perfect health, it is a realistic and sustainable dietary pattern that can help promote overall health and wellbeing when adopted as part of a balanced lifestyle.

Embrace a Healthy Lifestyle

The Mediterranean lifestyle is a way of life that is deeply rooted in the culture and traditions of the Mediterranean region, and it is often associated with a focus on healthy eating, physical activity, and social connectedness. This lifestyle is characterized by a slower pace of life, a love of fresh, seasonal produce, and a strong emphasis on community and social interactions.

One of the most important aspects of the Mediterranean lifestyle is its focus on healthy eating. The Mediterranean diet is rich in fresh fruits and vegetables, whole grains, lean proteins, and healthy fats, and it has been linked to numerous health benefits, including reduced risk of heart disease, stroke, and certain types of cancer. This diet also emphasizes the importance of enjoying meals with family and friends, and taking time to savor and appreciate the flavors and textures of food.

In addition to healthy eating, the Mediterranean lifestyle also places a strong emphasis on physical activity. Walking, cycling, swimming, and other forms of exercise are all common in Mediterranean communities, and are often integrated into daily routines. This focus on physical activity has been linked to a reduced risk of obesity, diabetes, and other chronic diseases.

Social connectedness is also an important aspect of the Mediterranean lifestyle, and it is often facilitated through daily interactions with family and friends, as well as community events and celebrations. This social support network can provide a sense of belonging and purpose, and has been linked to better mental health outcomes.

Overall, the Mediterranean lifestyle is characterized by a balanced approach to health and wellbeing, emphasizing healthy eating, physical activity, and social connectedness. It is a way of life that is deeply rooted in the traditions and culture of the Mediterranean region, and has been associated with numerous health benefits.

What to Expect with Mediterranean Diet?

The Mediterranean diet isn't just about filling your plate with deliciousness, it's a health ninja in disguise, ready to kick some serious butt! Adopting a Mediterranean diet has been linked to numerous health benefits, including:

1.Reduced risk of heart disease: Heart disease is one of the leading causes of death worldwide, and it is often linked to unhealthy lifestyle choices such as a diet high in saturated and trans fats, smoking, and lack of physical activity. One of the key benefits of adopting a Mediterranean diet is that it has been linked to a reduced risk of heart disease.

The Mediterranean diet is rich in healthy fats, such as olive oil, nuts, and fatty fish, which have been shown to improve cholesterol levels and reduce inflammation in the body. Inflammation is a key factor in the development of heart disease, and reducing inflammation through dietary changes is an important way to prevent the disease.

Additionally, the Mediterranean diet is high in fruits, vegetables, whole grains, and lean proteins, which are all important for overall heart health. These foods provide important vitamins and minerals, as well as fiber, which can help to lower blood pressure and reduce the risk of heart disease.

Studies have consistently shown that individuals who follow a Mediterranean diet have a lower risk of heart disease, stroke, and other cardiovascular diseases. In fact, one study published in the New England Journal of Medicine found that following a Mediterranean diet can reduce the risk of heart disease by up to 30%.

2.Improved brain function: Improved brain function is one of the many benefits of adopting a Mediterranean diet. The diet is high in nutrients such as omega-3 fatty acids, antioxidants, and flavonoids, which have been linked to improved cognitive function and a reduced risk of neurodegenerative diseases such as Alzheimer's.

Omega-3 fatty acids, which are found in fatty fish such as salmon and sardines, have been shown to support brain health by reducing inflammation and improving the health of brain cells. Antioxidants, such as those found in fruits and vegetables, can help to protect the brain from oxidative stress, which can contribute to cognitive decline. Flavonoids, which are found in foods such as berries, tea, and dark chocolate, have also been shown to have neuroprotective properties.

In addition to these specific nutrients, the Mediterranean diet as a whole is a healthy and balanced approach to eating that can support overall health and wellbeing. This can help to reduce the risk of chronic diseases that can impact brain health, such as heart disease and diabetes.

While the specific mechanisms by which the Mediterranean diet may improve brain function are still being studied, there is a growing body of evidence to suggest that it can be an effective way to support cognitive health and reduce the risk of neurodegenerative diseases. By emphasizing whole, nutrient-dense foods and limiting processed and refined foods, the Mediterranean diet can provide the nutrients and energy needed to support optimal brain function and overall health.

3.Lower risk of cancer: The Mediterranean diet has been associated with a lower risk of certain types of cancer. This is likely due to the fact that the diet is high in fruits, vegetables, and whole grains, which contain a variety of phytonutrients and antioxidants that can help to reduce inflammation and oxidative stress in the body.

For example, studies have shown that a higher intake of fruits and vegetables is associated with a lower risk of breast cancer, and that a diet rich in whole grains may reduce the risk of colon cancer. The Mediterranean diet also emphasizes healthy fats, such as olive oil and fatty fish, which have been linked to a reduced risk of prostate cancer.

In addition to specific foods, the Mediterranean lifestyle also emphasizes social connections and a relaxed pace of life, which can help to reduce stress and promote overall health. Chronic stress has been linked to an increased risk of certain types of cancer, so reducing stress levels may be another way in which the Mediterranean lifestyle helps to lower cancer risk.

While adopting a Mediterranean diet may not guarantee a complete absence of cancer, it can be a healthy and proactive step towards reducing the risk of certain types of cancer and promoting overall health and wellbeing.

4.Improved weight management: One of the benefits of adopting a Mediterranean diet is improved weight management. The diet emphasizes whole, nutrient-dense foods such as fruits, vegetables, whole grains, and lean proteins, while limiting processed and refined foods. This can help to promote satiety and reduce overall calorie intake, making it easier to achieve and maintain a healthy weight.

Additionally, the Mediterranean diet is rich in healthy fats, such as olive oil, nuts, and fatty fish, which can help to increase feelings of fullness and satisfaction. These fats also provide important nutrients and can help to reduce inflammation throughout the body, which has been linked to obesity and weight gain.

Another important aspect of the Mediterranean diet for weight management is its focus on mindful eating. The diet emphasizes the importance of taking time to savor and enjoy meals, and of eating in the company of others. This can help to reduce stress and promote a positive relationship with food, which can be beneficial for weight management.

While weight loss is not the primary focus of the Mediterranean diet, studies have shown that it can be effective for weight loss and weight management over the long term. In fact, research has suggested that following a Mediterranean diet may be more sustainable and effective for weight loss than other types of restrictive diets.

5.Better blood sugar control: Better blood sugar control is one of the many benefits of adopting a Mediterranean diet. This is because the diet emphasizes whole, nutrient-dense foods and limits processed and refined foods, which can help to improve blood sugar control and reduce the risk of type 2 diabetes.

The Mediterranean diet is low in added sugars, which can cause blood sugar levels to spike and then crash, leading to feelings of fatigue and hunger. Instead, the diet focuses on complex carbohydrates from whole grains, fruits, and vegetables, which are slowly digested and absorbed, providing a steady source of energy throughout the day.

The diet is also high in fiber, which slows down the absorption of glucose in the bloodstream and can help to improve insulin sensitivity. Insulin is a hormone that helps to regulate blood sugar levels, and when the body becomes less sensitive to insulin, it can lead to high blood sugar levels and an increased risk of type 2 diabetes.

The Mediterranean diet also includes healthy fats, such as olive oil and nuts, which have been shown to improve blood sugar control and reduce inflammation in the body. Inflammation can interfere with insulin sensitivity and contribute to the development of type 2 diabetes.

Reduced inflammation: Inflammation is a natural response of the immune system to protect the body from harmful stimuli, such as pathogens or injuries. However, chronic inflammation can be harmful and has been linked to a number of chronic diseases, including heart disease, cancer, and diabetes.

The Mediterranean diet is rich in anti-inflammatory foods, such as fruits, vegetables, and fatty fish. These foods are high in antioxidants and other compounds that have been shown to reduce inflammation in the body.

For example, fruits and vegetables are rich in polyphenols, which are powerful antioxidants that can help to reduce inflammation by scavenging free radicals in the body. Similarly, fatty fish, such as salmon and mackerel, are rich in omega-3 fatty acids, which have been shown to have anti-inflammatory effects.

In contrast, a diet high in processed and refined foods, such as sugary drinks and snacks, has been shown to increase inflammation in the body. These foods are often high in refined carbohydrates and unhealthy fats, which can lead to insulin resistance and chronic inflammation.

By adopting a Mediterranean diet, which emphasizes whole, nutrient-dense foods and limits processed and refined foods, individuals can help to reduce inflammation in the body and lower their risk of chronic diseases.

6.Better gut health: Better gut health refers to the overall health and balance of the gastrointestinal (GI) tract, which is home to trillions of microorganisms that make up the gut microbiome. A healthy gut microbiome is essential for good digestive health, as well as for overall health and wellbeing.

The Mediterranean diet is a way of eating that has been linked to improved gut health. This is because the diet is high in fiber, which helps to feed the beneficial bacteria in the gut and promote the growth of a diverse range of microorganisms. The diet is also rich in fermented foods, such as yogurt and sauerkraut, which contain live cultures of bacteria that can help to populate the gut with beneficial microbes.

A healthy gut microbiome is important for a number of reasons. For example, it helps to maintain the integrity of the GI tract, allowing nutrients to be absorbed and waste products to be eliminated efficiently. It also helps to regulate the immune system, reducing the risk of autoimmune and inflammatory conditions.

On the other hand, an imbalanced gut microbiome, also known as dysbiosis, has been linked to a number of health problems, including digestive disorders, allergies, and even mental health issues. Imbalances in the gut microbiome can be caused by factors such as antibiotics, a poor diet, stress, and lack of sleep.

In addition to eating a healthy diet, there are other steps that can be taken to improve gut health, such as getting regular exercise, managing stress, and avoiding smoking and excessive alcohol consumption. Overall, better gut health is an important aspect of overall health and wellbeing, and can be supported through a healthy diet and lifestyle choices.

Mediterranean Food Pyramid

The Mediterranean Food Pyramid is a visual representation of the traditional Mediterranean diet, which is based on the eating habits of people in countries such as Greece, Italy, and Spain. The pyramid emphasizes a plant-based diet that is rich in fruits, vegetables, whole grains, legumes, nuts, and seeds, with moderate amounts of fish, poultry, and dairy, and limited amounts of red meat and sweets.

At the base of the pyramid are plant-based foods, which are the foundation of the Mediterranean diet. These include fruits, vegetables, whole grains, legumes, nuts, and seeds, which provide a wide range of vitamins, minerals, fiber, and other nutrients. These foods are also rich in antioxidants, which have been linked to a reduced risk of chronic diseases.

The next level of the pyramid includes healthy fats, such as olive oil, nuts, and seeds, which are an important part of the Mediterranean diet. These foods are rich in monounsaturated and polyunsaturated fats, which have been linked to a reduced risk of heart disease and other chronic diseases.

The third level of the pyramid includes fish, poultry, eggs, and dairy, which are important sources of protein in the Mediterranean diet. These foods are typically consumed in moderation, with an emphasis on lean sources of protein, such as fish and poultry.

At the top of the pyramid are red meat and sweets, which should be consumed sparingly in the Mediterranean diet. These foods are high in saturated fat, added sugars, and other unhealthy ingredients, and can contribute to a range of health problems when consumed in excess.

Overall, the Mediterranean Food Pyramid emphasizes a plant-based diet that is rich in whole, nutrient-dense foods, and limits processed and refined foods. This way of eating has been linked to numerous health benefits, including a reduced risk of heart disease, improved brain function, better weight management, and improved gut health, making it a popular and highly recommended dietary pattern.

How to Adopt a Mediterranean Diet?

Adopting a Mediterranean diet can be a great way to improve your health and wellbeing, but it can also seem daunting if you're not sure where to start. Here are some tips on how to adopt a Mediterranean diet in a realistic and achievable way:

♦ Focus on plant-based foods: The foundation of the Mediterranean diet is plant-based foods such as fruits, vegetables, whole grains, legumes, nuts, and seeds. Make sure to include these in your meals as much as possible, and aim for at least five servings of fruits and vegetables per day.

♦ Use healthy fats: The Mediterranean diet emphasizes healthy fats such as olive oil, nuts, and seeds. Use olive oil as your primary cooking oil, and include nuts and seeds in your meals and snacks.

♦ Include fish and poultry: While the Mediterranean diet is primarily plant-based, it does include moderate amounts of fish and poultry. Aim to include these in your meals a few times per week.

♦ Limit red meat and sweets: The Mediterranean diet emphasizes limiting red meat and sweets, as these foods are high in saturated fat and added sugars. Save these foods for special occasions, and choose lean sources of protein such as fish and poultry instead.

♦ Embrace herbs and spices: The Mediterranean diet uses herbs and spices to add flavor to meals, instead of relying on salt and sugar. Experiment with different herbs and spices in your cooking to add variety and flavor.

♦ Practice mindful eating: In addition to what you eat, how you eat is also important in the Mediterranean diet. Take time to enjoy your meals, eat slowly, and savor the flavors and textures of your food.

♦ Make small changes: Adopting a new way of eating can be challenging, so start with small changes and build from there. For example, start by including one new plant-based food in your meals each week, and gradually increase the amount of healthy fats in your diet.

By making these simple changes, you can gradually adopt a Mediterranean diet and enjoy the health benefits that come with it. Remember to be patient with yourself and enjoy the journey towards a healthier lifestyle.

Some Useful Advice

♦ Start small: Don't try to change everything at once. Start by making small changes to your diet, such as swapping out unhealthy snacks for fruits and nuts, or using olive oil instead of butter.

♦ Make it tasty: The Mediterranean diet is known for its delicious and flavorful foods. Experiment with different herbs and spices, and try new recipes to keep things interesting.

♦ Don't be too strict: While it's important to stick to the core principles of the Mediterranean diet, it's also okay to indulge in moderation. If you're at a party and want to try a piece of cake, go for it! Just don't make it an everyday habit.

♦ Shop seasonally: In Mediterranean countries, people often eat foods that are in season. Not only does this support local farmers and reduce environmental impact, but it also ensures that you're getting the freshest and most flavorful foods.

♦ Embrace whole foods: The Mediterranean diet is based on whole, minimally processed foods. Focus on incorporating whole grains, fruits, vegetables, nuts, and seeds into your meals.

♦ Make it social: In Mediterranean cultures, meals are often a social occasion. Consider inviting friends and family over for a Mediterranean-inspired meal, or join a cooking class to learn new recipes and techniques.

♦ Be patient: Adopting a new way of eating takes time, and it's important to be patient with yourself. Don't get discouraged if you slip up, and focus on progress, not perfection.

Remember that the Mediterranean diet is not just a temporary diet, but a way of life. By adopting a few simple changes, you can incorporate the principles of the Mediterranean diet into your lifestyle and enjoy the many health benefits that come with it.

30-Day Meal Plan

DAYS	BREAKFAST	LUNCH	DINNER	SNACK/DESSERT
1	Butternut Squash and Ricotta Frittata	Farro Salad with Tomatoes and Olives	Eggplants Stuffed with Walnuts and Feta	Cinnamon-Apple Chips
2	Baked Peach Oatmeal	Lemon and Garlic Rice Pilaf	Moroccan Vegetable Tagine	Garlic-Mint Yogurt Dip
3	Red Pepper and Feta Frittata	Greek Chickpeas with Coriander and Sage	Ricotta, Basil, and Pistachio-Stuffed Zucchini	Lemon Shrimp with Garlic Olive Oil
4	Breakfast Farro with Dried Fruit and Nuts	Lentil Pâté	Farro with Roasted Tomatoes and Mushrooms	Roasted Mushrooms with Garlic
5	Lemon–Olive Oil Breakfast Cakes with Berry Syrup	Greek-Style Pea Casserole	Roasted Portobello Mushrooms with Kale and Red Onion	Black Bean Corn Dip
6	Spiced Potatoes with Chickpeas	Quinoa, Broccoli, and Baby Potatoes	Vegetable Burgers	Classic Hummus with Tahini
7	Summer Day Fruit Salad	Sweet Potato and Chickpea Moroccan Stew	Quinoa with Almonds and Cranberries	Honey-Rosemary Almonds
8	Egg and Pepper Pita	Cilantro Lime Rice	Mushroom Ragù with Parmesan Polenta	Italian Crepe with Herbs and Onion
9	Savory Sweet Potato Hash	White Beans with Garlic and Tomatoes	Moroccan Red Lentil and Pumpkin Stew	Buffalo Bites
10	Buckwheat Porridge with Fresh Fruit	Spanakorizo (Greek Spinach and Rice)	Tangy Asparagus and Broccoli	Spanish-Style Pan-Roasted Cod
11	Egg Salad with Red Pepper and Dill	Freekeh, Chickpea, and Herb Salad	Pistachio-Parmesan Kale-Arugula Salad	Rosemary-Grape Focaccia
12	Quinoa and Yogurt Breakfast Bowls	Crustless Spanakopita	Greek Black-Eyed Pea Salad	Crispy Green Bean Fries with Lemon-Yogurt Sauce
13	Honey-Apricot Granola with Greek Yogurt	Parmesan Artichokes	Spinach-Arugula Salad with Nectarines and Lemon Dressing	Domatosalata (Sweet-and-Spicy Tomato Sauce)
14	Peach Sunrise Smoothie	Cauliflower Rice-Stuffed Peppers	Watermelon Burrata Salad	Fried Baby Artichokes with Lemon-Garlic Aioli
15	Turkish Egg Bowl	Baked Mediterranean Tempeh with Tomatoes and Garlic	Roasted Cauliflower "Steak" Salad	Halloumi, Watermelon, Tomato Kebabs with Basil Oil Drizzle
16	Baklava Hot Porridge	Root Vegetable Soup with Garlic Aioli	Arugula Salad with Grapes, Goat Cheese, and Za'atar Croutons	Fruit Compote
17	Breakfast Panini with Eggs, Olives, and Tomatoes	Mediterranean Baked Chickpeas	Spinach Salad with Pomegranate, Lentils, and Pistachios	Crunchy Sesame Cookies
18	Whole Wheat Blueberry Muffins	Cauliflower Steaks with Olive Citrus Sauce	Spanish Potato Salad	Cocoa and Coconut Banana Slices

DAYS	BREAKFAST	LUNCH	DINNER	SNACK/DESSERT
19	Savory Feta, Spinach, and Red Pepper Muffins	Cheese Stuffed Zucchini	Taverna-Style Greek Salad	Grilled Stone Fruit with Whipped Ricotta
20	Spiced Antioxidant Granola Clusters	Caprese Eggplant Stacks	Cauliflower Tabbouleh Salad	Roasted Orange Rice Pudding
21	Sunshine Overnight Oats	Easy Greek Salad	Couscous with Apricots	Tortilla Fried Pies
22	Honey-Vanilla Greek Yogurt with Blueberries	Fruited Chicken Salad	Quinoa Salad with Chicken, Chickpeas, and Spinach	Pomegranate-Quinoa Dark Chocolate Bark
23	Creamy Cinnamon Porridge	Panzanella (Tuscan Tomato and Bread Salad)	Spiced Quinoa Salad	Minty Cantaloupe Granita
24	Almond Butter Banana Chocolate Smoothie	Arugula and Fennel Salad with Fresh Basil	Garbanzo and Pita No-Bake Casserole	S'mores
25	Egg Baked in Avocado	Yellow and White Hearts of Palm Salad	Brown Rice Pilaf with Golden Raisins	Fresh Figs with Chocolate Sauce
26	Veggie Hash with Eggs	Asparagus Salad	Wild Rice Pilaf with Pine Nuts	Almond Rice Pudding
27	Mediterranean Frittata	Endive with Shrimp	Black Lentil Dhal	Pumpkin-Ricotta Cheesecake
28	Mushroom-and-Tomato Stuffed Hash Browns	Greek Village Salad	Three-Bean Vegan Chili	Lemon Fool
29	Mediterranean-Inspired White Smoothie	Caprese Salad with Fresh Mozzarella	Bulgur Salad with Cucumbers, Olives, and Dill	Individual Meringues with Strawberries, Mint, and Toasted Coconut
30	Morning Buzz Iced Coffee	Wilted Kale Salad	Rice with Olives and Basil	Roasted Plums with Nut Crumble

Get to Cook Now

The Mediterranean lifestyle is a celebration of life itself. It's about leisurely family meals shared with laughter and love, long conversations over a glass of wine, and the joy of simple pleasures that nourish not just the body, but also the soul. It's a way of life that embraces the richness of nature's bounty, where farm-fresh produce, seasonal ingredients, and the golden elixir of olive oil take center stage.

So, whether you're a culinary connoisseur seeking new culinary horizons or a daring home cook looking to infuse your meals with Mediterranean flair, this cookbook is your culinary compass. Get ready to embark on a sensory odyssey that will transport you to the enchanting world of Mediterranean cuisine. So, roll up your sleeves, ignite your taste buds, and let's embark on this epicurean adventure together!

Chapter 1 Breakfasts

Butternut Squash and Ricotta Frittata

Prep time: 10 minutes | Cook time: 33 minutes | Serves 2 to 3

1 cup cubed (½-inch) butternut squash (5½ ounces / 156 g)
2 tablespoons olive oil
Kosher salt and freshly ground black pepper, to taste
4 fresh sage leaves, thinly sliced
6 large eggs, lightly beaten
½ cup ricotta cheese
Cayenne pepper

1. In a bowl, toss the squash with the olive oil and season with salt and black pepper until evenly coated. Sprinkle the sage on the bottom of a cake pan and place the squash on top. Place the pan in the air fryer and bake at 400ºF (204ºC) for 10 minutes. Stir to incorporate the sage, then cook until the squash is tender and lightly caramelized at the edges, about 3 minutes more. 2. Pour the eggs over the squash, dollop the ricotta all over, and sprinkle with cayenne. Bake at 300ºF (149ºC) until the eggs are set and the frittata is golden brown on top, about 20 minutes. Remove the pan from the air fryer and cut the frittata into wedges to serve.

Per Serving:

calories: 289 | fat: 22g | protein: 18g | carbs: 5g | fiber: 1g | sodium: 184mg

Smoked Salmon Egg Scramble with Dill and Chives

Prep time: 5 minutes | Cook time: 5 minutes | Serves 2

4 large eggs
1 tablespoon milk
1 tablespoon fresh chives, minced
1 tablespoon fresh dill, minced
¼ teaspoon kosher salt
⅛ teaspoon freshly ground black pepper
2 teaspoons extra-virgin olive oil
2 ounces (57 g) smoked salmon, thinly sliced

1. In a large bowl, whisk together the eggs, milk, chives, dill, salt, and pepper. 2. Heat the olive oil in a medium skillet or sauté pan over medium heat. Add the egg mixture and cook for about 3 minutes, stirring occasionally. 3. Add the salmon and cook until the eggs are set but moist, about 1 minute.

Per Serving:

calories: 325 | fat: 26g | protein: 23g | carbs: 1g | fiber: 0g | sodium: 455mg

Baked Peach Oatmeal

Prep time: 5 minutes | Cook time: 30 minutes | Serves 6

Olive oil cooking spray
2 cups certified gluten-free rolled oats
2 cups unsweetened almond milk
¼ cup raw honey, plus more for drizzling (optional)
½ cup nonfat plain Greek yogurt
1 teaspoon vanilla extract
½ teaspoon ground cinnamon
¼ teaspoon salt
1½ cups diced peaches, divided, plus more for serving (optional)

1. Preheat the air fryer to 380°F(193ºC). Lightly coat the inside of a 6-inch cake pan with olive oil cooking spray. 2. In a large bowl, mix together the oats, almond milk, honey, yogurt, vanilla, cinnamon, and salt until well combined. 3. Fold in ¾ cup of the peaches and then pour the mixture into the prepared cake pan. 4. Sprinkle the remaining peaches across the top of the oatmeal mixture. Bake in the air fryer for 30 minutes. 5. Allow to set and cool for 5 minutes before serving with additional fresh fruit and honey for drizzling, if desired.

Per Serving:

calories: 197 | fat: 3g | protein: 9g | carbs: 36g | fiber: 4g | sodium: 138mg

Breakfast Panini with Eggs, Olives, and Tomatoes

Prep time: 5 minutes | Cook time: 0 minutes | Serves 4

1 (12 ounces / 340 g) round whole-wheat pagnotta foggiana or other round, crusty bread
2 tablespoons olive oil
½ cup sliced pitted cured olives, such as Kalamata
8 hard-boiled eggs, peeled and sliced into rounds
2 medium tomatoes, thinly sliced into rounds
12 large leaves fresh basil

1. Split the bread horizontally and brush the cut sides with the olive oil. 2. Arrange the sliced olives on the bottom half of the bread in a single layer. Top with a layer of the egg slices, then the tomato slices, and finally the basil leaves. Cut the sandwich into quarters and serve immediately.

Per Serving:

calories: 427 | fat: 21g | protein: 23g | carbs: 39g | fiber: 7g | sodium: 674mg

Buckwheat Porridge with Fresh Fruit

Prep time: 10 minutes | Cook time: 6 minutes | Serves 4

1 cup buckwheat groats, rinsed and drained
3 cups water
½ cup chopped pitted dates
1 tablespoon light olive oil
¼ teaspoon ground cinnamon
¼ teaspoon salt
½ teaspoon vanilla extract
1 cup blueberries
1 cup raspberries
1 cup hulled and quartered strawberries
2 tablespoons balsamic vinegar

1. Place buckwheat, water, dates, oil, cinnamon, and salt in the Instant Pot® and stir well. Close lid and set steam release to Sealing. Press the Manual button and set time to 6 minutes. 2. When the timer beeps, let pressure release naturally, about 20 minutes. Open lid and stir in vanilla. 3. While buckwheat cooks, combine blueberries, raspberries, strawberries, and vinegar in a medium bowl. Stir well. Top porridge with berry mixture. Serve hot.

Per Serving:

calories: 318 | fat: 5g | protein: 6g | carbs: 64g | fiber: 9g | sodium: 151mg

Egg Salad with Red Pepper and Dill

Prep time: 5 minutes | Cook time: 10 minutes | Serves 6

6 large eggs
1 cup water
1 tablespoon olive oil
1 medium red bell pepper, seeded and chopped
¼ teaspoon salt
¼ teaspoon ground black pepper
½ cup low-fat plain Greek yogurt
2 tablespoons chopped fresh dill

1. Have ready a large bowl of ice water. Place rack or egg holder into bottom of the Instant Pot®. 2. Arrange eggs on rack or holder and add water to the Instant Pot®. Close lid, set steam release to Sealing, press the Manual button, and set time to 5 minutes. 3. When the timer beeps, let pressure release naturally for 5 minutes, then quick-release the remaining pressure until the float valve drops. Press the Cancel button and open lid. Carefully transfer eggs to the bowl of ice water. Let stand in ice water for 10 minutes, then peel, chop, and add eggs to a medium bowl. 4. Clean out pot, dry well, and return to machine. Press the Sauté button and heat oil. Add bell pepper, salt, and black pepper. Cook, stirring often, until bell pepper is tender, about 5 minutes. Transfer to bowl with eggs. 5. Add yogurt and dill to bowl, and fold to combine. Cover and chill for 1 hour before serving.

Per Serving:

calories: 111 | fat: 8g | protein: 8g | carbs: 3g | fiber: 0g | sodium: 178mg

Turkish Egg Bowl

Prep time: 10 minutes | Cook time: 15 minutes | Serves 2

2 tablespoons ghee
½–1 teaspoon red chile flakes
2 tablespoons extra-virgin olive oil
1 cup full-fat goat's or sheep's milk yogurt
1 clove garlic, minced
1 tablespoon fresh lemon juice
Salt and black pepper, to taste
Dash of vinegar
4 large eggs
Optional: pinch of sumac
2 tablespoons chopped fresh cilantro or parsley

1. In a skillet, melt the ghee over low heat. Add the chile flakes and let it infuse while you prepare the eggs. Remove from the heat and mix with the extra-virgin olive oil. Set aside. Combine the yogurt, garlic, lemon juice, salt, and pepper. 2. Poach the eggs. Fill a medium saucepan with water and a dash of vinegar. Bring to a boil over high heat. Crack each egg individually into a ramekin or a cup. Using a spoon, create a gentle whirlpool in the water; this will help the egg white wrap around the egg yolk. Slowly lower the egg into the water in the center of the whirlpool. Turn off the heat and cook for 3 to 4 minutes. Use a slotted spoon to remove the egg from the water and place it on a plate. Repeat for all remaining eggs. 3. To assemble, place the yogurt mixture in a bowl and add the poached eggs. Drizzle with the infused oil, and garnish with cilantro. Add a pinch of sumac, if using. Eat warm.

Per Serving:

calories: 576 | fat: 46g | protein: 27g | carbs: 17g | fiber: 4g | sodium: 150mg

Baklava Hot Porridge

Prep time: 5 minutes | Cook time: 5 minutes | Serves 2

2 cups riced cauliflower
¾ cup unsweetened almond, flax, or hemp milk
4 tablespoons extra-virgin olive oil, divided
2 teaspoons grated fresh orange peel (from ½ orange)
½ teaspoon ground cinnamon
½ teaspoon almond extract or vanilla extract
⅛ teaspoon salt
4 tablespoons chopped walnuts, divided
1 to 2 teaspoons liquid stevia, monk fruit, or other sweetener of choice (optional)

1. In medium saucepan, combine the riced cauliflower, almond milk, 2 tablespoons olive oil, grated orange peel, cinnamon, almond extract, and salt. Stir to combine and bring just to a boil over medium-high heat, stirring constantly. 2. Remove from heat and stir in 2 tablespoons chopped walnuts and sweetener (if using). Stir to combine. 3. Divide into bowls, topping each with 1 tablespoon of chopped walnuts and 1 tablespoon of the remaining olive oil.

Per Serving:

calories: 414 | fat: 38g | protein: 6g | carbs: 16g | fiber: 4g | sodium: 252mg

Breakfast Farro with Dried Fruit and Nuts

Prep time: 10 minutes | Cook time: 20 minutes | Serves 8

16 ounces (454 g) farro, rinsed and drained	1 cup dried mixed fruit
4½ cups water	½ cup chopped toasted mixed nuts
¼ cup maple syrup	2 cups almond milk
¼ teaspoon salt	

1. Place farro, water, maple syrup, and salt in the Instant Pot® and stir to combine. Close lid, set steam release to Sealing, press the Multigrain button, and set time to 20 minutes. When the timer beeps, let pressure release naturally, about 30 minutes. 2. Press the Cancel button, open lid, and add dried fruit. Close lid and let stand on the Keep Warm setting for 20 minutes. Serve warm with nuts and almond milk.

Per Serving:

calories: 347 | fat: 7g | protein: 9g | carbs: 65g | fiber: 9g | sodium: 145mg

Sunshine Overnight Oats

Prep time: 5 minutes | Cook time: 0 minutes | Serves 2

⅔ cup vanilla, unsweetened almond milk (not Silk brand)	1 teaspoon honey
⅓ cup rolled oats	¼ teaspoon turmeric
¼ cup raspberries	⅛ teaspoon ground cinnamon
	Pinch ground cloves

1. In a mason jar, combine the almond milk, oats, raspberries, honey, turmeric, cinnamon, and cloves and shake well. Store in the refrigerator for 8 to 24 hours, then serve cold or heated.

Per Serving:

calories: 82 | fat: 2g | protein: 2g | carbs: 14g | fiber: 3g | sodium: 98mg

Savory Sweet Potato Hash

Prep time: 15 minutes | Cook time: 18 minutes | Serves 6

2 medium sweet potatoes, peeled and cut into 1-inch cubes	2 tablespoons olive oil
½ green bell pepper, diced	1 garlic clove, minced
½ red onion, diced	½ teaspoon salt
4 ounces (113 g) baby bella mushrooms, diced	½ teaspoon black pepper
	½ tablespoon chopped fresh rosemary

1. Preheat the air fryer to 380°F(193°C). 2. In a large bowl, toss all ingredients together until the vegetables are well coated and seasonings distributed. 3. Pour the vegetables into the air fryer basket, making sure they are in a single even layer. (If using a smaller air fryer, you may need to do this in two batches.) 4. Roast for 9 minutes, then toss or flip the vegetables. Roast for 9 minutes more. 5. Transfer to a serving bowl or individual plates and enjoy.

Per Serving:

calories: 91 | fat: 5g | protein: 2g | carbs: 12g | fiber: 1g | sodium: 219mg

Peach Sunrise Smoothie

Prep time: 10 minutes | Cook time: 0 minutes | Serves 1

1 large unpeeled peach, pitted and sliced (about ½ cup)	peach low-fat Greek yogurt
6 ounces (170 g) vanilla or	2 tablespoons low-fat milk
	6 to 8 ice cubes

1. Combine all ingredients in a blender and blend until thick and creamy. Serve immediately.

Per Serving:

calories: 228 | fat: 3g | protein: 11g | carbs: 42g | fiber: 3g | sodium: 127mg

Whole Wheat Blueberry Muffins

Prep time: 10 minutes | Cook time: 15 minutes | Serves 6

Olive oil cooking spray	1½ cups plus 1 tablespoon whole wheat flour, divided
½ cup unsweetened applesauce	½ teaspoon baking soda
¼ cup raw honey	½ teaspoon baking powder
½ cup nonfat plain Greek yogurt	½ teaspoon salt
1 teaspoon vanilla extract	½ cup blueberries, fresh or frozen
1 large egg	

1. Preheat the air fryer to 360°F(182°C). Lightly coat the inside of six silicone muffin cups or a six-cup muffin tin with olive oil cooking spray. 2. In a large bowl, combine the applesauce, honey, yogurt, vanilla, and egg and mix until smooth. 3. Sift in 1½ cups of the flour, the baking soda, baking powder, and salt into the wet mixture, then stir until just combined. 4. In a small bowl, toss the blueberries with the remaining 1 tablespoon flour, then fold the mixture into the muffin batter. 5. Divide the mixture evenly among the prepared muffin cups and place into the basket of the air fryer. Bake for 12 to 15 minutes, or until golden brown on top and a toothpick inserted into the middle of one of the muffins comes out clean. 6. Allow to cool for 5 minutes before serving.

Per Serving:

calories: 186 | fat: 2g | protein: 7g | carbs: 38g | fiber: 4g | sodium: 318mg

Breakfast Polenta

Prep time: 5 minutes |Cook time: 10 minutes|

Serves: 6

2 (18-ounce / 510-g) tubes plain polenta

2¼ to 2½ cups 2% milk, divided

2 oranges, peeled and chopped

½ cup chopped pecans

¼ cup 2% plain Greek yogurt

8 teaspoons honey

1. Slice the polenta into rounds and place in a microwave-safe bowl. Heat in the microwave on high for 45 seconds. 2. Transfer the polenta to a large pot, and mash it with a potato masher or fork until coarsely mashed. Place the pot on the stove over medium heat. 3. In a medium, microwave-safe bowl, heat the milk in the microwave on high for 1 minute. Pour 2 cups of the warmed milk into the pot with the polenta, and stir with a whisk. Continue to stir and mash with the whisk, adding the remaining milk a few tablespoons at a time, until the polenta is fairly smooth and heated through, about 5 minutes. Remove from the stove. 4. Divide the polenta among four serving bowls. Top each bowl with one-quarter of the oranges, 2 tablespoons of pecans, 1 tablespoon of yogurt, and 2 teaspoons of honey before serving.

Per Serving:

calories: 319 | fat: 9g | protein: 8g | carbs: 54g | fiber: 4g | sodium: 428mg

Spiced Potatoes with Chickpeas

Prep time: 10 minutes | Cook time: 10 minutes |

Serves 4

¼ cup olive oil

3 medium potatoes, peeled and shredded

2 cups finely chopped baby spinach

1 medium onion, finely diced

1 tablespoon minced fresh ginger

1 teaspoon ground cumin

1 teaspoon ground coriander

½ teaspoon ground turmeric

½ teaspoon salt

1 (15 ounces / 425 g) can chickpeas, drained and rinsed

1 medium zucchini, diced

¼ cup chopped cilantro

1 cup plain yogurt

1. Heat the olive oil in a large skillet over medium heat. Add the potatoes, spinach, onions, ginger, cumin, coriander, turmeric, and salt and stir to mix well. Spread the mixture out into an even layer and let cook, without stirring, for about 5 minutes until the potatoes are crisp and browned on the bottom. 2. Add the chickpeas and zucchini and mix to combine, breaking up the layer of potatoes. Spread the mixture out again into an even layer and continue to cook, without stirring, for another 5 minutes or so, until the potatoes are crisp on the bottom. 3. To serve, garnish with cilantro and yogurt.

Per Serving:

calories: 679 | fat: 20g | protein: 28g | carbs: 100g | fiber: 24g | sodium: 388mg

Strawberry Collagen Smoothie

Prep time: 5 minutes | Cook time: 0 minutes | Serves 1

3 ounces (85 g) fresh or frozen strawberries

¾ cup unsweetened almond milk

¼ cup coconut cream or goat's cream

1 large egg

1 tablespoon chia seeds or flax meal

2 tablespoons grass-fed collagen powder

¼ teaspoon vanilla powder or 1 teaspoon unsweetened vanilla extract

Zest from ½ lemon

1 tablespoon macadamia oil

Optional: ice cubes, to taste

1. Place all of the ingredients in a blender and pulse until smooth and frothy. Serve immediately.

Per Serving:

calories: 515 | fat: 42g | protein: 10g | carbs: 30g | fiber: 4g | sodium: 202mg

Honey-Vanilla Greek Yogurt with Blueberries

Prep time: 2 minutes| Cook time: 0 minutes | Serves

2 to3

2 cups plain Greek yogurt

¼ to ½ cup honey

¾ teaspoon vanilla extract

1 cup blueberries

1. In a medium bowl, stir together the yogurt, honey (start with the smaller amount; you can always add more later), and vanilla. Taste and add additional honey, if needed. 2. To serve, spoon the sweetened yogurt mixture into bowls and top with the blueberries.

Per Serving:

calories: 295 | fat: 0g | protein: 23g | carbs: 55g | fiber: 2g | sodium: 82mg

Apple and Tahini Toast

Prep time: 10 minutes | Cook time: 0 minutes |

Serves 1

2 tablespoons tahini

2 slices whole-wheat bread, toasted

1 small apple of your choice, cored and thinly sliced

1 teaspoon honey

1. Spread the tahini on the toasted bread. 2. Lay the apples on the bread and drizzle with honey. Serve immediately.

Per Serving:

calories: 439 | fat: 19g | protein: 13g | carbs: 60g | fiber: 10g | sodium: 327mg

Egg and Pepper Pita

Prep time: 10 minutes | Cook time: 10 minutes | Serves 4

2 pita breads

2 tablespoons olive oil

1 red or yellow bell pepper, diced

2 zucchini, quartered lengthwise and sliced

4 large eggs, beaten

Sea salt

Freshly ground black pepper

Pinch dried oregano

2 avocados, sliced

½ to ¾ cup crumbled feta cheese

2 tablespoons chopped scallion, green part only, for garnish

Hot sauce, for serving

1. In a large skillet, heat the pitas over medium heat until warmed through and lightly toasted, about 2 minutes. Remove the pitas from the skillet and set aside. 2. In the same skillet, heat the olive oil over medium heat. Add the bell pepper and zucchini and sauté for 4 to 5 minutes. Add the eggs and season with salt, black pepper, and the oregano. Cook, stirring, for 2 to 3 minutes, until the eggs are cooked through. Remove from the heat. 3. Slice the pitas in half crosswise and fill each half with the egg mixture. Divide the avocado and feta among the pita halves. Garnish with the scallion and serve with hot sauce.

Per Serving:

calories: 476 | fat: 31g | protein: 17g | carbs: 36g | fiber: 11g | sodium: 455mg

Spinach and Swiss Frittata with Mushrooms

Prep time: 10 minutes | Cook time: 20 minutes | Serves 4

Olive oil cooking spray

8 large eggs

½ teaspoon salt

½ teaspoon black pepper

1 garlic clove, minced

2 cups fresh baby spinach

4 ounces (113 g) baby bella mushrooms, sliced

1 shallot, diced

½ cup shredded Swiss cheese, divided

Hot sauce, for serving (optional)

1. Preheat the air fryer to 360°F(182°C). Lightly coat the inside of a 6-inch round cake pan with olive oil cooking spray. 2. In a large bowl, beat the eggs, salt, pepper, and garlic for 1 to 2 minutes, or until well combined. 3. Fold in the spinach, mushrooms, shallot, and ¼ cup of the Swiss cheese. 4. Pour the egg mixture into the prepared cake pan, and sprinkle the remaining ¼ cup of Swiss over the top. 5. Place into the air fryer and bake for 18 to 20 minutes, or until the eggs are set in the center. 6. Remove from the air fryer and allow to cool for 5 minutes. Drizzle with hot sauce (if using) before serving.

Per Serving:

calories: 207 | fat: 13g | protein: 18g | carbs: 4g | fiber: 1g | sodium: 456mg

Creamy Cinnamon Porridge

Prep time: 10 minutes | Cook time: 10 minutes | Serves 2

¼ cup coconut milk

¾ cup unsweetened almond milk or water

¼ cup almond butter or hazelnut butter

1 tablespoon virgin coconut oil

2 tablespoons chia seeds

1 tablespoon flax meal

1 teaspoon cinnamon

¼ cup macadamia nuts

¼ cup hazelnuts

4 Brazil nuts

Optional: low-carb sweetener, to taste

¼ cup unsweetened large coconut flakes

1 tablespoon cacao nibs

1. In a small saucepan, mix the coconut milk and almond milk and heat over medium heat. Once hot (not boiling), take off the heat. Add the almond butter and coconut oil. Stir until well combined. If needed, use an immersion blender and process until smooth. 2. Add the chia seeds, flax meal, and cinnamon, and leave to rest for 5 to 10 minutes. Roughly chop the macadamias, hazelnuts, and Brazil nuts and stir in. Add sweetener, if using, and stir. Transfer to serving bowls. In a small skillet, dry-roast the coconut flakes over medium-high heat for 1 to 2 minutes, until lightly toasted and fragrant. Top the porridge with the toasted coconut flakes and cacao nibs (or you can use chopped 100% chocolate). Serve immediately or store in the fridge for up to 3 days.

Per Serving:

calories: 646 | fat: 61g | protein: 13g | carbs: 23g | fiber: 10g | sodium: 40mg

Summer Day Fruit Salad

Prep time: 5 minutes | Cook time: 0 minutes | Serves 8

2 cups cubed honeydew melon

2 cups cubed cantaloupe

2 cups red seedless grapes

1 cup sliced fresh strawberries

1 cup fresh blueberries

Zest and juice of 1 large lime

½ cup unsweetened toasted coconut flakes

¼ cup honey

¼ teaspoon sea salt

½ cup extra-virgin olive oil

1. Combine all of the fruits, the lime zest, and the coconut flakes in a large bowl and stir well to blend. Set aside. 2. In a blender, combine the lime juice, honey, and salt and blend on low. Once the honey is incorporated, slowly add the olive oil and blend until opaque. 3. Pour the dressing over the fruit and mix well. Cover and refrigerate for at least 4 hours before serving, stirring a few times to distribute the dressing.

Per Serving:

calories: 249 | fat: 15g | protein: 1g | carbs: 30g | fiber: 3g | sodium: 104mg

Spinach, Sun-Dried Tomato, and Feta Egg Wraps

Prep time: 10 minutes | Cook time: 7 minutes | Serves 2

1 tablespoon olive oil	1½ cups packed baby spinach
¼ cup minced onion	1 ounce (28 g) crumbled feta cheese
3 to 4 tablespoons minced sun-dried tomatoes in olive oil and herbs	Salt
3 large eggs, beaten	2 (8-inch) whole-wheat tortillas

1. In a large skillet, heat the olive oil over medium-high heat. Add the onion and tomatoes and sauté for about 3 minutes. 2. Turn the heat down to medium. Add the beaten eggs and stir to scramble them. 3. Add the spinach and stir to combine. Sprinkle the feta cheese over the eggs. Add salt to taste. 4. Warm the tortillas in the microwave for about 20 seconds each. 5. Fill each tortilla with half of the egg mixture. Fold in half or roll them up and serve.

Per Serving:

calories: 435 | fat: 28g | protein: 17g | carbs: 31g | fiber: 6g | sodium: 552mg

Mediterranean-Inspired White Smoothie

Prep time: 5 minutes | Cook time: 0 minutes | Serves

½ medium apple (any variety), peeled, halved, and seeded	banana before freezing)
5 roasted almonds	¼ cup full-fat Greek yogurt
½ medium frozen banana, sliced (be sure to peel the	½ cup low-fat 1% milk
	¼ teaspoon ground cinnamon
	½ teaspoon honey

1. Combine all the ingredients in a blender. Process until smooth. 2. Pour into a glass and serve promptly. (This recipe is best consumed fresh.)

Per Serving:

calories: 236 | fat: 7g | protein: 8g | carbs: 40g | fiber: 5g | sodium: 84mg

Quinoa and Yogurt Breakfast Bowls

Prep time: 10 minutes | Cook time: 12 minutes | Serves 8

2 cups quinoa, rinsed and drained	¼ teaspoon salt
4 cups water	2 cups low-fat plain Greek yogurt
1 teaspoon vanilla extract	2 cups blueberries

1 cup toasted almonds	½ cup pure maple syrup

1. Place quinoa, water, vanilla, and salt in the Instant Pot®. Close lid and set steam release to Sealing. Press the Rice button and set time to 12 minutes. 2. When the timer beeps, let pressure release naturally, about 20 minutes. Open lid and fluff quinoa with a fork. 3. Stir in yogurt. Serve warm, topped with berries, almonds, and maple syrup.

Per Serving:

calories: 376 | fat: 13g | protein: 16g | carbs: 52g | fiber: 6g | sodium: 105mg

Almond Butter Banana Chocolate Smoothie

Prep time: 5 minutes | Cook time: 0 minutes | Serves 1

¾ cup almond milk	1 tablespoon almond butter
½ medium banana, preferably frozen	1 tablespoon unsweetened cocoa powder
¼ cup frozen blueberries	1 tablespoon chia seeds

1. In a blender or Vitamix, add all the ingredients. Blend to combine.

Per Serving:

calories: 300 | fat: 16g | protein: 8g | carbs: 37g | fiber: 10g | sodium: 125mg

Egg Baked in Avocado

Prep time: 5 minutes | Cook time: 15 minutes | Serves 2

1 ripe large avocado	serving
2 large eggs	2 tablespoons chopped tomato, for serving
Salt	
Freshly ground black pepper	2 tablespoons crumbled feta, for serving (optional)
4 tablespoons jarred pesto, for	

1. Preheat the oven to 425°F(220ºC). 2. Slice the avocado in half and remove the pit. Scoop out about 1 to 2 tablespoons from each half to create a hole large enough to fit an egg. Place the avocado halves on a baking sheet, cut-side up. 3. Crack 1 egg in each avocado half and season with salt and pepper. 4. Bake until the eggs are set and cooked to desired level of doneness, 10 to 15 minutes. 5. Remove from oven and top each avocado with 2 tablespoons pesto, 1 tablespoon chopped tomato, and 1 tablespoon crumbled feta (if using).

Per Serving:

calories: 248 | fat: 23g | protein: 10g | carbs: 2g | fiber: 1g | sodium: 377mg

Morning Buzz Iced Coffee

Prep time: 10 minutes | Cook time: 0 minutes | Serves 1

1 cup freshly brewed strong black coffee, cooled slightly

1 tablespoon extra-virgin olive oil

1 tablespoon half-and-half or heavy cream (optional)

1 teaspoon MCT oil (optional)

⅛ teaspoon almond extract

⅛ teaspoon ground cinnamon

1. Pour the slightly cooled coffee into a blender or large glass (if using an immersion blender). 2. Add the olive oil, half-and-half (if using), MCT oil (if using), almond extract, and cinnamon. 3. Blend well until smooth and creamy. Drink warm and enjoy.

Per Serving:

calories: 124 | fat: 14g | protein: 0g | carbs: 0g | fiber: 0g | sodium: 5mg

Peachy Green Smoothie

Prep time: 10 minutes | Cook time: 0 minutes | Serves 2

1 cup almond milk

3 cups kale or spinach

1 banana, peeled

1 orange, peeled

1 small green apple

1 cup frozen peaches

¼ cup vanilla Greek yogurt

1. Put the ingredients in a blender in the order listed and blend on high until smooth. 2. Serve and enjoy.

Per Serving:

calories: 257 | fat: 5g | protein: 9g | carbs: 50g | fiber: 7g | sodium: 87mg

Savory Cottage Cheese Breakfast Bowl

Prep time: 10 minutes | Cook time: 0 minutes | Serves 4

2 cups low-fat cottage cheese

2 tablespoons chopped mixed fresh herbs, such as basil, dill, flat-leaf parsley, and oregano

½ teaspoon ground black pepper

1 large tomato, chopped

1 small cucumber, peeled and chopped

¼ cup pitted kalamata olives, halved

1 tablespoon extra-virgin olive oil

1. In a medium bowl, combine the cottage cheese, herbs, and pepper. Add the tomato, cucumber, and olives and gently stir to combine. Drizzle with the oil to serve.

Per Serving:

calories: 181 | fat: 10g | protein: 15g | carbs: 8g | fiber: 1g | sodium: 788mg

Chapter 2 Poultry

Deconstructed Greek Chicken Kebabs

Prep time: 20 minutes | Cook time: 6 to 8 hours |
Serves 4

2 pounds (907 g) boneless, skinless chicken thighs, cut into 1-inch cubes
2 zucchini (nearly 1 pound / 454 g), cut into 1-inch pieces
1 green bell pepper, seeded and cut into 1-inch pieces
1 red bell pepper, seeded and cut into 1-inch pieces
1 large red onion, chopped
2 tablespoons extra-virgin olive

oil
2 tablespoons freshly squeezed lemon juice
1 tablespoon red wine vinegar
2 garlic cloves, minced
1 teaspoon sea salt
1 teaspoon dried oregano
½ teaspoon dried basil
½ teaspoon dried thyme
¼ teaspoon freshly ground black pepper

1. In a slow cooker, combine the chicken, zucchini, green and red bell peppers, onion, olive oil, lemon juice, vinegar, garlic, salt, oregano, basil, thyme, and black pepper. Stir to mix well. 2. Cover the cooker and cook for 6 to 8 hours on Low heat.

Per Serving:
calories: 372 | fat: 17g | protein: 47g | carbs: 8g | fiber: 2g | sodium: 808mg

Greek-Style Roast Turkey Breast

Prep time: 10 minutes | Cook time: 7½ hours |
Serves 8

1 (4 pounds / 1.8 kg) turkey breast, trimmed of fat
½ cup chicken stock
2 tablespoons fresh lemon juice
2 cups chopped onions
½ cup pitted kalamata olives
½ cup oil-packed sun-dried tomatoes, drained and thinly sliced

1 clove garlic, minced
1 teaspoon dried oregano
½ teaspoon ground cinnamon
½ teaspoon ground dill
¼ teaspoon ground nutmeg
¼ teaspoon cayenne pepper
1 teaspoon sea salt
¼ teaspoon black pepper
3 tablespoons all-purpose flour

1. Place the turkey breast, ¼ cup of the chicken stock, lemon juice, onions, Kalamata olives, garlic, and sun-dried tomatoes into the slow cooker. Sprinkle with the oregano, cinnamon, dill, nutmeg, cayenne pepper, salt, and black pepper. Cover and cook on low for

7 hours. 2. Combine the remaining ¼ cup chicken stock and the flour in a small bowl. Whisk until smooth. Stir into the slow cooker. Cover and cook on low for an additional 30 minutes. 3. Serve hot over rice, pasta, potatoes, or another starch of your choice.

Per Serving:
calories: 386 | fat: 7g | protein: 70g | carbs: 8g | fiber: 2g | sodium: 601mg

Braised Chicken with Mushrooms and Tomatoes

Prep time: 20 minutes | Cook time: 25 minutes |
Serves 4

1 tablespoon extra-virgin olive oil
1 pound (454 g) portobello mushroom caps, gills removed, caps halved and sliced ½ inch thick
1 onion, chopped fine
¾ teaspoon salt, divided
4 garlic cloves, minced
1 tablespoon tomato paste
1 tablespoon all-purpose flour

2 teaspoons minced fresh sage
½ cup dry red wine
1 (14½ ounces / 411 g) can diced tomatoes, drained
4 (5 to 7 ounces / 142 to 198 g) bone-in chicken thighs, skin removed, trimmed
¼ teaspoon pepper
2 tablespoons chopped fresh parsley
Shaved Parmesan cheese

1. Using highest sauté function, heat oil in Instant Pot until shimmering. Add mushrooms, onion, and ¼ teaspoon salt. Partially cover and cook until mushrooms are softened and have released their liquid, about 5 minutes. Stir in garlic, tomato paste, flour, and sage and cook until fragrant, about 1 minute. Stir in wine, scraping up any browned bits, then stir in tomatoes. 2. Sprinkle chicken with remaining ½ teaspoon salt and pepper. Nestle chicken skinned side up into pot and spoon some of sauce on top. Lock lid in place and close pressure release valve. Select high pressure cook function and cook for 15 minutes. 3. Turn off Instant Pot and quick-release pressure. Carefully remove lid, allowing steam to escape away from you. Transfer chicken to serving dish, tent with aluminum foil, and let rest while finishing sauce. 4. Using highest sauté function, bring sauce to simmer and cook until thickened slightly, about 5 minutes. Season sauce with salt and pepper to taste. Spoon sauce over chicken and sprinkle with parsley and Parmesan. Serve.

Per Serving:
calories: 230 | fat: 7g | protein: 21g | carbs: 15g | fiber:2g | sodium: 730mg

Chicken and Artichoke Bake

Prep time: 10 minutes | Cook time: 6 to 8 hours |
Serves 2

1 teaspoon extra-virgin olive oil
2 bone-in, skinless chicken
breasts, about 8 ounces (227 g)
each
⅛ teaspoon sea salt
Freshly ground black pepper
1 (8 ounces / 227 g) jar low-
sodium artichoke hearts,
drained

2 fresh tomatoes, diced
½ red onion, halved and sliced
in thin rings
2 garlic cloves, minced
Zest of 1 lemon
Juice of 1 lemon
¼ cup fresh basil
2 tablespoons shredded smoked
mozzarella, for garnish

1. Grease the inside of the slow cooker with the olive oil. Season the chicken breasts with the salt and pepper and put them into the slow cooker. 2. Add the artichoke hearts, tomatoes, onion, garlic, lemon zest, lemon juice, and basil on top of the chicken. Do not stir the ingredients. 3. Cover and cook on low for 6 to 8 hours, until the chicken is cooked through and the vegetables are very tender. Garnish each serving with 1 tablespoon smoked mozzarella.

Per Serving:
calories: 394 | fat: 9g | protein: 59g | carbs: 21g | fiber: 8g | sodium: 426mg

Baked Chicken Caprese

Prep time: 5minutes |Cook time: 25 minutes|
Serves: 4

Nonstick cooking spray
1 pound (454 g) boneless,
skinless chicken breasts
2 tablespoons extra-virgin olive
oil
¼ teaspoon freshly ground
black pepper
¼ teaspoon kosher or sea salt
1 large tomato, sliced thinly

1 cup shredded mozzarella or 4
ounces (113 g) fresh mozzarella
cheese, diced
1 (14½ ounces / 411 g) can
low-sodium or no-salt-added
crushed tomatoes
2 tablespoons fresh torn basil
leaves
4 teaspoons balsamic vinegar

1. Set one oven rack about 4 inches below the broiler element. Preheat the oven to 450°F(235°C). Line a large, rimmed baking sheet with aluminum foil. Place a wire cooling rack on the aluminum foil, and spray the rack with nonstick cooking spray. Set aside. 2. Cut the chicken into 4 pieces (if they aren't already). Put the chicken breasts in a large zip-top plastic bag. With a rolling pin or meat mallet, pound the chicken so it is evenly flattened, about ¼-inch thick. Add the oil, pepper, and salt to the bag. Reseal the bag, and massage the ingredients into the chicken. Take the chicken out of the bag and place it on the prepared wire rack. 3. Cook the chicken for 15 to 18 minutes, or until the internal temperature of the chicken is 165°F(74ºC) on a meat thermometer and the juices run clear. Turn the oven to the high broiler setting. Layer the tomato slices on each chicken breast, and top with the mozzarella. Broil the chicken for another 2 to 3 minutes, or until the cheese is melted (don't let the chicken burn on the edges). Remove the chicken from the oven. 4. While the chicken is cooking, pour the crushed tomatoes into a small, microwave-safe bowl. Cover the bowl with a paper towel, and microwave for about 1 minute on high, until hot. When you're ready to serve, divide the tomatoes among four dinner plates. Place each chicken breast on top of the tomatoes. Top with the basil and a drizzle of balsamic vinegar.

Per Serving:
calories: 304 | fat: 15g | protein: 34g | carbs: 7g | fiber: 3g | sodium: 215mg

Chicken Gyros with Grilled Vegetables and Tzatziki Sauce

Prep time: 15 minutes | Cook time: 15 minutes |
Serves 2

For the chicken
2 tablespoons freshly squeezed
lemon juice
2 tablespoons olive oil, divided,
plus extra for oiling the grill
1 teaspoon minced fresh
oregano, or ½ teaspoon dry
oregano
½ teaspoon garlic powder
½ teaspoon salt, divided, plus
more to season vegetables
8 ounces (227 g) chicken

tenders
1 small zucchini, cut into
½-inch strips lengthwise
1 small eggplant, cut into 1-inch
strips lengthwise
½ red pepper, seeded and cut in
half lengthwise
¾ cup plain Greek yogurt
½ English cucumber, peeled
and minced
1 tablespoon minced fresh dill
2 (8-inch) pita breads

1. In a medium bowl, combine the lemon juice, 1 tablespoon of olive oil, the oregano, garlic powder, and ¼ teaspoon of salt. Add the chicken and marinate for 30 minutes. 2. Place the zucchini, eggplant, and red pepper in a large mixing bowl and sprinkle liberally with salt and the remaining 1 tablespoon of olive oil. Toss them well to coat. Let the vegetables rest while the chicken is marinating. 3. In a medium bowl, combine the yogurt, the cucumber, the remaining salt, and the dill. Stir well to combine and set aside in the refrigerator. 4. When ready to grill, heat the grill to medium-high and oil the grill grate. 5. Drain any liquid from the vegetables and place them on the grill. Remove the chicken tenders from the marinade and place them on the grill. 6. Cook chicken and vegetables for 3 minutes per side, or until the chicken is no longer pink inside and the vegetables have grill marks. 7. Remove the chicken and vegetables from the grill and set aside. On the grill, heat the pitas for about 30 seconds, flipping them frequently so they don't burn. 8. Divide the chicken tenders and vegetables between the pitas and top each with ¼ cup of the tzatziki sauce. Roll the pitas up like a cone to eat.

Per Serving:
calories: 584 | fat: 21g | protein: 38g | carbs: 64g | fiber: 12g | sodium: 762mg

Sheet Pan Lemon Chicken and Roasted Artichokes

Prep time: 10 minutes |Cook time: 20 minutes|

Serves: 4

2 large lemons	2 large artichokes
3 tablespoons extra-virgin olive oil, divided	4 (6 ounces / 170 g) bone-in, skin-on chicken thighs
½ teaspoon kosher or sea salt	

1. Put a large, rimmed baking sheet in the oven. Preheat the oven to 450°F (235°C) with the pan inside. Tear off four sheets of aluminum foil about 8-by-10 inches each; set aside. 2. Using a Microplane or citrus zester, zest 1 lemon into a large bowl. Halve both lemons and squeeze all the juice into the bowl with the zest. Whisk in 2 tablespoons of oil and the salt. Set aside. 3. Rinse the artichokes with cool water, and dry with a clean towel. Using a sharp knife, cut about 1½ inches off the tip of each artichoke. Cut about ¼ inch off each stem. Halve each artichoke lengthwise so each piece has equal amounts of stem. Immediately plunge the artichoke halves into the lemon juice and oil mixture (to prevent browning) and turn to coat on all sides. Lay one artichoke half flat-side down in the center of a sheet of aluminum foil, and close up loosely to make a foil packet. Repeat the process with the remaining three artichoke halves. Set the packets aside. 4. Put the chicken in the remaining lemon juice mixture and turn to coat. 5. Using oven mitts, carefully remove the hot baking sheet from the oven and pour on the remaining tablespoon of oil; tilt the pan to coat. Carefully arrange the chicken, skin-side down, on the hot baking sheet. Place the artichoke packets, flat-side down, on the baking sheet as well. (Arrange the artichoke packets and chicken with space between them so air can circulate around them.) 6. Roast for 20 minutes, or until the internal temperature of the chicken measures 165°F (74°C) on a meat thermometer and any juices run clear. Before serving, check the artichokes for doneness by pulling on a leaf. If it comes out easily, the artichoke is ready.

Per Serving:

calories: 566 | fat: 42g | protein: 35g | carbs: 13g | fiber: 6g | sodium: 524mg

Fajita-Stuffed Chicken Breast

Prep time: 15 minutes | Cook time: 25 minutes |

Serves 4

2 (6 ounces / 170 g) boneless, skinless chicken breasts	seeded and sliced
¼ medium white onion, peeled and sliced	1 tablespoon coconut oil
1 medium green bell pepper,	2 teaspoons chili powder
	1 teaspoon ground cumin
	½ teaspoon garlic powder

1. Slice each chicken breast completely in half lengthwise into two even pieces. Using a meat tenderizer, pound out the chicken until it's about ¼-inch thickness. 2. Lay each slice of chicken out and place three slices of onion and four slices of green pepper on the end closest to you. Begin rolling the peppers and onions tightly into the chicken. Secure the roll with either toothpicks or a couple pieces of butcher's twine. 3. Drizzle coconut oil over chicken. Sprinkle each side with chili powder, cumin, and garlic powder. Place each roll into the air fryer basket. 4. Adjust the temperature to 350°F (177°C) and air fry for 25 minutes. 5. Serve warm.

Per Serving:

calories: 168 | fat: 7g | protein: 25g | carbs: 3g | fiber: 1g | sodium: 320mg

Personal Cauliflower Pizzas

Prep time: 10 minutes | Cook time: 25 minutes |

Serves 2

1 (12 ounces / 340 g) bag frozen riced cauliflower	4 tablespoons no-sugar-added marinara sauce, divided
⅓ cup shredded Mozzarella cheese	4 ounces (113 g) fresh Mozzarella, chopped, divided
¼ cup almond flour	1 cup cooked chicken breast, chopped, divided
¼ grated Parmesan cheese	½ cup chopped cherry tomatoes, divided
1 large egg	
½ teaspoon salt	¼ cup fresh baby arugula, divided
1 teaspoon garlic powder	
1 teaspoon dried oregano	

1. Preheat the air fryer to 400°F (204°C). Cut 4 sheets of parchment paper to fit the basket of the air fryer. Brush with olive oil and set aside. 2. In a large glass bowl, microwave the cauliflower according to package directions. Place the cauliflower on a clean towel, draw up the sides, and squeeze tightly over a sink to remove the excess moisture. Return the cauliflower to the bowl and add the shredded Mozzarella along with the almond flour, Parmesan, egg, salt, garlic powder, and oregano. Stir until thoroughly combined. 3. Divide the dough into two equal portions. Place one piece of dough on the prepared parchment paper and pat gently into a thin, flat disk 7 to 8 inches in diameter. Air fry for 15 minutes until the crust begins to brown. Let cool for 5 minutes. 4. Transfer the parchment paper with the crust on top to a baking sheet. Place a second sheet of parchment paper over the crust. While holding the edges of both sheets together, carefully lift the crust off the baking sheet, flip it, and place it back in the air fryer basket. The new sheet of parchment paper is now on the bottom. Remove the top piece of paper and air fry the crust for another 15 minutes until the top begins to brown. Remove the basket from the air fryer. 5. Spread 2 tablespoons of the marinara sauce on top of the crust, followed by half the fresh Mozzarella, chicken, cherry tomatoes, and arugula. Air fry for 5 to 10 minutes longer, until the cheese is melted and beginning to brown. Remove the pizza from the oven and let it sit for 10 minutes before serving. Repeat with the remaining ingredients to make a second pizza.

Per Serving:

calories: 655 | fat: 35g | protein: 67g | carbs: 20g | fiber: 7g | sodium: 741mg

Savory Chicken Meatballs

Prep time: 20 minutes | Cook time: 20 minutes |
Serves 4

2 (1 pounds / 454 g) boxes frozen chopped spinach, thawed
1 medium shallot, grated
1 pound (454 g) ground chicken
¾ cup crumbled feta cheese
2 tablespoons za'atar seasoning
¼ cup extra-virgin olive oil
4 whole-wheat pita bread rounds, for serving
Tzatziki, for serving
⅓ seedless cucumber, peeled and chopped, for serving

1. Preheat the oven to 400°F(205°C). 2. While the oven preheats, squeeze all the water out of the spinach until it's completely dry. Use paper towels to blot it if necessary. 3. In a bowl, fluff the spinach with a fork to separate clumps and add the grated shallot to the spinach. Add the chicken, feta, and za'atar seasoning to the spinach and shallots and drizzle with the olive oil. 4. Combine all the ingredients and form the mixture into 10 to 15 meatballs. Lightly flatten the meatballs (just so that they won't roll around) and place on a nonstick baking sheet. 5. Bake for 10 to 12 minutes, or until the meatballs are golden brown and cooked thoroughly. 6. Serve in a pita, topped with tzatziki and cucumbers.

Per Serving:
calories: 514 | fat: 31g | protein: 36g | carbs: 29g | fiber: 9g | sodium: 631mg

Sheet Pan Pesto Chicken with Crispy Garlic Potatoes

Prep time: 15 minutes | Cook time: 50 minutes |
Serves 2

12 ounces (340 g) small red potatoes (3 or 4 potatoes)
1 tablespoon olive oil
¼ teaspoon salt
½ teaspoon garlic powder
1 (8 ounces / 227 g) boneless, skinless chicken breast
3 tablespoons prepared pesto

1. Preheat the oven to 425°F (220°C) and set the rack to the bottom position. Line a baking sheet with parchment paper. (Do not use foil, as the potatoes will stick.) 2. Scrub the potatoes and dry them well, then dice into 1-inch pieces. 3. In a medium bowl, combine the potatoes, olive oil, salt, and garlic powder. Toss well to coat. 4. Place the potatoes on the parchment paper and roast for 10 minutes. Flip the potatoes and return to the oven for another 10 minutes. 5. While the potatoes are roasting, place the chicken in the same bowl and toss with the pesto, coating the chicken evenly. 6. Check the potatoes to make sure they are golden brown on the top and bottom. Toss them again and add the chicken breast to the pan. 7. Turn the heat down to 350°F (180°C) and let the chicken and potatoes roast for 30 minutes. Check to make sure the chicken reaches an internal temperature of 165°F (74°C) and the potatoes are tender inside.

Per Serving:
calories: 377 | fat: 16g | protein: 30g | carbs: 31g | fiber: 4g | sodium: 426mg

Blackened Chicken

Prep time: 10 minutes | Cook time: 20 minutes |
Serves 4

1 large egg, beaten
¾ cup Blackened seasoning
2 whole boneless, skinless
chicken breasts (about 1 pound / 454 g each), halved
1 to 2 tablespoons oil

1. Place the beaten egg in one shallow bowl and the Blackened seasoning in another shallow bowl. 2. One at a time, dip the chicken pieces in the beaten egg and the Blackened seasoning, coating thoroughly. 3. Preheat the air fryer to 360°F (182°C). Line the air fryer basket with parchment paper. 4. Place the chicken pieces on the parchment and spritz with oil. 5. Cook for 10 minutes. Flip the chicken, spritz it with oil, and cook for 10 minutes more until the internal temperature reaches 165°F (74°C) and the chicken is no longer pink inside. Let sit for 5 minutes before serving.

Per Serving:
calories: 225 | fat: 10g | protein: 28g | carbs: 8g | fiber: 6g | sodium: 512mg

Whole Tandoori–Style Braised Chicken

Prep time: 10 minutes | Cook time: 4 to 8 hours |
Serves 6

1 tablespoon freshly grated ginger
5 garlic cloves, minced
2 fresh green chiles, finely chopped
⅔ cup Greek yogurt
2 tablespoons mustard oil
1 tablespoon Kashmiri chili powder
1 tablespoon dried fenugreek
leaves
1 tablespoon gram flour
2 teaspoons garam masala
1 teaspoon sea salt
1 teaspoon ground cumin
Juice of 1 large lemon
1 whole chicken, about 3⅓ pounds (1½ kg)
Handful fresh coriander leaves, chopped

1. Put the ginger, garlic, and green chiles in a spice grinder and grind to a paste. Empty into a large bowl and stir in all the other ingredients, except for the chicken and the coriander leaves. 2. Skin the chicken. Then, using a sharp knife, slash the chicken breasts and legs to allow the marinade to penetrate. 3. Marinate in the refrigerator for as long as you can leave it. (Overnight is fine.) 4. Preheat the slow cooker on high. My cooker has a stand I can sit meat on, but if you don't have one, scrunch up some foil and put it in the bottom of the cooker. Pour a few tablespoons of water in the bottom of the cooker and place the chicken on the foil. 5. Cook on high for 4 hours, or on low for 6 to 8 hours. 6. Remove the chicken from the cooker and cut it into pieces. Sprinkle the chopped coriander leaves over the chicken and serve.

Per Serving:
calories: 634 | fat: 45g | protein: 50g | carbs: 5g | fiber: 1g | sodium: 615mg

Jerk Chicken Thighs

Prep time: 30 minutes | Cook time: 15 to 20 minutes

| Serves 6

2 teaspoons ground coriander
1 teaspoon ground allspice
1 teaspoon cayenne pepper
1 teaspoon ground ginger
1 teaspoon salt
1 teaspoon dried thyme
½ teaspoon ground cinnamon
½ teaspoon ground nutmeg
2 pounds (907 g) boneless
chicken thighs, skin on
2 tablespoons olive oil

1. In a small bowl, combine the coriander, allspice, cayenne, ginger, salt, thyme, cinnamon, and nutmeg. Stir until thoroughly combined. 2. Place the chicken in a baking dish and use paper towels to pat dry. Thoroughly coat both sides of the chicken with the spice mixture. Cover and refrigerate for at least 2 hours, preferably overnight. 3. Preheat the air fryer to 360ºF (182ºC). 4. Working in batches if necessary, arrange the chicken in a single layer in the air fryer basket and lightly coat with the olive oil. Pausing halfway through the cooking time to flip the chicken, air fry for 15 to 20 minutes, until a thermometer inserted into the thickest part registers 165ºF (74ºC).

Per Serving:

calories: 227 | fat: 11g | protein: 30g | carbs: 1g | fiber: 0g | sodium: 532mg

Chicken with Lettuce

Prep time: 15 minutes | Cook time: 14 minutes |

Serves 4

1 pound (454 g) chicken breast tenders, chopped into bite-size pieces
½ onion, thinly sliced
½ red bell pepper, seeded and thinly sliced
½ green bell pepper, seeded and
thinly sliced
1 tablespoon olive oil
1 tablespoon fajita seasoning
1 teaspoon kosher salt
Juice of ½ lime
8 large lettuce leaves
1 cup prepared guacamole

1. Preheat the air fryer to 400ºF (204ºC). 2. In a large bowl, combine the chicken, onion, and peppers. Drizzle with the olive oil and toss until thoroughly coated. Add the fajita seasoning and salt and toss again. 3. Working in batches if necessary, arrange the chicken and vegetables in a single layer in the air fryer basket. Pausing halfway through the cooking time to shake the basket, air fry for 14 minutes, or until the vegetables are tender and a thermometer inserted into the thickest piece of chicken registers 165ºF (74ºC). 4. Transfer the mixture to a serving platter and drizzle with the fresh lime juice. Serve with the lettuce leaves and top with the guacamole.

Per Serving:

calories: 273 | fat: 15g | protein: 27g | carbs: 9g | fiber: 5g | sodium: 723mg

Curried Chicken and Lentil Salad

Prep time: 15 minutes | Cook time: 13 minutes |

Serves 8

1 teaspoon olive oil
2 pounds (907 g) boneless, skinless chicken breasts, cut into ½" pieces
1 cup dried lentils, rinsed and drained
2 cups water
2½ teaspoons curry powder, divided
2 small Golden Delicious apples, divided
1 teaspoon lemon juice
2 cups halved seedless grapes
1 cup roasted salted cashews
2 stalks celery, diced
½ small red onion, peeled and diced
¾ cup plain low-fat yogurt
¼ cup mayonnaise
11 ounces (312 g) baby salad greens

1. Press the Sauté button on the Instant Pot® and heat oil. Add chicken and cook for 5 minutes or until browned. Stir in lentils, water, and 1 teaspoon curry powder. Halve one of the apples; core and dice 1 half and add it to the pot. Coat the cut side of the other half of the apple with lemon juice to prevent it from turning brown and set aside. Press the Cancel button. 2. Close lid, set steam release to Sealing, press the Manual button, and set time to 8 minutes. When the timer beeps, let pressure release naturally, about 20 minutes. Open lid. 3. Transfer the contents of the Instant Pot® to a large bowl and set aside to cool. 4. Dice reserved apple half, and core and dice remaining apple. Add to chicken and lentil mixture along with grapes, cashews, celery, and red onion. 5. In a small bowl, mix together yogurt, mayonnaise, and remaining 1½ teaspoons curry powder. Drizzle over chicken and lentil mixture, and stir to combine. Serve over salad greens.

Per Serving:

calories: 404 | fat: 18g | protein: 41g | carbs: 21g | fiber: 3g | sodium: 177mg

Teriyaki Chicken Legs

Prep time: 12 minutes | Cook time: 18 to 20 minutes

| Serves 2

4 tablespoons teriyaki sauce
1 tablespoon orange juice
1 teaspoon smoked paprika
4 chicken legs
Cooking spray

1. Mix together the teriyaki sauce, orange juice, and smoked paprika. Brush on all sides of chicken legs. 2. Spray the air fryer basket with nonstick cooking spray and place chicken in basket. 3. Air fry at 360ºF (182ºC) for 6 minutes. Turn and baste with sauce. Cook for 6 more minutes, turn and baste. Cook for 6 to 8 minutes more, until juices run clear when chicken is pierced with a fork.

Per Serving:

calories: 392 | fat: 13g | protein: 59g | carbs: 7g | fiber: 1g | sodium: 641mg

Chicken Avgolemono

Prep time: 10 minutes | Cook time: 50 minutes |
Serves 4

1½ pounds (680 g) boneless, skinless chicken breasts

6 cups chicken broth, as needed

¾ cup dried Greek orzo

3 large eggs

Juice of 2 lemons

Sea salt

Freshly ground black pepper

1. Place the chicken in a stockpot and add enough broth to cover the chicken by 1 inch. Bring to a boil over high heat, then reduce the heat to low, cover, and simmer for 30 to 45 minutes, until the chicken is cooked through. Remove the chicken from the stockpot and set aside in a medium bowl. 2. Increase the heat to medium-high and bring the broth back to a boil. Add the orzo and cook for 7 to 10 minutes, until tender. 3. While the orzo is cooking, shred the chicken with two forks and return it to the pot when orzo is done. 4. Crack the eggs into a small bowl and whisk until frothy, then whisk in the lemon juice. While whisking continuously, slowly pour in 1 cup of the hot broth to temper the eggs. Pour the egg mixture back into the pot and stir. Simmer for 1 minute more, season with salt and pepper, and serve.

Per Serving:

calories: 391 | fat: 9g | protein: 46g | carbs: 29g | fiber: 1g | sodium: 171mg

Brazilian Tempero Baiano Chicken Drumsticks

Prep time: 30 minutes | Cook time: 20 minutes |
Serves 4

1 teaspoon cumin seeds

1 teaspoon dried oregano

1 teaspoon dried parsley

1 teaspoon ground turmeric

½ teaspoon coriander seeds

1 teaspoon kosher salt

½ teaspoon black peppercorns

½ teaspoon cayenne pepper

¼ cup fresh lime juice

2 tablespoons olive oil

1½ pounds (680 g) chicken drumsticks

1. In a clean coffee grinder or spice mill, combine the cumin, oregano, parsley, turmeric, coriander seeds, salt, peppercorns, and cayenne. Process until finely ground. 2. In a small bowl, combine the ground spices with the lime juice and oil. Place the chicken in a resealable plastic bag. Add the marinade, seal, and massage until the chicken is well coated. Marinate at room temperature for 30 minutes or in the refrigerator for up to 24 hours. 3. When you are ready to cook, place the drumsticks skin side up in the air fryer basket. Set the air fryer to 400ºF (204ºC) for 20 to 25 minutes, turning the legs halfway through the cooking time. Use a meat thermometer to ensure that the chicken has reached an internal temperature of 165ºF (74ºC). 4. Serve with plenty of napkins.

Per Serving:

calories: 267 | fat: 13g | protein: 33g | carbs: 2g | fiber: 1g | sodium: 777mg

Cajun-Breaded Chicken Bites

Prep time: 10 minutes | Cook time: 12 minutes |
Serves 4

1 pound (454 g) boneless, skinless chicken breasts, cut into 1-inch cubes

½ cup heavy whipping cream

½ teaspoon salt

¼ teaspoon ground black

pepper

1 ounce (28 g) plain pork rinds, finely crushed

¼ cup unflavored whey protein powder

½ teaspoon Cajun seasoning

1. Place chicken in a medium bowl and pour in cream. Stir to coat. Sprinkle with salt and pepper. 2. In a separate large bowl, combine pork rinds, protein powder, and Cajun seasoning. Remove chicken from cream, shaking off any excess, and toss in dry mix until fully coated. 3. Place bites into ungreased air fryer basket. Adjust the temperature to 400ºF (204ºC) and air fry for 12 minutes, shaking the basket twice during cooking. Bites will be done when golden brown and have an internal temperature of at least 165ºF (74ºC). Serve warm.

Per Serving:

calories: 272 | fat: 13g | protein: 35g | carbs: 2g | fiber: 1g | sodium: 513mg

Spanish Sautéed Lemon and Garlic Chicken

Prep time: 10 minutes | Cook time: 15 minutes |
Serves 3

2 large boneless, skinless chicken breasts

¼ cup extra virgin olive oil

3 garlic cloves, finely chopped

5 tablespoons fresh lemon juice

Zest of 1 lemon

½ cup chopped fresh parsley

¼ teaspoon fine sea salt

Pinch of freshly ground black pepper

1. Slice the chicken crosswise into very thin slices, each about ¼-inch thick. 2. In a pan large enough to hold the chicken in a single layer, heat the olive oil over medium heat. When the olive oil starts to shimmer, add the garlic and sauté for about 30 seconds, then add the chicken. Reduce the heat to medium-low and sauté for about 12 minutes, tossing the chicken breasts periodically until they begin to brown on the edges. 3. Add the lemon zest and lemon juice. Increase the heat to medium and bring to a boil. Cook for about 2 minutes while using a wooden spatula to scrape any browned bits from the bottom of the pan. 4. Add the parsley, stir, then remove the pan from the heat. 5. Transfer the chicken along with any juices to a platter. Season with the sea salt and black pepper, then serve promptly. Store in an airtight container in the refrigerator for up to 2 days.

Per Serving:

calories: 358 | fat: 22g | protein: 35g | carbs: 4g | fiber: 1g | sodium: 269mg

Chicken Skewers

¼ cup olive oil

Zest of 1 lemon

Juice of 2 lemons

2 tablespoons dried oregano

1 tablespoon dried thyme

2 garlic cloves, minced

Sea salt

Freshly ground black pepper

3 pounds (1.4 kg) boneless, skinless chicken breasts, cut into 2-inch cubes

1. In a large bowl, stir together the olive oil, lemon zest, lemon juice, oregano, thyme, and garlic. Season with salt and pepper and mix well. Add the chicken and stir to coat thoroughly. Cover the bowl and refrigerate for at least 20 to 30 minutes. 2. Remove the chicken from the refrigerator and thread the chicken pieces onto skewers, using 4 or 5 pieces per skewer. 3. Heat a cast-iron skillet over medium-high heat. Working in batches, place the skewers in the skillet, about 3 per batch, and cook, turning frequently, for 5 to 7 minutes, until the chicken is cooked through and has an internal temperature of 165ºF (74ºC). Repeat with the remaining skewers. Serve.

Per Serving:

calories: 504 | fat: 19g | protein: 76g | carbs: 4g | fiber: 1g | sodium: 214mg

Smoky Chicken Leg Quarters

½ cup avocado oil

2 teaspoons smoked paprika

1 teaspoon sea salt

1 teaspoon garlic powder

½ teaspoon dried rosemary

½ teaspoon dried thyme

½ teaspoon freshly ground black pepper

2 pounds (907 g) bone-in, skin-on chicken leg quarters

1. In a blender or small bowl, combine the avocado oil, smoked paprika, salt, garlic powder, rosemary, thyme, and black pepper. 2. Place the chicken in a shallow dish or large zip-top bag. Pour the marinade over the chicken, making sure all the legs are coated. Cover and marinate for at least 2 hours or overnight. 3. Place the chicken in a single layer in the air fryer basket, working in batches if necessary. Set the air fryer to 400ºF (204ºC) and air fry for 15 minutes. Flip the chicken legs, then reduce the temperature to 350ºF (177ºC). Cook for 8 to 12 minutes more, until an instant-read thermometer reads 160ºF (71ºC) when inserted into the thickest piece of chicken. 4. Allow to rest for 5 to 10 minutes before serving.

Per Serving:

calories: 347 | fat: 25g | protein: 29g | carbs: 1g | fiber: 0g | sodium: 534mg

Braised Duck with Fennel Root

¼ cup olive oil

1 whole duck, cleaned

3 teaspoon fresh rosemary

2 garlic cloves, minced

Sea salt and freshly ground pepper, to taste

3 fennel bulbs, cut into chunks

½ cup sherry

1. Preheat the oven to 375ºF (190ºC) 2. Heat the olive oil in a large stew pot or Dutch oven. 3. Season the duck, including the cavity, with the rosemary, garlic, sea salt, and freshly ground pepper. 4. Place the duck in the oil, and cook it for 10 to 15 minutes, turning as necessary to brown all sides. 5. Add the fennel bulbs and cook an additional 5 minutes. 6. Pour the sherry over the duck and fennel, cover the pot, and cook in the oven for 30 to 45 minutes, or until internal temperature of the duck is 150ºF (66ºC) at its thickest part. 7. Allow duck to sit for 15 minutes before serving.

Per Serving:

calories: 308 | fat: 23g | protein: 17g | carbs: 9g | fiber: 4g | sodium: 112mg

Punjabi Chicken Curry

2 tablespoons vegetable oil

3 onions, finely diced

6 garlic cloves, finely chopped

1 heaped tablespoon freshly grated ginger

1 (14 ounces / 397 g) can plum tomatoes

1 teaspoon salt

1 teaspoon turmeric

1 teaspoon chili powder

Handful coriander stems, finely

chopped

3 fresh green chiles, finely chopped

12 pieces chicken, mixed thighs and drumsticks, or a whole chicken, skinned, trimmed, and chopped

2 teaspoons garam masala

Handful fresh coriander leaves, chopped

1. Heat the oil in a frying pan (or in the slow cooker if you have a sear setting). Add the diced onions and cook for 5 minutes. Add the garlic and continue to cook for 10 minutes until the onions are brown. 2. Heat the slow cooker to high and add the onion-and-garlic mixture. Stir in the ginger, tomatoes, salt, turmeric, chili powder, coriander stems, and chiles. 3. Add the chicken pieces. Cover and cook on low for 6 hours, or on high for 4 hours. 4. Once cooked, check the seasoning, and then stir in the garam masala and coriander leaves.

Per Serving:

calories: 298 | fat: 9g | protein: 35g | carbs: 19g | fiber: 3g | sodium: 539mg

Chapter 3 Beans and Grains

Cilantro Lime Rice

Prep time: 10 minutes | Cook time: 32 minutes |

Serves 8

2 tablespoons extra-virgin olive oil	2 cups brown rice
½ medium yellow onion, peeled and chopped	2¼ cups water
	2 tablespoons lime juice
2 cloves garlic, peeled and minced	1 tablespoon grated lime zest
	¼ teaspoon salt
½ cup chopped fresh cilantro, divided	½ teaspoon ground black pepper

1. Press the Sauté button on the Instant Pot® and heat oil. Add onion and cook until soft, about 6 minutes. Add garlic and ¼ cup cilantro and cook until fragrant, about 30 seconds. Add rice and cook, stirring constantly, until well coated and starting to toast, about 3 minutes. Press the Cancel button. 2. Stir in water. Close lid, set steam release to Sealing, press the Manual button, and set time to 22 minutes. When the timer beeps, let pressure release naturally for 10 minutes, then quick-release the remaining pressure. Open lid and fluff rice with a fork. Fold in remaining ¼ cup cilantro, lime juice, lime zest, salt, and pepper. Serve warm.

Per Serving:

calories: 95 | fat: 4g | protein

Black Lentil Dhal

Prep time: 10 minutes | Cook time: 8 to 10 hours |

Serves 6

2 cups dry whole black lentils	2 teaspoons coriander seeds, ground
1 medium onion, finely chopped	
1 heaped tablespoon freshly grated ginger	1 teaspoon cumin seeds, ground
	1 teaspoon sea salt
3 garlic cloves, chopped	6⅓ cups water
3 fresh tomatoes, puréed, or	1 to 2 tablespoons butter
7 to 8 ounces (198 to 227 g) canned tomatoes, blended	(optional)
	1 teaspoon garam masala
2 fresh green chiles, chopped	1 teaspoon dried fenugreek
2 tablespoons ghee	leaves
½ teaspoon turmeric	Handful fresh coriander leaves, chopped
1 teaspoon chili powder	

1. Preheat the slow cooker on high. 2. Clean and wash the black lentils. 3. Put the lentils, onion, ginger, garlic, tomatoes, chiles, ghee, turmeric, chili powder, coriander seeds, cumin seeds, salt, and water into the slow cooker. Cover and cook for 10 hours on low or for 8 hours on high. 4. When the lentils are cooked and creamy, stir in the butter (if using), garam masala, and fenugreek leaves to make the dhal rich and delicious. Garnish with a sprinkle of fresh coriander leaves and serve.

Per Serving:

calories: 271 | fat: 3g | protein: 17g | carbs: 47g | fiber: 9g | sodium: 415mg

Greek Chickpeas with Coriander and Sage

Prep time: 20 minutes | Cook time: 22 minutes |

Serves 6 to 8

1½ tablespoons table salt, for brining	cracked
	¼ to ½ teaspoon red pepper flakes
1 pound (454 g) dried chickpeas, picked over and rinsed	2½ cups chicken broth
	¼ cup fresh sage leaves
2 tablespoons extra-virgin olive oil, plus extra for drizzling	2 bay leaves
	1½ teaspoons grated lemon zest
2 onions, halved and sliced thin	plus 2 teaspoons juice
¼ teaspoon table salt	2 tablespoons minced fresh
1 tablespoon coriander seeds,	parsley

1. Dissolve 1½ tablespoons salt in 2 quarts cold water in large container. Add chickpeas and soak at room temperature for at least 8 hours or up to 24 hours. Drain and rinse well. 2. Using highest sauté function, heat oil in Instant Pot until shimmering. Add onions and ¼ teaspoon salt and cook until onions are softened and well browned, 10 to 12 minutes. Stir in coriander and pepper flakes and cook until fragrant, about 30 seconds. Stir in broth, scraping up any browned bits, then stir in chickpeas, sage, and bay leaves. 3. Lock lid in place and close pressure release valve. Select low pressure cook function and cook for 10 minutes. Turn off Instant Pot and let pressure release naturally for 15 minutes. Quick-release any remaining pressure, then carefully remove lid, allowing steam to escape away from you. 4. Discard bay leaves. Stir lemon zest and juice into chickpeas and season with salt and pepper to taste. Sprinkle with parsley. Serve, drizzling individual portions with extra oil.

Per Serving:

calories: 190 | fat: 6g | protein: 11g | carbs: 40g | fiber: 1g | sodium: 360mg

Couscous with Apricots

Prep time: 10 minutes | Cook time: 15 minutes |
Serves 4

2 tablespoons olive oil
1 small onion, diced
1 cup whole-wheat couscous
2 cups water or broth
½ cup dried apricots, soaked in

water overnight
½ cup slivered almonds or
pistachios
½ teaspoon dried mint
½ teaspoon dried thyme

1. Heat the olive oil in a large skillet over medium-high heat. Add the onion and cook until translucent and soft. 2. Stir in the couscous and cook for 2–3 minutes. 3. Add the water or broth, cover, and cook for 8–10 minutes until the water is mostly absorbed. 4. Remove from the heat and let stand for a few minutes. 5. Fluff with a fork and fold in the apricots, nuts, mint, and thyme.

Per Serving:
calories: 294 | fat: 15g | protein: 8g | carbs: 38g | fiber: 6g | sodium: 6mg

Sweet Potato and Chickpea Moroccan Stew

Prep time: 10 minutes | Cook time: 40 minutes |
Serves 4

6 tablespoons extra virgin olive oil
2 medium red or white onions, finely chopped
6 garlic cloves, minced
3 medium carrots (about 8 ounces /227 g), peeled and cubed
1 teaspoon ground cumin
1 teaspoon ground coriander
½ teaspoon smoked paprika
½ teaspoon ground turmeric
1 cinnamon stick
½ pound (227 g) butternut squash, peeled and cut into

½-inch cubes
2 medium sweet potatoes, peeled and cut into ½-inch cubes
4 ounces (113 g) prunes, pitted
4 tomatoes (any variety), chopped, or 20 ounces (567g) canned chopped tomatoes
14 ounces (397 g) vegetable broth
14 ounces (397 g) canned chickpeas
½ cup chopped fresh parsley, for serving

1. Place a deep pan over medium heat and add the olive oil. When the oil is shimmering, add the onions and sauté for 5 minutes, then add the garlic and carrots, and sauté for 1 more minute. 2. Add the cumin, coriander, paprika, turmeric, and cinnamon stick. Continue cooking, stirring continuously, for 1 minute, then add the squash, sweet potatoes, prunes, tomatoes, and vegetable broth. Stir, cover, then reduce the heat to low and simmer for 20 minutes, stirring occasionally and checking the water levels, until the vegetables are cooked through. (If the stew appears to be drying out, add small amounts of hot water until the stew is thick.) 3. Add the chickpeas to the pan, stir, and continue simmering for 10 more minutes, adding more water if necessary. Remove the pan from the heat, discard the cinnamon stick, and set the stew aside to cool for 10 minutes. 4. When ready to serve, sprinkle the chopped parsley over the top of the stew. Store covered in the refrigerator for up to 4 days.

Per Serving:
calories: 471 | fat: 23g | protein: 9g | carbs: 63g | fiber: 12g | sodium: 651mg
: 1g | carbs: 14g | fiber: 1g | sodium: 94mg

White Beans with Garlic and Tomatoes

Prep time: 10 minutes | Cook time: 40 minutes |
Serves 6

1 cup dried cannellini beans, soaked overnight and drained
4 cups water
4 cups vegetable stock
1 tablespoon olive oil
1 teaspoon salt

2 cloves garlic, peeled and minced
½ cup diced tomato
½ teaspoon dried sage
½ teaspoon ground black pepper

1. Add beans and water to the Instant Pot®. Close lid, set steam release to Sealing, press the Bean button, and cook for default time of 30 minutes. When timer beeps, quick-release the pressure until the float valve drops. 2. Press the Cancel button, open lid, drain and rinse beans, and return to pot along with stock. Soak for 1 hour. 3. Add olive oil, salt, garlic, tomato, sage, and pepper to beans. Close lid, set steam release to Sealing, press the Manual button, and set time to 10 minutes. When the timer beeps, quick-release the pressure until the float valve drops and open lid. Serve hot.

Per Serving:
calories: 128 | fat: 2g | protein: 7g | carbs: 20g | fiber: 4g | sodium: 809mg

Quinoa, Broccoli, and Baby Potatoes

Prep time: 10 minutes | Cook time: 5 minutes |
Serves 4

2 tablespoons olive oil
1 cup baby potatoes, cut in half
1 cup broccoli florets
2 cups cooked quinoa

Zest of 1 lemon
Sea salt and freshly ground pepper, to taste

1. Heat the olive oil in a large skillet. 2. Add the potatoes and cook until tender and golden brown. Add the broccoli and cook until soft, about 3 minutes. 3. Remove from heat and add the quinoa and lemon zest. Season and serve.

Per Serving:
calories: 204 | fat: 9g | protein: 5g | carbs: 27g | fiber: 4g | sodium: 12mg

Lentil Pâté

2 tablespoons olive oil, divided
1 cup diced yellow onion
3 cloves garlic, peeled and minced
1 teaspoon red wine vinegar
2 cups dried green lentils,

rinsed and drained
4 cups water
1 teaspoon salt
¼ teaspoon ground black pepper

1. Press the Sauté button on the Instant Pot® and heat 1 tablespoon oil. Add onion and cook until translucent, about 3 minutes. Add garlic and vinegar, and cook for 30 seconds. Add lentils, water, remaining 1 tablespoon oil, and salt to pot and stir to combine. Press the Cancel button. 2. Close lid, set steam release to Sealing, press the Bean button, and allow to cook for default time of 30 minutes. When the timer beeps, let pressure release naturally for 10 minutes. Quick-release any remaining pressure until the float valve drops, then open lid. 3. Transfer lentil mixture to a food processor or blender, and blend until smooth. Season with pepper and serve warm.

Per Serving:

calories: 138 | fat: 3g | protein: 8g | carbs: 20g | fiber: 10g | sodium: 196mg

Wild Rice Pilaf with Pine Nuts

2 tablespoons extra-virgin olive oil
1 medium white onion, peeled and chopped
2 cups chopped baby bella mushrooms
3 cloves garlic, peeled and minced
2 cups wild rice

2½ cups vegetable broth
½ cup toasted pine nuts
¼ cup chopped fresh flat-leaf parsley
2 tablespoons chopped fresh chives
¼ teaspoon salt
½ teaspoon ground black pepper

1. Press the Sauté button on the Instant Pot® and heat oil. Add onion and mushrooms. Cook until soft, about 8 minutes. Add garlic and cook until fragrant, about 30 seconds. Add rice and press the Cancel button. 2. Stir in broth. Close lid, set steam release to Sealing, press the Manual button, and set time to 20 minutes. When the timer beeps, let pressure release naturally for 10 minutes, then quick-release the remaining pressure. Open lid and fluff rice with a fork. Fold in pine nuts, parsley, and chives. Season with salt and pepper. Serve warm.

Per Serving:

calories: 314 | fat: 18g | protein: 10g | carbs: 41g | fiber: 4g | sodium: 93mg

Garbanzo and Pita No-Bake Casserole

4 cups Greek yogurt
3 cloves garlic, minced
1 teaspoon salt
2 (16 ounces/ 454 g) cans garbanzo beans, rinsed and

drained
2 cups water
4 cups pita chips
5 tablespoons unsalted butter

1. In a large bowl, whisk together the yogurt, garlic, and salt. Set aside. 2. Put the garbanzo beans and water in a medium pot. Bring to a boil; let beans boil for about 5 minutes. 3. Pour the garbanzo beans and the liquid into a large casserole dish. 4. Top the beans with pita chips. Pour the yogurt sauce over the pita chip layer. 5. In a small saucepan, melt and brown the butter, about 3 minutes. Pour the brown butter over the yogurt sauce.

Per Serving:

calories: 772 | fat: 36g | protein: 39g | carbs: 73g | fiber: 13g | sodium: 1,003mg

Greek-Style Pea Casserole

⅓ cup extra virgin olive oil
1 medium onion (any variety), diced
1 medium carrot, peeled and sliced
1 medium white potato, peeled and cut into bite-sized pieces
1 pound (454 g) peas (fresh or frozen)
3 tablespoons chopped fresh

dill
2 medium tomatoes, grated, or 12 ounces (340 g) canned crushed tomatoes
½ teaspoon fine sea salt
¼ teaspoon freshly ground black pepper
½ cup hot water
Salt to taste

1. Add the olive oil to a medium pot over medium heat. When the oil starts to shimmer, add the onions and sauté for 2 minutes. Add the carrots and potatoes, and sauté for 3 more minutes. 2. Add the peas and dill. Stir until the peas are coated in the olive oil. 3. Add the tomatoes, sea salt, black pepper, and hot water. Mix well.Bring to the mixture to a boil, then cover, reduce the heat to low, and simmer for 40 minutes or until the peas and carrots are soft and the casserole has thickened. (Check the water levels intermittently, adding more hot water if the mixture appears to be getting too dry.) 4. Remove the casserole from the heat, uncover, and set aside for 20 minutes. Add salt to taste before serving. Store covered in the refrigerator for up to 3 days.

Per Serving:

calories: 439 | fat: 26g | protein: 12g | carbs: 45g | fiber: 13g | sodium: 429mg

Black Beans with Corn and Tomato Relish

½ pound (227 g) dried black beans, soaked overnight and drained

1 medium white onion, peeled and sliced in half

2 cloves garlic, peeled and lightly crushed

8 cups water

1 cup corn kernels

1 large tomato, seeded and chopped

½ medium red onion, peeled and chopped

¼ cup minced fresh cilantro

½ teaspoon ground cumin

¼ teaspoon smoked paprika

¼ teaspoon ground black pepper

¼ teaspoon salt

3 tablespoons extra-virgin olive oil

3 tablespoons lime juice

1. Add beans, white onion, garlic, and water to the Instant Pot®. Close lid, set steam release to Sealing, press the Bean button, and cook for the default time of 30 minutes. When the timer beeps, let pressure release naturally, about 20 minutes. 2. Open lid and remove and discard onion and garlic. Drain beans well and transfer to a medium bowl. Cool to room temperature, about 30 minutes. 3. In a separate small bowl, combine corn, tomato, red onion, cilantro, cumin, paprika, pepper, and salt. Toss to combine. Add to black beans and gently fold to mix. Whisk together olive oil and lime juice in a small bowl and pour over black bean mixture. Gently toss to coat. Serve at room temperature or refrigerate for at least 2 hours.

Per Serving:

calories: 216 | fat: 7g | protein: 8g | carbs: 28g | fiber: 6g | sodium: 192mg

Moroccan White Beans with Lamb

1½ tablespoons table salt, for brining

1 pound (454 g) dried great Northern beans, picked over and rinsed

1 (12 ounces/ 340 g) lamb shoulder chop (blade or round bone), ¾ to 1 inch thick, trimmed and halved

½ teaspoon table salt

2 tablespoons extra-virgin olive oil, plus extra for serving

1 onion, chopped

1 red bell pepper, stemmed, seeded, and chopped

2 tablespoons tomato paste

3 garlic cloves, minced

2 teaspoons paprika

2 teaspoons ground cumin

1½ teaspoons ground ginger

¼ teaspoon cayenne pepper

½ cup dry white wine

2 cups chicken broth

2 tablespoons minced fresh parsley

1. Dissolve 1½ tablespoons salt in 2 quarts cold water in large

container. Add beans and soak at room temperature for at least 8 hours or up to 24 hours. Drain and rinse well. 2. Pat lamb dry with paper towels and sprinkle with ½ teaspoon salt. Using highest sauté function, heat oil in Instant Pot for 5 minutes (or until just smoking). Brown lamb, about 5 minutes per side; transfer to plate. 3. Add onion and bell pepper to fat left in pot and cook, using highest sauté function, until softened, about 5 minutes. Stir in tomato paste, garlic, paprika, cumin, ginger, and cayenne and cook until fragrant, about 30 seconds. Stir in wine, scraping up any browned bits, then stir in broth and beans. 4. Nestle lamb into beans and add any accumulated juices. Lock lid in place and close pressure release valve. Select high pressure cook function and cook for 1 minute. Turn off Instant Pot and let pressure release naturally for 15 minutes. Quick-release any remaining pressure, then carefully remove lid, allowing steam to escape away from you. 5. Transfer lamb to cutting board, let cool slightly, then shred into bite-size pieces using 2 forks; discard excess fat and bones. Stir lamb and parsley into beans, and season with salt and pepper to taste. Drizzle individual portions with extra oil before serving.

Per Serving:

calories: 350 | fat: 12g | protein: 20g | carbs: 40g | fiber: 15g | sodium: 410mg

Quinoa Salad with Chicken, Chickpeas, and Spinach

4 tablespoons olive oil, divided

1 medium yellow onion, peeled and chopped

2 cloves garlic, peeled and minced

4 cups fresh baby spinach leaves

½ teaspoon salt

¼ teaspoon ground black pepper

1½ cups quinoa, rinsed and

drained

2 cups vegetable broth

1⅓ cups water

1 tablespoon apple cider vinegar

1 (15 ounces / 425 g) can chickpeas, drained and rinsed

1 (6 ounces / 170 g) boneless, skinless chicken breast, cooked and shredded

1. Press the Sauté button on the Instant Pot® and heat 2 tablespoons olive oil. Add onion and cook until tender, about 3 minutes. Add garlic, spinach, salt, and pepper and cook 3 minutes until spinach has wilted. Transfer spinach mixture to a large bowl. Press the Cancel button. 2. Add quinoa, broth, and water to the Instant Pot®. Close lid, set steam release to Sealing, press the Rice button, and set time to 12 minutes. 3. While quinoa cooks, add remaining 2 tablespoons olive oil, vinegar, chickpeas, and chicken to spinach mixture and toss to coat. Set aside. 4. When the timer beeps, let pressure release naturally, about 20 minutes. 5. Open lid and fluff quinoa with a fork. Press the Cancel button and let quinoa cool 10 minutes, then transfer to the bowl with chicken mixture. Mix well. Serve warm, at room temperature, or cold.

Per Serving:

calories: 232 | fat: 12g | protein: 14g | carbs: 20g | fiber: 6g | sodium: 463mg

Spiced Quinoa Salad

Prep time: 15 minutes | Cook time: 17 minutes | Serves 6

2 tablespoons vegetable oil
1 medium white onion, peeled and chopped
2 cloves garlic, peeled and minced
½ teaspoon ground cumin
½ teaspoon ground coriander
½ teaspoon smoked paprika
½ teaspoon salt
¼ teaspoon ground black

pepper
1½ cups quinoa, rinsed and drained
2 cups vegetable broth
1⅓ cups water
2 cups fresh baby spinach leaves
2 plum tomatoes, seeded and chopped

1. Press the Sauté button on the Instant Pot® and heat oil. Add onion and cook until tender, about 3 minutes. Add garlic, cumin, coriander, paprika, salt, and pepper, and cook 30 seconds until garlic and spices are fragrant. 2. Add quinoa and toss to coat in spice mixture. Cook 2 minutes to lightly toast quinoa. Add broth and water, making sure to scrape bottom and sides of pot to loosen any brown bits. Press the Cancel button. 3. Close lid and set steam release to Sealing. Press the Rice button and set time to 12 minutes. 4. When the timer beeps, let pressure release naturally, about 20 minutes. Open lid, add spinach and tomatoes, and fluff quinoa with a fork. Serve warm, at room temperature, or cold.

Per Serving:

calories: 215 | fat: 7g | protein: 7g | carbs: 32g | fiber: 4g | sodium: 486mg

Quinoa Salad with Tomatoes

Prep time: 10 minutes | Cook time: 22 minutes | Serves 4

2 tablespoons olive oil
2 cloves garlic, peeled and minced
1 cup diced fresh tomatoes
¼ cup chopped fresh Italian flat-leaf parsley

1 tablespoon lemon juice
1 cup quinoa, rinsed and drained
2 cups water
1 teaspoon salt

1. Press the Sauté button on the Instant Pot® and heat oil. Add garlic and cook 30 seconds, then add tomatoes, parsley, and lemon juice. Cook an additional 1 minute. Transfer mixture to a small bowl and set aside. Press the Cancel button. 2. Add quinoa and water to the Instant Pot®. Close lid, set steam release to Sealing, press the Multigrain button, and set time to 20 minutes. 3. When timer beeps, let pressure release naturally, about 20 minutes, then open lid. Fluff with a fork and stir in tomato mixture and salt. Serve immediately.

Per Serving:

calories: 223 | fat: 10g | protein: 6g | carbs: 29g | fiber: 3g | sodium: 586mg

Three-Bean Vegan Chili

Prep time: 20 minutes | Cook time: 30 minutes | Serves 12

1 cup dried pinto beans, soaked overnight and drained
1 cup dried red beans, soaked overnight and drained
1 cup dried black beans, soaked overnight and drained
2 medium white onions, peeled and chopped
2 medium red bell peppers, seeded and chopped
2 stalks celery, chopped
1 (28 ounces / 794 g) can diced

tomatoes
1 (15 ounces / 425 g) can tomato sauce
¼ cup chili powder
2 tablespoons smoked paprika
1 teaspoon ground cumin
1 teaspoon ground coriander
½ teaspoon salt
½ teaspoon ground black pepper
3 cups vegetable broth
1 cup water

1. Place all ingredients in the Instant Pot® and stir to combine. Close lid, set steam release to Sealing, press the Chili button, and cook for the default time of 30 minutes. 2. When the timer beeps, quick-release the pressure until the float valve drops, then open lid and stir well. If chili is too thin, press the Cancel button and then press the Sauté button and let chili simmer, uncovered, until desired thickness is reached. Serve warm.

Per Serving:

calories: 195 | fat: 1g | protein: 10g | carbs: 35g | fiber: 10g | sodium: 521mg

Farro Salad with Tomatoes and Olives

Prep time: 10 minutes | Cook time: 20 minutes | Serves 6

10 ounces (283 g) farro, rinsed and drained
4 cups water
4 Roma tomatoes, seeded and chopped
4 scallions, green parts only, thinly sliced

½ cup sliced black olives
¼ cup minced fresh flat-leaf parsley
¼ cup extra-virgin olive oil
2 tablespoons balsamic vinegar
¼ teaspoon ground black pepper

1. Place farro and water in the Instant Pot®. Close lid and set steam release to Sealing. Press the Multigrain button and set time to 20 minutes. When the timer beeps, let pressure release naturally, about 30 minutes. 2. Open lid and fluff with a fork. Transfer to a bowl and cool 30 minutes. Add tomatoes, scallions, black olives, and parsley and mix well. 3. In a small bowl, whisk together oil, balsamic vinegar, and pepper. Pour over salad and toss to evenly coat. Refrigerate for at least 4 hours before serving. Serve chilled or at room temperature.

Per Serving:

calories: 288 | fat: 14g | protein: 7g | carbs: 31g | fiber: 3g | sodium: 159mg

Vegetarian Dinner Loaf

Prep time: 10 minutes | Cook time: 45 minutes |
Serves 6

1 cup dried pinto beans, soaked overnight and drained	1 large egg, beaten
8 cups water, divided	¾ cup ketchup
1 tablespoon vegetable oil	1 teaspoon garlic powder
1 teaspoon salt	1 teaspoon dried basil
1 cup diced onion	1 teaspoon dried parsley
1 cup chopped walnuts	½ teaspoon salt
½ cup rolled oats	½ teaspoon ground black pepper

1. Add beans and 4 cups water to the Instant Pot®. Close lid, set steam release to Sealing, press the Manual button, and set time to 1 minute. When the timer beeps, quick-release the pressure until the float valve drops. Press the Cancel button. 2. Open lid, then drain and rinse beans and return to the pot with remaining 4 cups water. Soak for 1 hour. 3. Preheat oven to 350ºF. 4. Add the oil and salt to pot. Close lid, set steam release to Sealing, press the Manual button, and set time to 11 minutes. When the timer beeps, let pressure release naturally, about 25 minutes, and open lid. Drain beans and pour into a large mixing bowl. 5. Stir in onion, walnuts, oats, egg, ketchup, garlic powder, basil, parsley, salt, and pepper. Spread the mixture into a loaf pan and bake for 30 to 35 minutes. Cool for 20 minutes in pan before slicing and serving.

Per Serving:

calories: 278 | fat: 17g | protein: 9g | carbs: 27g | fiber: 6g | sodium: 477mg

Red Lentil and Goat Cheese Stuffed Tomatoes

Prep time: 10 minutes | Cook time: 15 minutes |
Serves 4

4 tomatoes	¼ teaspoon salt
½ cup cooked red lentils	¼ teaspoon black pepper
1 garlic clove, minced	4 ounces (113 g) goat cheese
1 tablespoon minced red onion	2 tablespoons shredded Parmesan cheese
4 basil leaves, minced	

1. Preheat the air fryer to 380°F (193ºC). 2. Slice the top off of each tomato. 3. Using a knife and spoon, cut and scoop out half of the flesh inside of the tomato. Place it into a medium bowl. 4. To the bowl with the tomato, add the cooked lentils, garlic, onion, basil, salt, pepper, and goat cheese. Stir until well combined. 5. Spoon the filling into the scooped-out cavity of each of the tomatoes, then top each one with ½ tablespoon of shredded Parmesan cheese. 6. Place the tomatoes in a single layer in the air fryer basket and bake for 15 minutes.

Per Serving:

calories: 249 | fat: 12g | protein: 16g | carbs: 22g | fiber: 4g | sodium: 318mg

Bulgur Salad with Cucumbers, Olives, and Dill

Prep time: 10 minutes | Cook time: 12 minutes |
Serves 4

1 cup bulgur wheat	½ teaspoon salt
2 cups water	1 large English cucumber, chopped
¼ cup olive oil	½ medium red onion, peeled and diced
2 tablespoons balsamic vinegar	
1 clove garlic, peeled and minced	¼ cup chopped salt-cured olives
½ teaspoon ground black pepper	¼ cup chopped fresh dill

1. Add bulgur and water to the Instant Pot® and stir well. Close lid, set steam release to Sealing, press the Rice button, adjust pressure to Low, and set time to 12 minutes. When the timer beeps, quick-release the pressure until the float valve drops. Open lid and fluff bulgur with a fork. Transfer to a medium bowl and set aside to cool to room temperature, about 40 minutes. 2. Stir in oil, vinegar, garlic, pepper, salt, cucumber, onion, olives, and dill, and toss well. Refrigerate for 4 hours before serving.

Per Serving:

calories: 290 | fat: 27g | protein: 2g | carbs: 11g | fiber: 2g | sodium: 352mg

Rice with Olives and Basil

Prep time: 10 minutes | Cook time: 32 minutes |
Serves 8

2 tablespoons extra-virgin olive oil	2¼ cups water
1 medium yellow onion, peeled and chopped	1 cup pitted Kalamata olives
	½ cup torn basil
2 cloves garlic, peeled and minced	1 tablespoon lemon juice
	2 teaspoons grated lemon zest
2 cups brown rice	½ teaspoon ground black pepper

1. Press the Sauté button on the Instant Pot® and heat oil. Add onion and cook until soft, about 6 minutes. Add garlic and cook until fragrant, about 30 seconds. Add rice and cook, stirring constantly, until well coated and starting to toast, about 3 minutes. Press the Cancel button. 2. Stir in water. Close lid, set steam release to Sealing, press the Manual button, and set time to 22 minutes. When the timer beeps, let pressure release naturally for 10 minutes, then quick-release the remaining pressure until the float valve drops. Open lid and fluff rice with a fork. Fold in olives, basil, lemon juice, lemon zest, and pepper. Serve warm.

Per Serving:

calories: 182 | fat: 11g | protein: 1g | carbs: 18g | fiber: 1g | sodium: 355mg

Brown Rice Pilaf with Golden Raisins

Prep time: 5 minutes |Cook time: 15 minutes|

Serves: 6

1 tablespoon extra-virgin olive oil	½ teaspoon ground cinnamon
1 cup chopped onion (about ½ medium onion)	2 cups instant brown rice
	1¾ cups 100% orange juice
½ cup shredded carrot (about 1 medium carrot)	¼ cup water
	1 cup golden raisins
1 teaspoon ground cumin	½ cup shelled pistachios
	Chopped fresh chives (optional)

1. In a medium saucepan over medium-high heat, heat the oil. Add the onion and cook for 5 minutes, stirring frequently. Add the carrot, cumin, and cinnamon, and cook for 1 minute, stirring frequently. Stir in the rice, orange juice, and water. Bring to a boil, cover, then lower the heat to medium-low. Simmer for 7 minutes, or until the rice is cooked through and the liquid is absorbed. 2. Stir in the raisins, pistachios, and chives (if using) and serve.

Per Serving:

calories: 337 | fat: 8.5g | protein: 7.4g | carbs: 71.3g | fiber: 5g | sodium: 154mg

Lemon and Garlic Rice Pilaf

Prep time: 10 minutes | Cook time: 34 minutes |

Serves 8

2 tablespoons olive oil	1 teaspoon dried thyme
1 medium yellow onion, peeled and chopped	1 teaspoon dried oregano
	¼ teaspoon salt
4 cloves garlic, peeled and minced	2 tablespoons white wine
	2 tablespoons lemon juice
1 tablespoon grated lemon zest	2 cups brown rice
½ teaspoon ground black pepper	2 cups vegetable broth

1. Press the Sauté button on the Instant Pot® and heat oil. Add onion and cook until soft, about 6 minutes. Add garlic and cook until fragrant, about 30 seconds. Add lemon zest, pepper, thyme, oregano, and salt. Cook until fragrant, about 1 minute. 2. Add wine and lemon juice and cook, stirring well, until liquid has almost evaporated, about 1 minute. Add rice and cook, stirring constantly, until coated and starting to toast, about 3 minutes. Press the Cancel button. 3. Stir in broth. Close lid, set steam release to Sealing, press the Manual button, and set time to 22 minutes. 4. When the timer beeps, let pressure release naturally for 10 minutes, then quick-release the remaining pressure until the float valve drops. Open lid and fluff rice with a fork. Serve warm.

Per Serving:

calories: 202 | fat: 5g | protein: 4g | carbs: 37g | fiber: 1g | sodium: 274mg

Sun-Dried Tomato Rice

Prep time: 10 minutes | Cook time: 30 minutes |

Serves 8

2 tablespoons extra-virgin olive oil	1 tablespoon tomato paste
	2 cups brown rice
½ medium yellow onion, peeled and chopped	2¼ cups water
	½ cup chopped fresh basil
2 cloves garlic, peeled and minced	¼ teaspoon salt
	½ teaspoon ground black pepper
1 cup chopped sun-dried tomatoes in oil, drained	

1. Press the Sauté button on the Instant Pot® and heat oil. Add onion and cook until soft, about 6 minutes. Add garlic and sun-dried tomatoes and cook until fragrant, about 30 seconds. Add tomato paste, rice, and water, and stir well. Press the Cancel button. 2. Close lid, set steam release to Sealing, press the Manual button, and set time to 22 minutes. When the timer beeps, let pressure release naturally for 10 minutes, then quick-release the remaining pressure. Open lid and fold in basil. Season with salt and pepper. Serve warm.

Per Serving:

calories: 114 | fat: 4g | protein: 2g | carbs: 18g | fiber: 2g | sodium: 112mg

Garlic Shrimp with Quinoa

Prep time: 10 minutes | Cook time: 30 minutes |

Serves 4

4 cups chicken broth	Sea salt
2 cups uncooked quinoa, rinsed	Freshly ground black pepper
5 tablespoons olive oil	1½ pounds (680 g) medium shrimp (36/40 count), peeled and deveined
½ red onion, chopped	
6 garlic cloves, minced	
1 tablespoon tomato paste	½ cup crumbled feta cheese, for garnish
1 teaspoon chili powder	

1. In a large stockpot, combine the broth and quinoa and bring to a boil over high heat. Reduce the heat to low, cover, and simmer for 20 to 25 minutes, until the quinoa is cooked. Drain the quinoa and set aside in a medium bowl. 2. Rinse and dry the pot. Pour in the olive oil and heat over medium heat. Add the onion, garlic, tomato paste, and chili powder and cook for 1 minute. Season with salt and pepper and stir to combine. Add the shrimp and cook until the shrimp are pink and just cooked through, 5 to 7 minutes. 3. Return the quinoa to the pot and stir everything together. Remove from the heat. 4. Serve topped with the feta.

Per Serving:

calories: 712 | fat: 28g | protein: 54g | carbs: 62g | fiber: 7g | sodium: 474mg

Chapter 4 Beef, Pork, and Lamb

Cheesy Low-Carb Lasagna

Prep time: 10 minutes | Cook time: 10 minutes | Serves 4

Meat Layer:
Extra-virgin olive oil
1 pound (454 g) 85% lean ground beef
1 cup prepared marinara sauce
¼ cup diced celery
¼ cup diced red onion
½ teaspoon minced garlic
Kosher salt and black pepper, to taste

Cheese Layer:
8 ounces (227 g) ricotta cheese
1 cup shredded Mozzarella cheese
½ cup grated Parmesan cheese
2 large eggs
1 teaspoon dried Italian seasoning, crushed
½ teaspoon each minced garlic, garlic powder, and black pepper

1. For the meat layer: Grease a cake pan with 1 teaspoon olive oil. 2. In a large bowl, combine the ground beef, marinara, celery, onion, garlic, salt, and pepper. Place the seasoned meat in the pan. 3. Place the pan in the air fryer basket. Set the air fryer to 375ºF (191ºC) for 10 minutes. 4. Meanwhile, for the cheese layer: In a medium bowl, combine the ricotta, half the Mozzarella, the Parmesan, lightly beaten eggs, Italian seasoning, minced garlic, garlic powder, and pepper. Stir until well blended. 5. At the end of the cooking time, spread the cheese mixture over the meat mixture. Sprinkle with the remaining ½ cup Mozzarella. Set the air fryer to 375ºF (191ºC) for 10 minutes, or until the cheese is browned and bubbling. 6. At the end of the cooking time, use a meat thermometer to ensure the meat has reached an internal temperature of 160ºF (71ºC). 7. Drain the fat and liquid from the pan. Let stand for 5 minutes before serving.

Per Serving:
calories: 555 | fat: 36g | protein: 45g | carbs: 10g | fiber: 2g | sodium: 248mg

Kofta with Vegetables in Tomato Sauce

Prep time: 15 minutes | Cook time: 6 to 8 hours | Serves 4

1 pound (454 g) raw ground beef
1 small white or yellow onion, finely diced
2 garlic cloves, minced
1 tablespoon dried parsley
2 teaspoons ground coriander

1 teaspoon ground cumin
½ teaspoon sea salt
½ teaspoon freshly ground black pepper
¼ teaspoon ground nutmeg
¼ teaspoon dried mint
¼ teaspoon paprika

1 (28 ounces/ 794 g) can no-salt-added diced tomatoes
2 or 3 zucchini, cut into 1½-inch-thick rounds

4 ounces (113 g) mushrooms
1 large red onion, chopped
1 green bell pepper, seeded and chopped

1. In large bowl, mix together the ground beef, white or yellow onion, garlic, parsley, coriander, cumin, salt, pepper, nutmeg, mint, and paprika until well combined and all of the spices and onion are well blended into the meat. Form the meat mixture into 10 to 12 oval patties. Set aside. 2. In a slow cooker, combine the tomatoes, zucchini, mushrooms, red onion, and bell pepper. Stir to mix well. 3. Place the kofta patties on top of the tomato mixture. 4. Cover the cooker and cook for 6 to 8 hours on Low heat.

Per Serving:
calories: 263 | fat: 9g | protein: 27g | carbs: 23g | fiber: 7g | sodium: 480mg

Greek Meatball Soup

Prep time: 20 minutes | Cook time: 45 minutes | Serves 5

1 pound (454 g) ground beef
⅓ cup orzo
4 large eggs
1 onion, finely chopped
2 garlic cloves, minced
2 tablespoons finely chopped

fresh Italian parsley
Sea salt
Freshly ground black pepper
½ cup all-purpose flour
5 to 6 cups chicken broth
Juice of 2 lemons

1. In a large bowl, combine the ground beef, orzo, 1 egg, the onion, garlic, and parsley and stir until well mixed. Season with salt and pepper and mix again. 2. Place the flour in a small bowl. 3. Roll the meat mixture into a ball about the size of a golf ball and dredge it in the flour to coat, shaking off any excess. Place the meatball in a stockpot and repeat with the remaining meat mixture. 4. Pour enough broth into the pot to cover the meatballs by about 1 inch. Bring the broth to a boil over high heat. Reduce the heat to low, cover, and simmer for 30 to 45 minutes, until the meatballs are cooked through. 5. While the meatballs are simmering, in a small bowl, whisk the 3 remaining eggs until frothy. Add the lemon juice and whisk well. 6. When the meatballs are cooked, while whisking continuously, slowly pour 1½ cups of the hot broth into the egg mixture. Pour the egg mixture back into the pot and mix well. Bring back to a simmer, then remove from the heat and serve.

Per Serving:
calories: 297 | fat: 9g | protein: 27g | carbs: 28g | fiber: 1g | sodium: 155mg

Italian Pot Roast

Prep time: 15 minutes | Cook time: 6 hours | Serves 8

1 (3 pounds / 1.4 kg) beef chuck roast, trimmed and halved crosswise
4 cloves garlic, halved lengthwise
1½ teaspoons coarse sea salt
1 teaspoon black pepper
1 tablespoon olive oil
1 large yellow onion, cut into 8 wedges
1¼ pounds (567 g) small white potatoes
1 (28 ounces / 794 g) can whole tomatoes in purée
1 tablespoon chopped fresh rosemary leaves (or 1 teaspoon dried and crumbled rosemary)

1. With a sharp paring knife, cut four slits in each of the beef roast halves, and stuff the slits with one-half of the garlic halves. Generously season the beef with the salt and pepper. 2. In a large skillet, heat the olive oil over medium-high heat, swirling to coat the bottom of the pan. Cook the beef until browned on all sides, about 5 minutes. 3. Combine the beef, onion, potatoes, tomatoes, rosemary, and the remaining garlic in the slow cooker. 4. Cover and cook until the meat is fork-tender, on high for about 6 hours. 5. Transfer the meat to a cutting board. Thinly slice, and discard any fat or gristle. 6. Skim the fat from the top of the sauce in the slow cooker. 7. Serve hot, dividing the beef and vegetables among the eight bowls, and generously spooning the sauce over the top.

Per Serving:

calories: 317 | fat: 12g | protein: 37g | carbs: 17g | fiber: 4g | sodium: 605mg

Pork and Cabbage Egg Roll in a Bowl

Prep time: 10 minutes | Cook time: 10 minutes | Serves 6

1 tablespoon light olive oil
1 pound (454 g) ground pork
1 medium yellow onion, peeled and chopped
1 clove garlic, peeled and minced
2 teaspoons minced fresh ginger
¼ cup low-sodium chicken broth
2 tablespoons soy sauce
2 (10-ounce/ 283-g) bags shredded coleslaw mix
1 teaspoon sesame oil
1 teaspoon garlic chili sauce

1. Press the Sauté button on the Instant Pot® and heat olive oil. Add pork and sauté until cooked through, about 8 minutes. Add onion, garlic, and ginger, and cook until fragrant, about 2 minutes. Stir in chicken broth and soy sauce. Press the Cancel button. 2. Spread coleslaw mix over pork, but do not mix. Close lid, set steam release to Sealing, press the Manual button, and set time to 0 minutes. 3. When the timer beeps, quick-release the pressure until the float valve drops and open lid. Stir in sesame oil and garlic chili sauce. Serve hot.

Per Serving:

calories: 283 | fat: 24g | protein: 12g | carbs: 5g | fiber: 2g | sodium: 507mg

Seasoned Beef Kebabs

Prep time: 15 minutes | Cook time: 10 minutes | Serves 6

2 pounds beef fillet
1½ teaspoons salt
1 teaspoon freshly ground black pepper
½ teaspoon ground allspice
½ teaspoon ground nutmeg
⅓ cup extra-virgin olive oil
1 large onion, cut into 8 quarters
1 large red bell pepper, cut into 1-inch cubes

1. Preheat a grill, grill pan, or lightly oiled skillet to high heat. 2. Cut the beef into 1-inch cubes and put them in a large bowl. 3. In a small bowl, mix together the salt, black pepper, allspice, and nutmeg. 4. Pour the olive oil over the beef and toss to coat the beef. Then evenly sprinkle the seasoning over the beef and toss to coat all pieces. 5. Skewer the beef, alternating every 1 or 2 pieces with a piece of onion or bell pepper. 6. To cook, place the skewers on the grill or skillet, and turn every 2 to 3 minutes until all sides have cooked to desired doneness, 6 minutes for medium-rare, 8 minutes for well done. Serve warm.

Per Serving:

calories: 326 | fat: 21g | protein: 32g | carbs: 4g | fiber: 1g | sodium: 714mg

Marinated Steak Tips with Mushrooms

Prep time: 30 minutes | Cook time: 10 minutes | Serves 4

1½ pounds (680 g) sirloin, trimmed and cut into 1-inch pieces
8 ounces (227 g) brown mushrooms, halved
¼ cup Worcestershire sauce
1 tablespoon Dijon mustard
1 tablespoon olive oil
1 teaspoon paprika
1 teaspoon crushed red pepper flakes
2 tablespoons chopped fresh parsley (optional)

1. Place the beef and mushrooms in a gallon-size resealable bag. In a small bowl, whisk together the Worcestershire, mustard, olive oil, paprika, and red pepper flakes. Pour the marinade into the bag and massage gently to ensure the beef and mushrooms are evenly coated. Seal the bag and refrigerate for at least 4 hours, preferably overnight. Remove from the refrigerator 30 minutes before cooking. 2. Preheat the air fryer to 400°F (204°C). 3. Drain and discard the marinade. Arrange the steak and mushrooms in the air fryer basket. Air fry for 10 minutes, pausing halfway through the baking time to shake the basket. Transfer to a serving plate and top with the parsley, if desired.

Per Serving:

calories: 383 | fat: 23g | protein: 37g | carbs: 7g | fiber: 1g | sodium: 307mg

Greek-Style Ground Beef Pita Sandwiches

Prep timePrep Time: 15 minutes | Cook Time: 10 minutes | Serves 2

For the beef

1 tablespoon olive oil

½ medium onion, minced

2 garlic cloves, minced

6 ounces (170 g) lean ground beef

1 teaspoon dried oregano

For the yogurt sauce

⅓ cup plain Greek yogurt

1 ounce (28 g) crumbled feta cheese (about 3 tablespoons)

1 tablespoon minced fresh

parsley

1 tablespoon minced scallion

1 tablespoon freshly squeezed lemon juice

Pinch salt

For the sandwiches

2 large Greek-style pitas

½ cup cherry tomatoes, halved

1 cup diced cucumber

Salt

Freshly ground black pepper

Make the beef Heat the olive oil in a sauté pan over medium high-heat. Add the onion, garlic, and ground beef and sauté for 7 minutes, breaking up the meat well. When the meat is no longer pink, drain off any fat and stir in the oregano. Turn off the heat. Make the yogurt sauce In a small bowl, combine the yogurt, feta, parsley, scallion, lemon juice, and salt. To assemble the sandwiches 1. Warm the pitas in the microwave for 20 seconds each. 2. To serve, spread some of the yogurt sauce over each warm pita. Top with the ground beef, cherry tomatoes, and diced cucumber. Season with salt and pepper. Add additional yogurt sauce if desired.

Per Serving:

calories: 541 | fat: 21g | protein: 29g | carbs: 57g | fiber: 4g | sodium: 694mg

Stewed Pork with Greens

Prep time: 10 minutes | Cook time: 1 hour 40 minutes | Serves 3

¾ teaspoon fine sea salt, divided

½ teaspoon freshly ground black pepper, divided

1¼ pounds (567g) pork shoulder, trimmed and cut into 1½-inch chunks

6 tablespoons extra virgin olive oil, divided

1 bay leaf

3 allspice berries

2 tablespoons dry red wine

1 medium onion (any variety), chopped

2 spring onions, sliced (white parts only)

1 leek, sliced (white parts only)

¼ cup chopped fresh dill

1 pound (454 g) Swiss chard, roughly chopped

3 tablespoons fresh lemon juice plus more for serving

1. Sprinkle ¼ teaspoon of the sea salt and ¼ teaspoon of the black pepper over the pork. Rub the seasonings into the meat. 2. Add 1 tablespoon of the olive oil to a heavy pan over medium-high heat.

Add the bay leaf and allspice berries, then add the meat and brown for 2–3 minutes per side. 3. Add the red wine and let it bubble, then use a wooden spatula to scrape the browned bits from the pan. Continue simmering until the liquid has evaporated, about 3 minutes, then transfer the meat and juices to a plate. Set aside. 4. Heat 4 tablespoons of the olive oil in a large pot placed over medium heat. Add the onion, spring onions, and leeks, and sauté until soft, about 5 minutes, then add the dill and sauté for 1–2 minutes more. 5. Add the meat and juices to the pot and sprinkle another ¼ teaspoon sea salt and ¼ teaspoon black pepper over the meat. Add just enough hot water to cover the meat halfway (start with less water), then cover and reduce the heat to low. Simmer for about 1 hour or until the meat is tender. 6. Remove the lid and add the chard and lemon juice. Use tongs to toss the chard and mix well. Continue simmering for about 5 minutes, then drizzle in the last tablespoon of olive oil and mix again. Cover and simmer for another 20 minutes, mixing occasionally, until the greens are wilted, then remove the pot from the heat. 7. Let stand covered for 10 minutes, then add a squeeze of lemon before serving. Allow to cool completely before covering and storing in the refrigerator for up to 2 days.

Per Serving:

calories: 565 | fat: 38g | protein: 39g | carbs: 15g | fiber: 4g | sodium: 592mg

Lebanese Ground Meat with Rice

Prep time: 10 minutes | Cook time: 35 minutes | Serves 6

3 tablespoons olive oil, divided

4 ounces (113 g) cremini (baby bella) mushrooms, sliced

½ red onion, finely chopped

2 garlic cloves, minced

1 pound (454 g) lean ground beef

¾ teaspoon ground cinnamon

¼ teaspoon ground cloves

¼ teaspoon ground nutmeg

Sea salt

Freshly ground black pepper

1½ cups basmati rice

2¾ cups chicken broth

½ cup pine nuts

½ cup coarsely chopped fresh Italian parsley

1. In a sauté pan, heat 2 tablespoons of olive oil over medium-high heat. Add the mushrooms, onion, and garlic and sauté until the mushrooms release their liquid and the onion becomes translucent, about 5 minutes. Add the ground beef, cinnamon, cloves, and nutmeg and season with salt and pepper. Reduce the heat to medium and cook, stirring often, for 5 to 7 minutes, until the meat is cooked through. Remove the beef mixture from the pan with a slotted spoon and set aside in a medium bowl. 2. In the same pan, heat the remaining 1 tablespoon of olive oil over medium-high heat. Add the rice and fry for about 5 minutes. Return the meat mixture to the pan and mix well to combine with the rice. Add the broth and bring to a boil, then reduce the heat to low, cover, and simmer for 15 minutes, or until you can fluff the rice with a fork. 3. Add the pine nuts and mix well. Garnish with the parsley and serve.

Per Serving:

calories: 422 | fat: 19g | protein: 22g | carbs: 43g | fiber: 2g | sodium: 81mg

Pork with Orzo

Prep time: 10 minutes | Cook time: 30 minutes | Serves 4

2 tablespoons olive oil

2 yellow squash, diced

2 carrots, chopped

½ red onion, chopped

2 garlic cloves, minced

1 pound (454 g) boneless pork loin chops, cut into 2-inch pieces

1 teaspoon Italian seasoning

2 cups chicken broth

1 cup dried orzo

2 cups arugula

Sea salt

Freshly ground black pepper

Grated Parmesan cheese (optional)

1. In a Dutch oven, heat the olive oil over medium-high heat. Add the squash, carrots, onion, and garlic and sauté for 5 minutes, or until softened. Add the pork and Italian seasoning and sauté, stirring occasionally, for 3 to 5 minutes, until browned. 2. Increase the heat to high, add the broth, and bring to a boil. Add the orzo, reduce the heat to medium-low, and simmer, stirring occasionally, for 8 minutes. Add the arugula and stir until wilted. Turn off the heat, cover, and let sit for 5 minutes. 3. Season with salt and pepper and serve topped with Parmesan, if desired.

Per Serving:

calories: 423 | fat: 11g | protein: 31g | carbs: 48g | fiber: 4g | sodium: 127mg

Steak Gyro Platter

Prep time: 30 minutes | Cook time: 8 to 10 minutes | Serves 4

1 pound (454 g) flank steak

1 teaspoon garlic powder

1 teaspoon ground cumin

½ teaspoon sea salt

½ teaspoon freshly ground black pepper

5 ounces (142 g) shredded romaine lettuce

½ cup crumbled feta cheese

½ cup peeled and diced cucumber

⅓ cup sliced red onion

¼ cup seeded and diced tomato

2 tablespoons pitted and sliced black olives

Tzatziki sauce, for serving

1. Pat the steak dry with paper towels. In a small bowl, combine the garlic powder, cumin, salt, and pepper. Sprinkle this mixture all over the steak, and allow the steak to rest at room temperature for 45 minutes. 2. Preheat the air fryer to 400ºF (204ºC). Place the steak in the air fryer basket and air fry for 4 minutes. Flip the steak and cook 4 to 6 minutes more, until an instant-read thermometer reads 120ºF (49ºC) at the thickest point for medium-rare (or as desired). Remove the steak from the air fryer and let it rest for 5 minutes. 3. Divide the romaine among plates. Top with the feta, cucumber, red onion, tomato, and olives.

Per Serving:

calories: 229 | fat: 10g | protein: 28g | carbs: 5g | fiber: 2g | sodium: 559mg

Smoky Herb Lamb Chops and Lemon-Rosemary Dressing

Prep time: 1 hour 35 minutes | Cook time: 10 minutes | Serves 6

4 large cloves garlic

1 cup lemon juice

⅓ cup fresh rosemary

1 cup extra-virgin olive oil

1½ teaspoons salt

1 teaspoon freshly ground black pepper

6 (1-inch-thick) lamb chops

1. In a food processor or blender, blend the garlic, lemon juice, rosemary, olive oil, salt, and black pepper for 15 seconds. Set aside. 2. Put the lamb chops in a large plastic zip-top bag or container. Cover the lamb with two-thirds of the rosemary dressing, making sure that all of the lamb chops are coated with the dressing. Let the lamb marinate in the fridge for 1 hour. 3. When you are almost ready to eat, take the lamb chops out of the fridge and let them sit on the counter-top for 20 minutes. Preheat a grill, grill pan, or lightly oiled skillet to high heat. 4. Cook the lamb chops for 3 minutes on each side. To serve, drizzle the lamb with the remaining dressing.

Per Serving:

calories: 484 | fat: 42g | protein: 24g | carbs: 5g | fiber: 1g | sodium: 655mg

Fajita Meatball Lettuce Wraps

Prep time: 10 minutes | Cook time: 10 minutes | Serves 4

1 pound (454 g) ground beef (85% lean)

½ cup salsa, plus more for serving if desired

¼ cup chopped onions

¼ cup diced green or red bell peppers

1 large egg, beaten

1 teaspoon fine sea salt

½ teaspoon chili powder

½ teaspoon ground cumin

1 clove garlic, minced

For Serving (Optional):

8 leaves Boston lettuce

Pico de gallo or salsa

Lime slices

1. Spray the air fryer basket with avocado oil. Preheat the air fryer to 350ºF (177ºC). 2. In a large bowl, mix together all the ingredients until well combined. 3. Shape the meat mixture into eight 1-inch balls. Place the meatballs in the air fryer basket, leaving a little space between them. Air fry for 10 minutes, or until cooked through and no longer pink inside and the internal temperature reaches 145ºF (63ºC). 4. Serve each meatball on a lettuce leaf, topped with pico de gallo or salsa, if desired. Serve with lime slices if desired. 5. Store leftovers in an airtight container in the fridge for 3 days or in the freezer for up to a month. Reheat in a preheated 350ºF (177ºC) air fryer for 4 minutes, or until heated through.

Per Serving:

calories: 289 | fat: 20g | protein: 24g | carbs: 4g | fiber: 1g | sodium: 815mg

Spicy Lamb Burgers with Harissa Mayo

Prep timePrep Time: 15 minutes | Cook Time: 10 minutes | Serves 2

½ small onion, minced

1 garlic clove, minced

2 teaspoons minced fresh parsley

2 teaspoons minced fresh mint

¼ teaspoon salt

Pinch freshly ground black pepper

1 teaspoon cumin

1 teaspoon smoked paprika

¼ teaspoon coriander

8 ounces (227 g) lean ground lamb

2 tablespoons olive oil mayonnaise

½ teaspoon harissa paste (more or less to taste)

2 hamburger buns or pitas, fresh greens, tomato slices (optional, for serving)

1. Preheat the grill to medium-high and oil the grill grate. Alternatively, you can cook these in a heavy pan (cast iron is best) on the stovetop. 2. In a large bowl, combine the onion, garlic, parsley, mint, salt, pepper, cumin, paprika, and coriander. Add the lamb and, using your hands, combine the meat with the spices so they are evenly distributed. Form meat mixture into 2 patties. 3. Grill the burgers for 4 minutes per side, or until the internal temperature registers 160°F (71°C) for medium. 4. If cooking on the stovetop, heat the pan to medium-high and oil the pan. Cook the burgers for 5 to 6 minutes per side, or until the internal temperature registers 160°F(71°C). 5. While the burgers are cooking, combine the mayonnaise and harissa in a small bowl. 6. Serve the burgers with the harissa mayonnaise and slices of tomato and fresh greens on a bun or pita—or skip the bun altogether.

Per Serving:

calories: 381 | fat: 20g | protein: 22g | carbs: 27g | fiber: 2g | sodium: 653mg

Kheema Meatloaf

Prep time: 10 minutes | Cook time: 15 minutes | Serves 4

1 pound (454 g) 85% lean ground beef

2 large eggs, lightly beaten

1 cup diced yellow onion

¼ cup chopped fresh cilantro

1 tablespoon minced fresh ginger

1 tablespoon minced garlic

2 teaspoons garam masala

1 teaspoon kosher salt

1 teaspoon ground turmeric

1 teaspoon cayenne pepper

½ teaspoon ground cinnamon

⅛ teaspoon ground cardamom

1. In a large bowl, gently mix the ground beef, eggs, onion, cilantro, ginger, garlic, garam masala, salt, turmeric, cayenne, cinnamon, and cardamom until thoroughly combined. 2. Place the seasoned meat in a baking pan. Place the pan in the air fryer basket. Set the air fryer to 350°F (177°C) for 15 minutes. Use a meat thermometer to ensure the meat loaf has reached an internal temperature of 160°F

/ 71°C (medium). 3. Drain the fat and liquid from the pan and let stand for 5 minutes before slicing. 4. Slice and serve hot.

Per Serving:

calories: 205 | fat: 8g | protein: 28g | carbs: 5g | fiber: 1g | sodium: 696mg

Filipino Crispy Pork Belly

Prep time: 20 minutes | Cook time: 30 minutes | Serves 4

1 pound (454 g) pork belly

3 cups water

6 garlic cloves

2 tablespoons soy sauce

1 teaspoon kosher salt

1 teaspoon black pepper

2 bay leaves

1. Cut the pork belly into three thick chunks so it will cook more evenly. 2. Place the pork, water, garlic, soy sauce, salt, pepper, and bay leaves in the inner pot of an Instant Pot or other electric pressure cooker. Seal and cook at high pressure for 15 minutes. Let the pressure release naturally for 10 minutes, then manually release the remaining pressure. (If you do not have a pressure cooker, place all the ingredients in a large saucepan. Cover and cook over low heat until a knife can be easily inserted into the skin side of pork belly, about 1 hour.) Using tongs, very carefully transfer the meat to a wire rack over a rimmed baking sheet to drain and dry for 10 minutes. 3. Cut each chunk of pork belly into two long slices. Arrange the slices in the air fryer basket. Set the air fryer to 400ºF (204ºC) for 15 minutes, or until the fat has crisped. 4. Serve immediately.

Per Serving:

calories: 619 | fat: 62g | protein: 12g | carbs: 4g | fiber: 0g | sodium: 743mg

Pork Souvlaki

Prep time: 1 hour 15 minutes | Cook time: 10 minutes | Serves 4

1 (1½ pounds / 680 g) pork loin

2 tablespoons garlic, minced

⅓ cup extra-virgin olive oil

⅓ cup lemon juice

1 tablespoon dried oregano

1 teaspoon salt

Pita bread and tzatziki, for serving (optional)

1. Cut the pork into 1-inch cubes and put them into a bowl or plastic zip-top bag. 2. In a large bowl, mix together the garlic, olive oil, lemon juice, oregano, and salt. 3. Pour the marinade over the pork and let it marinate for at least 1 hour. 4. Preheat a grill, grill pan, or lightly oiled skillet to high heat. Using wood or metal skewers, thread the pork onto the skewers. 5. Cook the skewers for 3 minutes on each side, for 12 minutes in total. 6. Serve with pita bread and tzatziki sauce, if desired.

Per Serving:

calories: 393 | fat: 25g | protein: 38g | carbs: 3g | fiber: 0g | sodium: 666mg

Lamb Stew

Prep time: 20 minutes | Cook time: 2 hours 20 minutes | Serves 6

3 carrots, peeled and sliced

2 onions, minced

2 cups white wine

½ cup flat-leaf parsley, chopped

2 garlic cloves, minced

3 bay leaves

1 teaspoon dried rosemary leaves

¼ teaspoon nutmeg

¼ teaspoon ground cloves

2 pounds (907 g) boneless lamb, cut into 1-inch pieces

¼ cup olive oil

1 package frozen artichoke hearts

Sea salt and freshly ground pepper, to taste

1. Combine the carrots, onion, white wine, parsley, garlic, bay leaves, and seasonings in a plastic bag or shallow dish. 2. Add the lamb and marinate overnight. 3. Drain the lamb, reserving the marinade, and pat dry. 4. Heat the olive oil in a large stew pot. Brown the lamb meat, turning frequently. 5. Pour the marinade into the stew pot, cover, and simmer on low for 2 hours. 6. Add the artichoke hearts and simmer an additional 20 minutes. Season with sea salt and freshly ground pepper.

Per Serving:

calories: 399 | fat: 18g | protein: 33g | carbs: 13g | fiber: 3g | sodium: 167mg

Spiced Oven-Baked Meatballs with Tomato Sauce

Prep time: 25 minutes | Cook time: 1 hour 5 minutes | Serves 4

For the Meatballs:

1 pound (454 g) ground chuck

¼ cup unseasoned breadcrumbs

2 garlic cloves, minced

1 teaspoon salt

½ teaspoon black pepper

1 teaspoon ground cumin

3 tablespoons chopped fresh parsley

1 egg, lightly beaten

3 tablespoons extra virgin olive oil

1 teaspoon tomato paste

1 teaspoon red wine vinegar

2 tablespoons dry red wine

1 teaspoon fresh lemon juice

For the sauce

3 medium tomatoes, chopped, or 1 (15 ounces / 425 g) can chopped tomatoes

1 tablespoon plus 1 teaspoon tomato paste

¼ cup extra virgin olive oil

1 teaspoon fine sea salt

¼ teaspoon black pepper

¼ teaspoon granulated sugar

1¾ cups hot water

1. Begin making the meatballs by combining all the ingredients in a large bowl. Knead the mixture for 3 minutes or until all the ingredients are well incorporated. Cover the bowl with plastic wrap and transfer the mixture to the refrigerator to rest for at least 20 minutes. 2. While the meatball mixture is resting, preheat the oven to 350°F (180°C) and begin making the sauce by placing all the ingredients except the hot water in a food processor. Process until smooth and then transfer the mixture to a small pan over medium heat. Add the hot water and mix well. Let the mixture come to a boil and then reduce the heat to low and simmer for 10 minutes. 3. Remove the meatball mixture from the refrigerator and shape it into 24 oblong meatballs. 4. Spread 3 tablespoons of the sauce into the bottom of a large baking dish and place the meatballs in a single layer on top of the sauce. Pour the remaining sauce over the top of the meatballs. 5. Bake for 45 minutes or until the meatballs are lightly brown and then turn the meatballs and bake for an additional 10 minutes. (If the sauce appears to be drying out, add another ¼ cup hot water to the baking dish.) 6. Transfer the meatballs to a serving platter. Spoon the sauce over the meatballs before serving. Store covered in the refrigerator for up to 3 days or in an airtight container in the freezer for up to 3 months.

Per Serving:

calories: 221 | fat: 16g | protein: 14g | carbs: 5g | fiber: 1g | sodium: 661mg

Moroccan Meatballs

Prep time: 10 minutes |Cook time: 20 minutes| Serves: 4

¼ cup finely chopped onion (about ⅛ onion)

¼ cup raisins, coarsely chopped

1 teaspoon ground cumin

½ teaspoon ground cinnamon

¼ teaspoon smoked paprika

1 large egg

1 pound (454 g) ground beef (93% lean) or ground lamb

⅓ cup panko bread crumbs

1 teaspoon extra-virgin olive oil

1 (28 ounces/ 794 g) can low-sodium or no-salt-added crushed tomatoes

Chopped fresh mint, feta cheese, and/or fresh orange or lemon wedges, for serving (optional)

1. In a large bowl, combine the onion, raisins, cumin, cinnamon, smoked paprika, and egg. Add the ground beef and bread crumbs and mix gently with your hands. Divide the mixture into 20 even portions, then wet your hands and roll each portion into a ball. Wash your hands. 2. In a large skillet over medium-high heat, heat the oil. Add the meatballs and cook for 8 minutes, rolling around every minute or so with tongs or a fork to brown them on most sides. (They won't be cooked through.) Transfer the meatballs to a paper towel–lined plate. Drain the fat out of the pan, and carefully wipe out the hot pan with a paper towel. 3. Return the meatballs to the pan, and pour the tomatoes over the meatballs. Cover and cook on medium-high heat until the sauce begins to bubble. Lower the heat to medium, cover partially, and cook for 7 to 8 more minutes, until the meatballs are cooked through. Garnish with fresh mint, feta cheese, and/or a squeeze of citrus, if desired, and serve.

Per Serving:

calories: 351 | fat: 18g | protein: 28g | carbs: 23g | fiber: 5g | sodium: 170mg

Beef Burger

1¼ pounds (567 g) lean ground beef	½ teaspoon cumin powder
1 tablespoon coconut aminos	¼ cup scallions, minced
1 teaspoon Dijon mustard	⅓ teaspoon sea salt flakes
A few dashes of liquid smoke	⅓ teaspoon freshly cracked
1 teaspoon shallot powder	mixed peppercorns
1 clove garlic, minced	1 teaspoon celery seeds
	1 teaspoon parsley flakes

1. Mix all of the above ingredients in a bowl; knead until everything is well incorporated. 2. Shape the mixture into four patties. Next, make a shallow dip in the center of each patty to prevent them puffing up during air frying. 3. Spritz the patties on all sides using nonstick cooking spray. Cook approximately 12 minutes at 360ºF (182ºC). 4. Check for doneness, an instant-read thermometer should read 160ºF (71ºC). Bon appétit!

Per Serving:

calories: 193 | fat: 7g | protein: 31g | carbs: 1g | fiber: 0g | sodium: 304mg

Balsamic Beef and Vegetable Stew

1 pound (454 g) beef stew meat, cut into 1" pieces	minced
2 tablespoons all-purpose flour	4 sprigs thyme
¼ teaspoon salt	2 tablespoons chopped fresh oregano
¼ teaspoon ground black pepper	2 bay leaves
2 tablespoons olive oil, divided	¼ cup balsamic vinegar
2 medium carrots, peeled and sliced	1½ cups beef broth
2 stalks celery, sliced	1 (14½ ounces / 411 g) can diced tomatoes, drained
1 medium onion, peeled and chopped	1 medium russet potato, cut into 1" pieces
8 ounces (227 g) whole crimini mushrooms, quartered	1 (6 ounces / 170 g) can large black olives, drained and quartered
3 cloves garlic, peeled and	¼ cup chopped fresh parsley

1. In a medium bowl, add beef, flour, salt, and pepper. Toss meat with seasoned flour until thoroughly coated. Set aside. 2. Press the Sauté button on the Instant Pot® and heat 1 tablespoon oil. Place half of the beef pieces in a single layer, leaving space between each piece to prevent steaming, and brown well on all sides, about 3 minutes per side. Transfer beef to a medium bowl and repeat with remaining 1 tablespoon oil and beef. 3. Add carrots, celery, and onion to the pot. Cook until tender, about 8 minutes. Add mushrooms, garlic, thyme, oregano, and bay leaves. Stir well. 4. Slowly add balsamic vinegar and beef broth, scraping bottom of pot

well to release any brown bits. Add tomatoes, potato, and browned beef along with any juices. Press the Cancel button. 5. Close lid, set steam release to Sealing, press the Stew button, and set time to 40 minutes. When the timer beeps, quick-release the pressure until the float valve drops, open lid, and stir well. Remove and discard thyme and bay leaves. Stir in olives and parsley. Serve immediately.

Per Serving:

calories: 332| fat: 17g | protein: 16g | carbs: 15g | fiber: 5g | sodium: 404mg

Mediterranean Beef Steaks

2 tablespoons coconut aminos	pepper
3 heaping tablespoons fresh chives	½ teaspoon dried basil
2 tablespoons olive oil	½ teaspoon dried rosemary
3 tablespoons dry white wine	1 teaspoon freshly ground black pepper
4 small-sized beef steaks	1 teaspoon sea salt, or more to taste
2 teaspoons smoked cayenne	

1. Firstly, coat the steaks with the cayenne pepper, black pepper, salt, basil, and rosemary. 2. Drizzle the steaks with olive oil, white wine, and coconut aminos. 3. Finally, roast in the air fryer for 20 minutes at 340ºF (171ºC). Serve garnished with fresh chives. Bon appétit!

Per Serving:

calories: 320 | fat: 17g | protein: 37g | carbs: 5g | fiber: 1g | sodium: 401mg

Pork Loin Roast

1½ pounds (680 g) boneless pork loin roast, washed	¾ teaspoon sea salt flakes
1 teaspoon mustard seeds	1 teaspoon red pepper flakes, crushed
1 teaspoon garlic powder	2 dried sprigs thyme, crushed
1 teaspoon porcini powder	2 tablespoons lime juice
1 teaspoon shallot powder	

1. Firstly, score the meat using a small knife; make sure to not cut too deep. 2. In a small-sized mixing dish, combine all seasonings in the order listed above; mix to combine well. 3. Massage the spice mix into the pork meat to evenly distribute. Drizzle with lemon juice. 4. Set the air fryer to 360ºF (182ºC). Place the pork in the air fryer basket; roast for 25 to 30 minutes. Pause the machine, check for doneness and cook for 25 minutes more.

Per Serving:

calories: 157 | fat: 5g | protein: 26g | carbs: 1g | fiber: 0g | sodium: 347mg

Chapter 5 Fish and Seafood

Steamed Clams

Prep time: 10 minutes | Cook time: 8 minutes | Serves 4

2 pounds (907 g) fresh clams, rinsed

1 tablespoon olive oil

1 small white onion, peeled and diced

1 clove garlic, peeled and quartered

½ cup Chardonnay

½ cup water

1. Place clams in the Instant Pot® steamer basket. Set aside. 2. Press the Sauté button and heat oil. Add onion and cook until tender, about 3 minutes. Add garlic and cook about 30 seconds. Pour in Chardonnay and water. Insert steamer basket with clams. Press the Cancel button. 3. Close lid, set steam release to Sealing, press the Manual button, and set time to 4 minutes. When the timer beeps, quick-release the pressure until the float valve drops. Open lid. 4. Transfer clams to four bowls and top with a generous scoop of cooking liquid.

Per Serving:

calories: 205 | fat: 6g | protein: 30g | carbs: 7g | fiber: 0g | sodium: 135mg

Southern-Style Catfish

Prep time: 10 minutes | Cook time: 12 minutes | Serves 4

4 (7 ounces / 198 g) catfish fillets

⅓ cup heavy whipping cream

1 tablespoon lemon juice

1 cup blanched finely ground

almond flour

2 teaspoons Old Bay seasoning

½ teaspoon salt

¼ teaspoon ground black pepper

1. Place catfish fillets into a large bowl with cream and pour in lemon juice. Stir to coat. 2. In a separate large bowl, mix flour and Old Bay seasoning. 3. Remove each fillet and gently shake off excess cream. Sprinkle with salt and pepper. Press each fillet gently into flour mixture on both sides to coat. 4. Place fillets into ungreased air fryer basket. Adjust the temperature to 400ºF (204ºC) and air fry for 12 minutes, turning fillets halfway through cooking. Catfish will be golden brown and have an internal temperature of at least 145ºF (63ºC) when done. Serve warm.

Per Serving:

calories: 438 | fat: 28g | protein: 41g | carbs: 7g | fiber: 4g | sodium: 387mg

Garlicky Broiled Sardines

Prep time: 5 minutes | Cook time: 3 minutes | Serves 4

4 (3¼ ounces / 92 g) cans sardines (about 16 sardines), packed in water or olive oil

2 tablespoons extra-virgin olive oil (if sardines are packed in water)

4 garlic cloves, minced

½ teaspoon red pepper flakes

½ teaspoon salt

¼ teaspoon freshly ground black pepper

1. Preheat the broiler. Line a baking dish with aluminum foil. Arrange the sardines in a single layer on the foil. 2. Combine the olive oil (if using), garlic, and red pepper flakes in a small bowl and spoon over each sardine. Season with salt and pepper. 3. Broil just until sizzling, 2 to 3 minutes. 4. To serve, place 4 sardines on each plate and top with any remaining garlic mixture that has collected in the baking dish.

Per Serving:

calories: 197 | fat: 11g | protein: 23g | carbs: 1g | fiber: 0g | sodium: 574mg

Crispy Fish Sticks

Prep time: 15 minutes | Cook time: 10 minutes | Serves 4

1 ounce (28 g) pork rinds, finely ground

¼ cup blanched finely ground almond flour

½ teaspoon Old Bay seasoning

1 tablespoon coconut oil

1 large egg

1 pound (454 g) cod fillet, cut into ¾-inch strips

1. Place ground pork rinds, almond flour, Old Bay seasoning, and coconut oil into a large bowl and mix together. In a medium bowl, whisk egg. 2. Dip each fish stick into the egg and then gently press into the flour mixture, coating as fully and evenly as possible. Place fish sticks into the air fryer basket. 3. Adjust the temperature to 400ºF (204ºC) and air fry for 10 minutes or until golden. 4. Serve immediately.

Per Serving:

calories: 223 | fat: 14g | protein: 21g | carbs: 2g | fiber: 1g | sodium: 390mg

Tilapia with Pecans

Prep time: 20 minutes | Cook time: 16 minutes | Serves 5

2 tablespoons ground flaxseeds

1 teaspoon paprika

Sea salt and white pepper, to taste

1 teaspoon garlic paste

2 tablespoons extra-virgin olive oil

½ cup pecans, ground

5 tilapia fillets, sliced into halves

1. Combine the ground flaxseeds, paprika, salt, white pepper, garlic paste, olive oil, and ground pecans in a Ziploc bag. Add the fish fillets and shake to coat well. 2. Spritz the air fryer basket with cooking spray. Cook in the preheated air fryer at 400ºF (204ºC) for 10 minutes; turn them over and cook for 6 minutes more. Work in batches. 3. Serve with lemon wedges, if desired. Enjoy!

Per Serving:

calories: 252 | fat: 17g | protein: 25g | carbs: 3g | fiber: 2g | sodium: 65mg

Oregano Tilapia Fingers

Prep time: 15 minutes | Cook time: 9 minutes | Serves 4

1 pound (454 g) tilapia fillet

½ cup coconut flour

2 eggs, beaten

½ teaspoon ground paprika

1 teaspoon dried oregano

1 teaspoon avocado oil

1. Cut the tilapia fillets into fingers and sprinkle with ground paprika and dried oregano. 2. Then dip the tilapia fingers in eggs and coat in the coconut flour. 3. Sprinkle fish fingers with avocado oil and cook in the air fryer at 370ºF (188ºC) for 9 minutes.

Per Serving:

calories: 187 | fat: 9g | protein: 26g | carbs: 2g | fiber: 1g | sodium: 92mg

Seared Scallops with Braised Dandelion Greens

Prep time: 5 minutes | Cook time: 15 minutes | Serves 4

3 tablespoons olive oil, divided

2 cloves garlic, thinly sliced

1 pound (454 g) dandelion greens

1 cup low-sodium chicken broth or water

½ teaspoon kosher salt, divided

¼ teaspoon ground black

pepper, divided

1 cup chopped fresh mint

1 cup chopped fresh flat-leaf parsley

1 pound (454 g) scallops, muscle tabs removed

Lemon wedges, for serving

1. In a large skillet over medium-high heat, warm 1 tablespoon of the oil. Cook the garlic until softened, about 2 minutes. Add the dandelion greens and broth or water and bring to a boil. Cover and cook until the greens are wilted, 2 minutes. Season with ¼ teaspoon of the salt and ⅛ teaspoon of the pepper. Cover and cook until the greens are tender, 5 to 10 minutes. Stir in the mint and parsley. 2. Meanwhile, pat the scallops dry and season with the remaining ¼ teaspoon salt and the remaining ⅛ teaspoon pepper. In a large nonstick skillet over medium heat, warm 1 tablespoon of the oil. Add the scallops in a single layer and cook without disturbing until browned, 1 to 2 minutes. Add the remaining 1 tablespoon oil to the skillet, flip the scallops, and cook until browned on the other side, 1 to 2 minutes. Serve the scallops over the braised greens and with the lemon wedges.

Per Serving:

calories: 235 | fat: 12g | protein: 18g | carbs: 17g | fiber: 5g | sodium: 850mg

Apple Cider Mussels

Prep time: 10 minutes | Cook time: 2 minutes | Serves 5

2 pounds (907 g) mussels, cleaned, peeled

1 teaspoon onion powder

1 teaspoon ground cumin

1 tablespoon avocado oil

¼ cup apple cider vinegar

1. Mix mussels with onion powder, ground cumin, avocado oil, and apple cider vinegar. 2. Put the mussels in the air fryer and cook at 395ºF (202ºC) for 2 minutes.

Per Serving:

calories: 187 | fat: 7g | protein: 22g | carbs: 7g | fiber: 0g | sodium: 521mg

Sesame-Crusted Tuna Steak

Prep time: 5 minutes | Cook time: 8 minutes | Serves 2

2 (6 ounces / 170 g) tuna steaks

1 tablespoon coconut oil, melted

½ teaspoon garlic powder

2 teaspoons white sesame seeds

2 teaspoons black sesame seeds

1. Brush each tuna steak with coconut oil and sprinkle with garlic powder. 2. In a large bowl, mix sesame seeds and then press each tuna steak into them, covering the steak as completely as possible. Place tuna steaks into the air fryer basket. 3. Adjust the temperature to 400ºF (204ºC) and air fry for 8 minutes. 4. Flip the steaks halfway through the cooking time. Steaks will be well-done at 145ºF (63ºC) internal temperature. Serve warm.

Per Serving:

calories: 281 | fat: 11g | protein: 43g | carbs: 1g | fiber: 1g | sodium: 80mg

Tomato-Stewed Calamari

Prep time: 15 minutes | Cook time: 16 minutes |
Serves 6

2 tablespoons olive oil	1 (28 ounces / 794 g) can diced
1 small carrot, peeled and	tomatoes
grated	½ cup white wine
1 stalk celery, finely diced	⅓ cup water
1 small white onion, peeled and	1 teaspoon dried parsley
diced	1 teaspoon dried basil
3 cloves garlic, peeled and	½ teaspoon salt
minced	½ teaspoon ground black
2½ pounds (1.1 kg) calamari	pepper

1. Press the Sauté button on the Instant Pot® and heat oil. Add carrot and celery, and cook until just tender, about 2 minutes. 2. Add onion and cook until tender, about 3 minutes. Stir in garlic and cook until fragrant, about 30 seconds. Press the Cancel button. 3. Add calamari, tomatoes, wine, water, parsley, basil, salt, and pepper to the Instant Pot®. Close lid, set steam release to Sealing, press the Manual button, and set time to 10 minutes. When the timer beeps, quick-release the pressure until the float valve drops and open lid. Serve immediately.

Per Serving:

calories: 394 | fat: 7g | protein: 62g | carbs: 12g | fiber: 3g | sodium: 505mg

Wild Cod Oreganata

Prep time: 10 minutes | Cook time: 20 minutes |
Serves 2

10 ounces (283 g) wild cod (1	pepper
large piece or 2 smaller ones)	1 tablespoon olive oil
⅓ cup panko bread crumbs	2 tablespoons freshly squeezed
1 tablespoon dried oregano	lemon juice
Zest of 1 lemon	2 tablespoons white wine
½ teaspoon salt	1 tablespoon minced fresh
Pinch freshly ground black	parsley

1. Preheat the oven to 350°F(180°C). Place the cod in a baking dish and pat it dry with a paper towel. 2. In a small bowl, combine the panko, oregano, lemon zest, salt, pepper, and olive oil and mix well. Pat the panko mixture onto the fish. 3. Combine the lemon juice and wine in a small bowl and pour it around the fish. 4. Bake the fish for 20 minutes, or until it flakes apart easily and reaches an internal temperature of 145°F(63°C). 5. Garnish with fresh minced parsley.

Per Serving:

calories: 203 | fat: 8g | protein: 23g | carbs: 9g | fiber: 2g | sodium: 149mg

Italian Halibut with Grapes and Olive Oil

Prep time: 15 minutes | Cook time: 20 minutes |
Serves 4

¼ cup extra-virgin olive oil	2 cups seedless green grapes
4 boneless halibut fillets, 4	A handful of fresh basil leaves,
ounces (113 g) each	roughly torn
4 cloves garlic, roughly	½ teaspoon unrefined sea salt or
chopped	salt
1 small red chile pepper, finely	Freshly ground black pepper
chopped	

1. Heat the olive oil in a large, heavy-bottomed skillet over medium-high heat. Add the halibut, followed by the garlic, chile pepper, grapes, basil, and the salt and pepper. Pour in 1¾ cups of water, turn the heat down to medium-low, cover, and cook the fish until opaque, or for 7 minutes on each side. 2. Remove the fish from the pan and place on a large serving dish. Raise the heat, cook the sauce for 30 seconds to concentrate the flavors slightly. Taste and adjust salt and pepper. Pour sauce over the fish.

Per Serving:

calories: 389 | fat: 29g | protein: 17g | carbs: 15g | fiber: 1g | sodium: 384mg

Fish Chili

Prep time: 10 minutes | Cook time: 5 to 7 hours |
Serves 6

1 (28 ounces / 794 g) can no-salt-added diced tomatoes	1 small onion, diced
1 (15 ounces / 425 g) can reduced sodium white beans, drained and rinsed	1 bell pepper, any color, seeded and diced
1 (10 ounces / 283 g) can no-salt-added diced tomatoes with green chiles	2 tablespoons chili powder
	2 teaspoons ground cumin
	1½ teaspoons paprika
1 (8 ounces / 227 g) can no-salt-added tomato sauce	1 teaspoon sea salt
	1 teaspoon dried oregano
3 garlic cloves, minced	2 pounds (907 g) fresh or frozen fish fillets of your choice, cut into 2-inch pieces

1. In a slow cooker, combine the tomatoes, beans, tomatoes with green chiles, tomato sauce, garlic, onion, bell pepper, chili powder, cumin, paprika, salt, and oregano. Stir to mix well. 2. Cover the cooker and cook for 5 to 7 hours on Low heat. 3. Stir in the fish, replace the cover on the cooker, and cook for 30 minutes on Low heat.

Per Serving:

calories: 292 | fat: 2g | protein: 41g | carbs: 27g | fiber: 9g | sodium: 611mg

Baked Swordfish with Herbs

Prep time: 10 minutes | Cook time: 20 minutes | Serves 4

Olive oil spray	¼ cup extra-virgin olive oil
1 cup fresh Italian parsley	½ teaspoon salt
¼ cup fresh thyme	4 swordfish steaks (each 5 to 7
¼ cup lemon juice	ounces / 142 to 198 g)
2 cloves garlic	

1. Preheat the oven to 450ºF (235ºC). Coat a large baking dish with olive oil spray. 2. In a food processor, pulse the parsley, thyme, lemon juice, garlic, olive oil, and salt 10 times. 3. Place the swordfish in the prepared baking dish. Spoon the parsley mixture over the steaks. 4. Put the fish in the oven to bake for 17 to 20 minutes.

Per Serving:

calories: 397 | fat: 22g | protein: 44g | carbs: 3g | fiber: 1g | sodium: 495mg

Paprika-Spiced Fish

Prep time: 5 minutes | Cook time: 10 minutes | Serves 4

4 (5 ounces / 142 g) sea bass fillets	1 tablespoon smoked paprika
½ teaspoon salt	3 tablespoons unsalted butter
	Lemon wedges

1. Season the fish on both sides with the salt. Repeat with the paprika. 2. Preheat a skillet over high heat. Melt the butter. 3. Once the butter is melted, add the fish and cook for 4 minutes on each side. 4. Once the fish is done cooking, move to a serving dish and squeeze lemon over the top.

Per Serving:

calories: 257 | fat: 34g | protein: 34g | carbs: 1g | fiber: 1g | sodium: 416mg

Italian Breaded Shrimp

Prep time: 10 minutes | Cook time: 5 minutes | Serves 4

2 large eggs	1 cup flour
2 cups seasoned Italian breadcrumbs	1 pound (454 g) large shrimp (21-25), peeled and deveined
1 teaspoon salt	Extra-virgin olive oil

1. In a small bowl, beat the eggs with 1 tablespoon water, then transfer to a shallow dish. 2. Add the breadcrumbs and salt to a separate shallow dish; mix well. 3. Place the flour into a third shallow dish. 4. Coat the shrimp in the flour, then egg, and finally the breadcrumbs. Place on a plate and repeat with all of the shrimp. 5. Preheat a skillet over high heat. Pour in enough olive oil to coat the bottom of the skillet. Cook the shrimp in the hot skillet for 2 to 3 minutes on each side. Take the shrimp out and drain on a paper towel. Serve warm.

Per Serving:

calories: 459 | fat: 6g | protein: 36g | carbs: 63g | fiber: 3g | sodium: 617mg

Whitefish with Lemon and Capers

Prep time: 5 minutes | Cook time: 20 minutes | Serves 4

4 (4 to 5 ounces / 113 to 142 g) cod fillets (or any whitefish)	butter
	2 tablespoons capers, drained
1 tablespoon extra-virgin olive oil	3 tablespoons lemon juice
	½ teaspoon freshly ground
1 teaspoon salt, divided	black pepper
4 tablespoons (½ stick) unsalted	

1. Preheat the oven to 450°F(235ºC). Put the cod in a large baking dish and drizzle with the olive oil and ½ teaspoon of salt. Bake for 15 minutes. 2. Right before the fish is done cooking, melt the butter in a small saucepan over medium heat. Add the capers, lemon juice, remaining ½ teaspoon of salt, and pepper; simmer for 30 seconds. 3. Place the fish in a serving dish once it is done baking; spoon the caper sauce over the fish and serve.

Per Serving:

calories: 255 | fat: 16g | protein: 26g | carbs: 1g | fiber: 0g | sodium: 801mg

Flounder with Tomatoes and Basil

Prep time: 10 minutes | Cook time: 20 minutes | Serves 4

1 pound (454 g) cherry tomatoes	ribbons
	½ teaspoon kosher salt
4 garlic cloves, sliced	¼ teaspoon freshly ground
2 tablespoons extra-virgin olive oil	black pepper
	4 (5 to 6 ounces / 142 to 170 g)
2 tablespoons lemon juice	flounder fillets
2 tablespoons basil, cut into	

1. Preheat the oven to 425ºF (220ºC). 2. In a baking dish, combine the tomatoes, garlic, olive oil, lemon juice, basil, salt, and black pepper; mix well. Bake for 5 minutes. 3. Remove the baking dish from the oven and arrange the flounder on top of the tomato mixture. Bake until the fish is opaque and begins to flake, about 10 to 15 minutes, depending on thickness.

Per Serving:

calories: 215 | fat: 9g | protein: 28g | carbs: 6g | fiber: 2g | sodium: 261mg

Cucumber and Salmon Salad

Prep time: 10 minutes | Cook time: 8 to 10 minutes |

Serves 2

1 pound (454 g) salmon fillet
1½ tablespoons olive oil, divided
1 tablespoon sherry vinegar
1 tablespoon capers, rinsed and drained
1 seedless cucumber, thinly

sliced
¼ Vidalia onion, thinly sliced
2 tablespoons chopped fresh parsley
Salt and freshly ground black pepper, to taste

1. Preheat the air fryer to 400°F (204°C). 2. Lightly coat the salmon with ½ tablespoon of the olive oil. Place skin-side down in the air fryer basket and air fry for 8 to 10 minutes until the fish is opaque and flakes easily with a fork. Transfer the salmon to a plate and let cool to room temperature. Remove the skin and carefully flake the fish into bite-size chunks. 3. In a small bowl, whisk the remaining 1 tablespoon olive oil and the vinegar until thoroughly combined. Add the flaked fish, capers, cucumber, onion, and parsley. Season to taste with salt and freshly ground black pepper. Toss gently to coat. Serve immediately or cover and refrigerate for up to 4 hours.

Per Serving:

calories: 399 | fat: 20g | protein: 47g | carbs: 4g | fiber: 1g | sodium: 276mg

Lemon and Herb Fish Packets

Prep time: 10 minutes | Cook time: 5 minutes |

Serves 4

1 cup water
4 (4 ounces / 113 g) halibut or other white fish fillets
½ teaspoon salt
½ teaspoon ground black pepper
1 small lemon, thinly sliced

¼ cup chopped fresh dill
¼ cup chopped fresh chives
2 tablespoons chopped fresh tarragon
2 tablespoons extra-virgin olive oil

1. Add water to the Instant Pot® and place the rack inside. 2. Season fish fillets with salt and pepper. Measure out four pieces of foil large enough to wrap around fish fillets. Lay fish fillets on foil. Top with lemon, dill, chives, and tarragon, and drizzle each with olive oil. Carefully wrap fish loosely in foil. 3. Place packets on rack. Close lid, set steam release to Sealing, press the Steam button, and set time to 5 minutes. 4. When the timer beeps, quick-release the pressure until the float valve drops. Press the Cancel button and open lid. Serve immediately.

Per Serving:

calories: 185 | fat: 9g | protein: 23g | carbs: 0g | fiber: 0g | sodium: 355mg

Seasoned Steamed Crab

Prep time: 10 minutes | Cook time: 3 minutes |

Serves 2

1 tablespoon extra-virgin olive oil
½ teaspoon Old Bay seafood seasoning
½ teaspoon smoked paprika
¼ teaspoon cayenne pepper

2 cloves garlic, peeled and minced
2 (2 pounds / 907 g) Dungeness crabs
1 cup water

1. In a medium bowl, combine oil, seafood seasoning, smoked paprika, cayenne pepper, and garlic. Mix well. Coat crabs in seasoning mixture and place in the steamer basket. 2. Add water to the Instant Pot® and place steamer basket inside. Close lid, set steam release to Sealing, press the Manual button, and set time to 3 minutes. 3. When the timer beeps, quick-release the pressure until the float valve drops. Press the Cancel button and open lid. Transfer crabs to a serving platter. Serve hot.

Per Serving:

calories: 185 | fat: 8g | protein: 25g | carbs: 1g | fiber: 0g | sodium: 434mg

Marinated Swordfish Skewers

Prep time: 30 minutes | Cook time: 6 to 8 minutes |

Serves 4

1 pound (454 g) filleted swordfish
¼ cup avocado oil
2 tablespoons freshly squeezed lemon juice
1 tablespoon minced fresh

parsley
2 teaspoons Dijon mustard
Sea salt and freshly ground black pepper, to taste
3 ounces (85 g) cherry tomatoes

1. Cut the fish into 1½-inch chunks, picking out any remaining bones. 2. In a large bowl, whisk together the oil, lemon juice, parsley, and Dijon mustard. Season to taste with salt and pepper. Add the fish and toss to coat the pieces. Cover and marinate the fish chunks in the refrigerator for 30 minutes. 3. Remove the fish from the marinade. Thread the fish and cherry tomatoes on 4 skewers, alternating as you go. 4. Set the air fryer to 400°F (204°C). Place the skewers in the air fryer basket and air fry for 3 minutes. Flip the skewers and cook for 3 to 5 minutes longer, until the fish is cooked through and an instant-read thermometer reads 140°F (60°C).

Per Serving:

calories: 291 | fat: 21g | protein: 23g | carbs: 2g | fiber: 0g | sodium: 121mg

Snapper with Shallot and Tomato

Prep time: 20 minutes | Cook time: 15 minutes | Serves 2

2 snapper fillets
1 shallot, peeled and sliced
2 garlic cloves, halved
1 bell pepper, sliced
1 small-sized serrano pepper, sliced
1 tomato, sliced

1 tablespoon olive oil
¼ teaspoon freshly ground black pepper
½ teaspoon paprika
Sea salt, to taste
2 bay leaves

1. Place two parchment sheets on a working surface. Place the fish in the center of one side of the parchment paper. 2. Top with the shallot, garlic, peppers, and tomato. Drizzle olive oil over the fish and vegetables. Season with black pepper, paprika, and salt. Add the bay leaves. 3. Fold over the other half of the parchment. Now, fold the paper around the edges tightly and create a half moon shape, sealing the fish inside. 4. Cook in the preheated air fryer at 390ºF (199ºC) for 15 minutes. Serve warm.

Per Serving:

calories: 325 | fat: 10g | protein: 47g | carbs: 11g | fiber: 2g | sodium: 146mg

Sesame-Ginger Cod

Prep time: 10 minutes | Cook time: 4 to 6 hours | Serves 4

¼ cup low-sodium soy sauce
2 tablespoons balsamic vinegar
1 tablespoon freshly squeezed lemon juice
2 teaspoons extra-virgin olive oil
1 tablespoon ground ginger
½ teaspoon sea salt

¼ teaspoon freshly ground black pepper
Nonstick cooking spray
2 pounds (907 g) fresh cod fillets
½ teaspoon sesame seeds
4 scallions, green parts only, cut into 3-inch lengths

1. In a small bowl, whisk together the soy sauce, vinegar, lemon juice, olive oil, ginger, salt, and pepper until combined. Set aside. 2. Coat a slow-cooker insert with cooking spray and place the cod in the prepared slow cooker. Pour the soy sauce mixture over the cod. 3. Cover the cooker and cook for 4 to 6 hours on Low heat. 4. Garnish with sesame seeds and scallions for serving.

Per Serving:

calories: 282 | fat: 4g | protein: 52g | carbs: 4g | fiber: 1g | sodium: 869mg

Flounder Fillets

Prep time: 10 minutes | Cook time: 5 to 8 minutes | Serves 4

1 egg white
1 tablespoon water
1 cup panko bread crumbs
2 tablespoons extra-light virgin olive oil

4 (4 ounces / 113 g) flounder fillets
Salt and pepper, to taste
Oil for misting or cooking spray

1. Preheat the air fryer to 390ºF (199ºC). 2. Beat together egg white and water in shallow dish. 3. In another shallow dish, mix panko crumbs and oil until well combined and crumbly (best done by hand). 4. Season flounder fillets with salt and pepper to taste. Dip each fillet into egg mixture and then roll in panko crumbs, pressing in crumbs so that fish is nicely coated. 5. Spray the air fryer basket with nonstick cooking spray and add fillets. Air fry at 390ºF (199ºC) for 3 minutes. 6. Spray fish fillets but do not turn. Cook 2 to 5 minutes longer or until golden brown and crispy. Using a spatula, carefully remove fish from basket and serve.

Per Serving:

calories: 252 | fat: 10g | protein: 19g | carbs: 19g | fiber: 1g | sodium: 212mg

Mustard-Crusted Fish Fillets

Prep time: 5 minutes | Cook time: 8 to 11 minutes | Serves 4

5 teaspoons low-sodium yellow mustard
1 tablespoon freshly squeezed lemon juice
4 (3½ ounces / 99 g) sole fillets
½ teaspoon dried thyme

½ teaspoon dried marjoram
⅛ teaspoon freshly ground black pepper
1 slice low-sodium whole-wheat bread, crumbled
2 teaspoons olive oil

1. In a small bowl, mix the mustard and lemon juice. Spread this evenly over the fillets. Place them in the air fryer basket. 2. In another small bowl, mix the thyme, marjoram, pepper, bread crumbs, and olive oil. Mix until combined. 3. Gently but firmly press the spice mixture onto the top of each fish fillet. 4. Bake at 320ºF (160ºC) for 8 to 11 minutes, or until the fish reaches an internal temperature of at least 145ºF (63ºC) on a meat thermometer and the topping is browned and crisp. Serve immediately.

Per Serving:

calories: 4 | fat: 5g | protein: 15g | carbs: 4g | fiber: 1g | sodium: 441mg

Lemon Pepper Shrimp

Prep time: 15 minutes | Cook time: 8 minutes |

Serves 2

Oil, for spraying

12 ounces (340 g) medium raw shrimp, peeled and deveined

3 tablespoons lemon juice

1 tablespoon olive oil

1 teaspoon lemon pepper

¼ teaspoon paprika

¼ teaspoon granulated garlic

1. Preheat the air fryer to 400ºF (204ºC). Line the air fryer basket with parchment and spray lightly with oil. 2. In a medium bowl, toss together the shrimp, lemon juice, olive oil, lemon pepper, paprika, and garlic until evenly coated. 3. Place the shrimp in the prepared basket. 4. Cook for 6 to 8 minutes, or until pink and firm. Serve immediately.

Per Serving:

calories: 211 | fat: 8g | protein: 34g | carbs: 2g | fiber: 0g | sodium: 203mg

Lemon Pesto Salmon

Prep time: 5 minutes | Cook time: 10 minutes |

Serves 2

10 ounces (283 g) salmon fillet (1 large piece or 2 smaller ones)

Salt

Freshly ground black pepper

2 tablespoons prepared pesto sauce

1 large fresh lemon, sliced

1. Oil the grill grate and heat the grill to medium-high heat. Alternatively, you can roast the salmon in a 350ºF (180ºC) oven. 2. Prepare the salmon by seasoning with salt and freshly ground black pepper, and then spread the pesto sauce on top. 3. Make a bed of fresh lemon slices about the same size as your fillet on the hot grill (or on a baking sheet if roasting), and rest the salmon on top of the lemon slices. Place any additional lemon slices on top of the salmon. 4. Grill the salmon for 6 to 10 minutes, or until it's opaque and flakes apart easily. If roasting, it will take about 20 minutes. There is no need to flip the fish over.

Per Serving:

calories: 315 | fat: 21g | protein: 29g | carbs: 1g | fiber: 0g | sodium: 176mg

Burgundy Salmon

Prep time: 10 minutes | Cook time: 26 minutes |

Serves 4

4 salmon steaks

Sea salt and freshly ground pepper, to taste

1 tablespoon olive oil

1 shallot, minced

2 cups high-quality Burgundy

wine

½ cup beef stock

2 tablespoons tomato paste

1 teaspoon fresh thyme, chopped

1. Preheat the oven to 350ºF (180ºC). 2. Season the salmon steaks with sea salt and freshly ground pepper. Wrap the salmon steaks in aluminum foil and bake for 10–13 minutes. 3. Heat the olive oil in a deep skillet on medium heat. Add the shallot and cook for 3 minutes, or until tender. 4. Add the wine, beef stock, and tomato paste, and simmer for 10 minutes, or until sauce thickens and reduces by ⅓. 5. Place the fish on a serving platter and spoon the sauce over it. Sprinkle the fish with the fresh thyme, and serve.

Per Serving:

calories: 546 | fat: 17g | protein: 66g | carbs: 6g | fiber: 0g | sodium: 303mg

Baked Halibut with Cherry Tomatoes

Prep time: 5 minutes | Cook time: 15 minutes |

Serves 4

4 (5 ounces / 142 g) pieces of boneless halibut, skin on

1 pint (2 cups) cherry tomatoes

3 tablespoons garlic, minced

½ cup lemon juice

¼ cup extra-virgin olive oil

1 teaspoon salt

1. Preheat the oven to 425°F(220ºC). 2. Put the halibut in a large baking dish; place the tomatoes around the halibut. 3. In a small bowl, combine the garlic, lemon juice, olive oil, and salt. 4. Pour the sauce over the halibut and tomatoes. Put the baking dish in the oven and bake for 15 minutes. Serve immediately.

Per Serving:

calories: 350 | fat: 18g | protein: 39g | carbs: 8g | fiber: 1g | sodium: 687mg

Chapter 6 Snacks and Appetizers

Classic Hummus with Tahini

Prep time: 5 minutes | Cook time: 0 minutes | Makes about 2 cups

2 cups drained canned chickpeas, liquid reserved	1 tablespoon ground cumin
½ cup tahini	Salt
¼ cup olive oil, plus more for garnish	Freshly ground black pepper
2 cloves garlic, peeled, or to taste	1 teaspoon paprika, for garnish
Juice of 1 lemon, plus more as needed	2 tablespoons chopped flat-leaf parsley, for garnish
	4 whole-wheat pita bread or flatbread rounds, warmed

1. In a food processor, combine the chickpeas, tahini, oil, garlic, lemon juice, and cumin. Season with salt and pepper, and process until puréed. With the food processor running, add the reserved chickpea liquid until the mixture is smooth and reaches the desired consistency. 2. Spoon the hummus into a serving bowl, drizzle with a bit of olive oil, and sprinkle with the paprika and parsley. 3. Serve immediately, with warmed pita bread or flatbread, or cover and refrigerate for up to 2 days. Bring to room temperature before serving.

Per Serving:

¼ cup: calories: 309 | fat: 16g | protein: 9g | carbs: 36g | fiber: 7g | sodium: 341mg

Buffalo Bites

Prep time: 15 minutes | Cook time: 11 to 12 minutes per batch | Makes 16 meatballs

1½ cups cooked jasmine or sushi rice	sauce
¼ teaspoon salt	2 ounces (57 g) Gruyère cheese, cut into 16 cubes
1 pound (454 g) ground chicken	1 tablespoon maple syrup
8 tablespoons buffalo wing	

1. Mix 4 tablespoons buffalo wing sauce into all the ground chicken. 2. Shape chicken into a log and divide into 16 equal portions. 3. With slightly damp hands, mold each chicken portion around a cube of cheese and shape into a firm ball. When you have shaped 8 meatballs, place them in air fryer basket. 4. Air fry at 390ºF (199ºC) for approximately 5 minutes. Shake basket, reduce temperature to 360ºF (182ºC), and cook for 5 to 6 minutes longer. 5. While the first batch is cooking, shape remaining chicken and cheese into 8 more meatballs. 6. Repeat step 4 to cook second batch of meatballs. 7. In a medium bowl, mix the remaining 4 tablespoons of buffalo wing sauce with the maple syrup. Add all the cooked meatballs and toss to coat. 8. Place meatballs back into air fryer basket and air fry at 390ºF (199ºC) for 2 to 3 minutes to set the glaze. Skewer each with a toothpick and serve.

Per Serving:

calories: 85 | fat: 4g | protein: 7g | carbs: 6g | fiber: 0g | sodium: 236mg

Spanish-Style Pan-Roasted Cod

Prep time: 15 minutes | Cook time: 25 minutes | Serves 4

4 tablespoons olive oil	Spanish olives, sliced (about ⅓ cup)
8 garlic cloves, minced	4 tablespoons finely chopped fresh parsley
½ small onion, finely chopped	4 (4-ounce / 113-g) cod fillets, about 1 inch thick
½ pound (227 g) small red or new potatoes, quartered	Salt and freshly ground black pepper (optional)
1 (14½ ounces / 411 g) can low-sodium diced tomatoes, with their juices	
16 pimiento-stuffed low-salt	

1. In a 10-inch skillet, heat 2 tablespoons of the olive oil and the garlic over medium heat. Cook, being careful not to let the garlic burn, until it becomes fragrant, 1 to 2 minutes. 2. Raise the temperature to medium-high heat, and add the onion, potatoes, tomatoes with their juices, olives, and 3 tablespoons of the parsley. Bring to a boil. Reduce the heat to maintain a simmer, cover, and cook for 15 to 18 minutes, until the potatoes are tender. Transfer the mixture from the skillet to a large bowl; keep warm. Wipe out the skillet and return it to the stovetop. 3. Heat the remaining 2 tablespoons olive oil in the skillet over medium-high heat. Season the cod with salt and pepper, if desired, and add it to the pan. Cook for 2 to 3 minutes, then carefully flip the fish and cook for 2 to 3 minutes more, until the fish flakes easily with a fork. 4. Divide the tomato mixture evenly among four plates and top each with a cod fillet. Sprinkle evenly with the remaining 1 tablespoon parsley and serve.

Per Serving:

1 cup: calories: 297 | fat: 20g | protein: 9g | carbs: 20g | fiber: 4g | sodium: 557mg

Cinnamon-Apple Chips

Prep time: 10 minutes | Cook time: 32 minutes | Serves 4

Oil, for spraying
2 Red Delicious or Honeycrisp apples

¼ teaspoon ground cinnamon, divided

1. Line the air fryer basket with parchment and spray lightly with oil. 2. Trim the uneven ends off the apples. Using a mandoline on the thinnest setting or a sharp knife, cut the apples into very thin slices. Discard the cores. 3. Place half of the apple slices in a single layer in the prepared basket and sprinkle with half of the cinnamon. 4. Place a metal air fryer trivet on top of the apples to keep them from flying around while they are cooking. 5. Air fry at 300ºF (149ºC) for 16 minutes, flipping every 5 minutes to ensure even cooking. Repeat with the remaining apple slices and cinnamon. 6. Let cool to room temperature before serving. The chips will firm up as they cool.

Per Serving:

calories: 63 | fat: 0g | protein: 0g | carbs: 15g | fiber: 3g | sodium: 1mg

Garlic-Mint Yogurt Dip

Prep time: 5 minutes | Cook time: 0 minutes | Serves 4 to 6

1 cup plain Greek yogurt
Zest and juice of 1 lemon
1 garlic clove, minced
3 tablespoons chopped fresh mint

¼ teaspoon Aleppo pepper or cayenne pepper
¼ teaspoon salt
Freshly ground black pepper (optional)

1. In a small bowl, stir together all the ingredients until well combined. Season with black pepper, if desired. Refrigerate until ready to serve.

Per Serving:

1 cup: calories: 52 | fat: 2g | protein: 2g | carbs: 7g | fiber: 0g | sodium: 139mg

Roasted Mushrooms with Garlic

Prep time: 3 minutes | Cook time: 22 to 27 minutes | Serves 4

16 garlic cloves, peeled
2 teaspoons olive oil, divided
16 button mushrooms
½ teaspoon dried marjoram

⅛ teaspoon freshly ground black pepper
1 tablespoon white wine or low-sodium vegetable broth

1. In a baking pan, mix the garlic with 1 teaspoon of olive oil.

Roast in the air fryer at 350ºF (177ºC) for 12 minutes. 2. Add the mushrooms, marjoram, and pepper. Stir to coat. Drizzle with the remaining 1 teaspoon of olive oil and the white wine. 3. Return to the air fryer and roast for 10 to 15 minutes more, or until the mushrooms and garlic cloves are tender. Serve.

Per Serving:

calories: 57 | fat: 3g | protein: 3g | carbs: 7g | fiber: 1g | sodium: 6mg

Black Bean Corn Dip

Prep time: 10 minutes | Cook time: 10 minutes | Serves 4

½ (15 ounces / 425 g) can black beans, drained and rinsed
½ (15 ounces / 425 g) can corn, drained and rinsed
¼ cup chunky salsa
2 ounces (57 g) reduced-fat cream cheese, softened

¼ cup shredded reduced-fat Cheddar cheese
½ teaspoon ground cumin
½ teaspoon paprika
Salt and freshly ground black pepper, to taste

1. Preheat the air fryer to 325ºF (163ºC). 2. In a medium bowl, mix together the black beans, corn, salsa, cream cheese, Cheddar cheese, cumin, and paprika. Season with salt and pepper and stir until well combined. 3. Spoon the mixture into a baking dish. 4. Place baking dish in the air fryer basket and bake until heated through, about 10 minutes. 5. Serve hot.

Per Serving:

calories: 119 | fat: 2g | protein: 8g | carbs: 19g | fiber: 6g | sodium: 469mg

Honey-Rosemary Almonds

Prep time: 5 minutes |Cook time: 10 minutes| Serves: 6

1 cup raw, whole, shelled almonds
1 tablespoon minced fresh rosemary

¼ teaspoon kosher or sea salt
1 tablespoon honey
Nonstick cooking spray

1. In a large skillet over medium heat, combine the almonds, rosemary, and salt. Stir frequently for 1 minute. 2. Drizzle in the honey and cook for another 3 to 4 minutes, stirring frequently, until the almonds are coated and just starting to darken around the edges. 3. Remove from the heat. Using a spatula, spread the almonds onto a pan coated with nonstick cooking spray. Cool for 10 minutes or so. Break up the almonds before serving.

Per Serving:

calories: 149 | fat: 12g | protein: 5g | carbs: 8g | fiber: 3g | sodium: 97mg

Domatosalata (Sweet-and-Spicy Tomato Sauce)

Prep time: 10 minutes | Cook time: 50 minutes |
Serves 8

2 tablespoons olive oil
1 large onion, finely chopped
2 (28 ounces / 794 g) cans no-salt added diced tomatoes, with their juices
2 tablespoons tomato paste
1½ teaspoons ground cinnamon
1 garlic clove, minced

½ teaspoon freshly ground black pepper
⅛ teaspoon cayenne pepper
½ teaspoon kosher salt, or to taste
2 tablespoons honey
2 tablespoons red wine vinegar

1. In a large, heavy skillet, heat the olive oil over medium heat. Add the onion and sauté until soft, about 8 minutes. Add the diced tomatoes and their juices, tomato paste, cinnamon, garlic, black pepper, cayenne, and salt. Cook, stirring occasionally, for 30 minutes, or until most of the liquid has evaporated. The tomato mixture should have thickened to a jam-like consistency. 2. Add the honey, reduce the heat to give a slow simmer, and cook, stirring occasionally, for 8 to 10 minutes more, until slightly syrupy. Do not let it burn. 3. Remove from the heat; stir in the vinegar. 4. Serve warm or at room temperature.

Per Serving:

1 cup: calories: 75 | fat: 4g | protein: 2g | carbs: 11g | fiber: 3g | sodium: 159mg

Greek Yogurt Deviled Eggs

Prep time: 15 minutes | Cook time: 15 minutes |
Serves 4

4 eggs
¼ cup nonfat plain Greek yogurt
1 teaspoon chopped fresh dill
⅛ teaspoon salt

⅛ teaspoon paprika
⅛ teaspoon garlic powder
Chopped fresh parsley, for garnish

1. Preheat the air fryer to 260°F(127°C). 2. Place the eggs in a single layer in the air fryer basket and cook for 15 minutes. 3. Quickly remove the eggs from the air fryer and place them into a cold water bath. Let the eggs cool in the water for 10 minutes before removing and peeling them. 4. After peeling the eggs, cut them in half. 5. Spoon the yolk into a small bowl. Add the yogurt, dill, salt, paprika, and garlic powder and mix until smooth. 6. Spoon or pipe the yolk mixture into the halved egg whites. Serve with a sprinkle of fresh parsley on top.

Per Serving:

calories: 74 | fat: 4g | protein: 7g | carbs: 2g | fiber: 0g | sodium: 152mg

Herbed Labneh Vegetable Parfaits

Prep time: 15 minutes | Cook time: 0 minutes |
Serves 2

For the Labneh:
8 ounces (227 g) plain Greek yogurt (full-fat works best)
Generous pinch salt
1 teaspoon za'atar seasoning
1 teaspoon freshly squeezed lemon juice

Pinch lemon zest
For the Parfaits:
½ cup peeled, chopped cucumber
½ cup grated carrots
½ cup cherry tomatoes, halved

Make the Labneh: 1. Line a strainer with cheesecloth and place it over a bowl. 2. Stir together the Greek yogurt and salt and place in the cheesecloth. Wrap it up and let it sit for 24 hours in the refrigerator. 3. When ready, unwrap the labneh and place it into a clean bowl. Stir in the za'atar, lemon juice, and lemon zest. Make the Parfaits: 1. Divide the cucumber between two clear glasses. 2. Top each portion of cucumber with about 3 tablespoons of labneh. 3. Divide the carrots between the glasses. 4. Top with another 3 tablespoons of the labneh. 5. Top parfaits with the cherry tomatoes.

Per Serving:

calories: 143 | fat: 7g | protein: 5g | carbs: 16g | fiber: 2g | sodium: 187mg

Cheesy Dates

Prep time: 15 minutes | Cook time: 10 minutes |
Serves 12 to 15

1 cup pecans, shells removed
1 (8 ounces / 227 g) container

mascarpone cheese
20 Medjool dates

1. Preheat the oven to 350°F(180°C). Put the pecans on a baking sheet and bake for 5 to 6 minutes, until lightly toasted and aromatic. Take the pecans out of the oven and let cool for 5 minutes. 2. Once cooled, put the pecans in a food processor fitted with a chopping blade and chop until they resemble the texture of bulgur wheat or coarse sugar. 3. Reserve ¼ cup of ground pecans in a small bowl. Pour the remaining chopped pecans into a larger bowl and add the mascarpone cheese. 4. Using a spatula, mix the cheese with the pecans until evenly combined. 5. Spoon the cheese mixture into a piping bag. 6. Using a knife, cut one side of the date lengthwise, from the stem to the bottom. Gently open and remove the pit. 7. Using the piping bag, squeeze a generous amount of the cheese mixture into the date where the pit used to be. Close up the date and repeat with the remaining dates. 8. Dip any exposed cheese from the stuffed dates into the reserved chopped pecans to cover it up. 9. Set the dates on a serving plate; serve immediately or chill in the fridge until you are ready to serve.

Per Serving:

calories: 253 | fat: 4g | protein: 2g | carbs: 31g | fiber: 4g | sodium: 7mg

Marinated Mushrooms and Pearl Onions

Prep time: 10 minutes | Cook time: 4 minutes |

Serves 10

3 pounds (1.4 kg) button mushrooms, trimmed

1 (15 ounces / 425 g) bag frozen pearl onions, thawed

3 cloves garlic, peeled and minced

1 cup vegetable broth

¼ cup balsamic vinegar

¼ cup red wine

2 tablespoons olive oil

2 sprigs fresh thyme

½ teaspoon ground black pepper

¼ teaspoon crushed red pepper flakes

1. Place all ingredients in the Instant Pot® and mix well. 2. Close lid, set steam release to Sealing, press the Manual button, and set time to 4 minutes. 3. When the timer beeps, quick-release the pressure until the float valve drops and open lid. Transfer mixture to a bowl and serve warm.

Per Serving:

calories: 90 | fat: 3g | protein: 4g | carbs: 9g | fiber: 2g | sodium: 92mg

Greek Potato Skins with Olives and Feta

Prep time: 5 minutes | Cook time: 45 minutes |

Serves 4

2 russet potatoes

3 tablespoons olive oil, divided, plus more for drizzling (optional)

1 teaspoon kosher salt, divided

¼ teaspoon black pepper

2 tablespoons fresh cilantro, chopped, plus more for serving

¼ cup Kalamata olives, diced

¼ cup crumbled feta

Chopped fresh parsley, for garnish (optional)

1. Preheat the air fryer to 380°F(193°C). 2. Using a fork, poke 2 to 3 holes in the potatoes, then coat each with about ½ tablespoon olive oil and ½ teaspoon salt. 3. Place the potatoes into the air fryer basket and bake for 30 minutes. 4. Remove the potatoes from the air fryer, and slice in half. Using a spoon, scoop out the flesh of the potatoes, leaving a ½-inch layer of potato inside the skins, and set the skins aside. 5. In a medium bowl, combine the scooped potato middles with the remaining 2 tablespoons of olive oil, ½ teaspoon of salt, black pepper, and cilantro. Mix until well combined. 6. Divide the potato filling into the now-empty potato skins, spreading it evenly over them. Top each potato with a tablespoon each of the olives and feta. 7. Place the loaded potato skins back into the air fryer and bake for 15 minutes. 8. Serve with additional chopped cilantro or parsley and a drizzle of olive oil, if desired.

Per Serving:

calories: 209 | fat: 13g | protein: 4g | carbs: 20g | fiber: 2g | sodium: 635mg

Spanish Home Fries with Spicy Tomato Sauce

Prep time: 5 minutes | Cook time: 1 hour | Serves 6

4 russet potatoes, peeled, cut into large dice

¼ cup olive oil plus 1 tablespoon, divided

½ cup crushed tomatoes

1½ teaspoons red wine

1 teaspoon hot smoked paprika

1 serrano chile, seeded and chopped

½ teaspoon salt

¼ teaspoon freshly ground black pepper

1. Preheat the oven to 425°F(220°C). 2. Toss the potatoes with ¼ cup of olive oil and spread on a large baking sheet. Season with salt and pepper and roast in the preheated oven for about 50 to 60 minutes, turning once in the middle, until the potatoes are golden brown and crisp. 3. Meanwhile, make the sauce by combining the tomatoes, the remaining 1 tablespoon olive oil, wine, paprika, chile, salt, and pepper in a food processor or blender and process until smooth. 4. Serve the potatoes hot with the sauce on the side for dipping or spooned over the top.

Per Serving:

calories: 201 | fat: 11g | protein: 3g | carbs: 25g | fiber: 4g | sodium: 243mg

Mediterranean Mini Spinach Quiche

Prep time: 15 minutes | Cook time: 25 minutes |

Serves 5

2 teaspoons extra virgin olive oil plus extra for greasing pan

3 eggs

3 ounces (85 g) crumbled feta

4 tablespoons grated Parmesan cheese, divided

¼ teaspoon freshly ground

black pepper

6 ounces (170 g) frozen spinach, thawed and chopped

1 tablespoon chopped fresh mint

1 tablespoon chopped fresh dill

1. Preheat the oven to 375°F (190°C). Liberally grease a 10-cup muffin pan with olive oil. 2. In a medium bowl, combine the eggs, feta, 3 tablespoons of the Parmesan, black pepper, and 2 teaspoons of the olive oil. Mix well. Add the spinach, mint, and dill, and mix to combine. 3. Fill each muffin cup with 1 heaping tablespoon of the batter. Sprinkle the remaining Parmesan over the quiche. 4. Bake for 25 minutes or until the egg is set and the tops are golden. Set aside to cool for 3 minutes, then remove the quiche from the pan by running a knife around the edges of each muffin cup. Transfer the quiche to a wire rack to cool completely. 5. Store in the refrigerator for up to 3 days or freeze for up to 3 months. (If freezing, individually wrap each quiche in plastic wrap and then in foil.)

Per Serving:

calories: 129 | fat: 9g | protein: 8g | carbs: 4g | fiber: 1g | sodium: 291mg

Lemon Shrimp with Garlic Olive Oil

Prep time: 5 minutes | Cook time: 6 minutes | Serves 4

1 pound (454 g) medium shrimp, cleaned and deveined
¼ cup plus 2 tablespoons olive oil, divided
Juice of ½ lemon
3 garlic cloves, minced and divided
½ teaspoon salt
¼ teaspoon red pepper flakes
Lemon wedges, for serving (optional)
Marinara sauce, for dipping (optional)

1. Preheat the air fryer to 380°F(193°C). 2. In a large bowl, combine the shrimp with 2 tablespoons of the olive oil, as well as the lemon juice, ⅓ of the minced garlic, salt, and red pepper flakes. Toss to coat the shrimp well. 3. In a small ramekin, combine the remaining ¼ cup of olive oil and the remaining minced garlic. 4. Tear off a 12-by-12-inch sheet of aluminum foil. Pour the shrimp into the center of the foil, then fold the sides up and crimp the edges so that it forms an aluminum foil bowl that is open on top. Place this packet into the air fryer basket. 5. Roast the shrimp for 4 minutes, then open the air fryer and place the ramekin with oil and garlic in the basket beside the shrimp packet. Cook for 2 more minutes. 6. Transfer the shrimp on a serving plate or platter with the ramekin of garlic olive oil on the side for dipping. You may also serve with lemon wedges and marinara sauce, if desired.

Per Serving:
calories: 283 | fat: 21g | protein: 23g | carbs: 1g | fiber: 0g | sodium: 427mg

Zucchini Feta Roulades

Prep time: 10 minutes | Cook time: 10 minutes | Serves 6

½ cup feta
1 garlic clove, minced
2 tablespoons fresh basil, minced
1 tablespoon capers, minced
⅛ teaspoon salt
⅛ teaspoon red pepper flakes
1 tablespoon lemon juice
2 medium zucchini
12 toothpicks

1. Preheat the air fryer to 360°F (182°C).(If using a grill attachment, make sure it is inside the air fryer during preheating.) 2. In a small bowl, combine the feta, garlic, basil, capers, salt, red pepper flakes, and lemon juice. 3. Slice the zucchini into ⅛-inch strips lengthwise. (Each zucchini should yield around 6 strips.) 4. Spread 1 tablespoon of the cheese filling onto each slice of zucchini, then roll it up and secure it with a toothpick through the middle. 5. Place the zucchini roulades into the air fryer basket in a single layer, making sure that they don't touch each other. 6. Bake or grill in the air fryer for 10 minutes. 7. Remove the zucchini roulades from the air fryer and gently remove the toothpicks before serving.

Per Serving:
calories: 36 | fat: 3g | protein: 2g | carbs: 1g | fiber: 0g | sodium: 200mg

Greens Chips with Curried Yogurt Sauce

Prep time: 10 minutes | Cook time: 5 to 6 minutes | Serves 4

1 cup low-fat Greek yogurt
1 tablespoon freshly squeezed lemon juice
1 tablespoon curry powder
½ bunch curly kale, stemmed, ribs removed and discarded,
leaves cut into 2- to 3-inch pieces
½ bunch chard, stemmed, ribs removed and discarded, leaves cut into 2- to 3-inch pieces
1½ teaspoons olive oil

1. In a small bowl, stir together the yogurt, lemon juice, and curry powder. Set aside. 2. In a large bowl, toss the kale and chard with the olive oil, working the oil into the leaves with your hands. This helps break up the fibers in the leaves so the chips are tender. 3. Air fry the greens in batches at 390°F (199°C) for 5 to 6 minutes, until crisp, shaking the basket once during cooking. Serve with the yogurt sauce.

Per Serving:
calories: 98 | fat: 4g | protein: 7g | carbs: 13g | fiber: 4g | sodium: 186mg

Halloumi, Watermelon, Tomato Kebabs with Basil Oil Drizzle

Prep time: 20 minutes | Cook time: 10 minutes | Serves 8

¼ cup coarsely chopped fresh basil
3 tablespoons extra-virgin olive oil
1 small clove garlic, chopped
¼ teaspoon kosher salt
¼ teaspoon ground black pepper
32 cubes watermelon (from 1 melon)
32 cherry tomatoes (about 1½ pints)
1 package (8 to 10 ounces / 227 to 283 g) Halloumi cheese, cut into 32 cubes

1. Soak 16 skewers in water. 2. In a blender or food processor, combine the basil, oil, garlic, salt, and pepper. Blend until the basil is finely chopped and the mixture is well combined. 3. Alternately thread the watermelon, tomatoes, and cheese onto the skewers. Brush with half the basil oil. Coat a grill rack or grill pan with olive oil and prepare the grill to medium-high heat. 4. Grill the kebabs, covered, until good grill marks form on the cheese, about 8 minutes, turning once. 5. Set kebabs on a platter and drizzle with the remaining basil oil.

Per Serving:
calories: 178 | fat: 15g | protein: 7g | carbs: 6g | fiber: 1g | sodium: 365mg

Tirokafteri (Spicy Feta and Yogurt Dip)

Prep time: 10 minutes | Cook time: 0 minutes |

Serves 8

1 teaspoon red wine vinegar	oil
1 small green chili, seeded and sliced	9 ounces (255 g) full-fat feta
2 teaspoons extra virgin olive	¾ cup full-fat Greek yogurt

1. Combine the vinegar, chili, and olive oil in a food processor. Blend until smooth. 2. In a small bowl, combine the feta and Greek yogurt, and use a fork to mash the ingredients until a paste is formed. Add the pepper mixture and stir until blended. 3. Cover and transfer to the refrigerator to chill for at least 1 hour before serving. Store covered in the refrigerator for up to 3 days.

Per Serving:

calories: 109 | fat: 8g | protein: 6g | carbs: 4g | fiber: 0g | sodium: 311mg

Cherry Tomato Bruschetta

Prep time: 15 minutes | Cook time: 0 minutes |

Serves 4

8 ounces (227 g) assorted cherry tomatoes, halved	¼ teaspoon kosher salt
⅓ cup fresh herbs, chopped (such as basil, parsley, tarragon, dill)	⅛ teaspoon freshly ground black pepper
1 tablespoon extra-virgin olive oil	¼ cup ricotta cheese
	4 slices whole-wheat bread, toasted

1. Combine the tomatoes, herbs, olive oil, salt, and black pepper in a medium bowl and mix gently. 2. Spread 1 tablespoon of ricotta cheese onto each slice of toast. Spoon one-quarter of the tomato mixture onto each bruschetta. If desired, garnish with more herbs.

Per Serving:

calories: 100 | fat: 1g | protein: 4g | carbs: 10g | fiber: 2g | sodium: 135mg

No-Mayo Tuna Salad Cucumber Bites

Prep time: 5 minutes | Cook time: 0 minutes | Serves 3

1 (5-ounce / 142-g) can water-packed tuna, drained	spring onion (white parts only)
⅓ cup full-fat Greek yogurt	1 tablespoon chopped fresh dill
½ teaspoon extra virgin olive oil	Pinch of coarse sea salt
1 tablespoon finely chopped	¼ teaspoon freshly ground black pepper
	1 medium cucumber, cut into

15 (¼-inch) thick slices   1 teaspoon red wine vinegar

1. In a medium bowl, combine the tuna, yogurt, olive oil, spring onion, dill, sea salt, and black pepper. Mix well. 2. Arrange the cucumber slices on a plate and sprinkle the vinegar over the slices. 3. Place 1 heaping teaspoon of the tuna salad on top of each cucumber slice 4. Serve promptly. Store the tuna salad mixture covered in the refrigerator for up to 1 day.

Per Serving:

calories: 80 | fat: 3g | protein: 11g | carbs: 4g | fiber: 1g | sodium: 131mg

Sfougato

Prep time: 10 minutes | Cook time: 8 minutes |

Serves 4

½ cup crumbled feta cheese	½ teaspoon salt
¼ cup bread crumbs	½ teaspoon ground black pepper
1 medium onion, peeled and minced	1 tablespoon dried thyme
4 tablespoons all-purpose flour	6 large eggs, beaten
2 tablespoons minced fresh mint	1 cup water

1. In a medium bowl, mix cheese, bread crumbs, onion, flour, mint, salt, pepper, and thyme. Stir in eggs. 2. Spray an 8" round baking dish with nonstick cooking spray. Pour egg mixture into dish. 3. Place rack in the Instant Pot® and add water. Fold a long piece of foil in half lengthwise. Lay foil over rack to form a sling and top with dish. Cover loosely with foil. Close lid, set steam release to Sealing, press the Manual button, and set time to 8 minutes. 4. When the timer beeps, quick-release the pressure until the float valve drops. Open lid. Let stand 5 minutes, then remove dish from pot.

Per Serving:

calories: 226 | fat: 12g | protein: 14g | carbs: 15g | fiber: 1g | sodium: 621mg

Mediterranean Trail Mix

Prep time: 5 minutes | Cook time: 0 minutes | Serves 6

1 cup roughly chopped unsalted walnuts	½ cup shelled salted pistachios
½ cup roughly chopped salted almonds	½ cup roughly chopped apricots
	½ cup roughly chopped dates
	⅓ cup dried figs, sliced in half

1. In a large zip-top bag, combine the walnuts, almonds, pistachios, apricots, dates, and figs and mix well.

Per Serving:

calories: 348 | fat: 24g | protein: 9g | carbs: 33g | fiber: 7g | sodium: 95mg

Turmeric-Spiced Crunchy Chickpeas

Prep time: 15 minutes | Cook time: 30 minutes | Serves 4

2 (15 ounces / 425 g) cans organic chickpeas, drained and rinsed

3 tablespoons extra-virgin olive oil

2 teaspoons Turkish or smoked paprika

2 teaspoons turmeric

½ teaspoon dried oregano

½ teaspoon salt

¼ teaspoon ground ginger

⅛ teaspoon ground white pepper (optional)

1. Preheat the oven to 400°F(205°C). Line a baking sheet with parchment paper and set aside. 2. Completely dry the chickpeas. Lay the chickpeas out on a baking sheet, roll them around with paper towels, and allow them to air-dry. I usually let them dry for at least 2½ hours, but can also be left to dry overnight. 3. In a medium bowl, combine the olive oil, paprika, turmeric, oregano, salt, ginger, and white pepper (if using). 4. Add the dry chickpeas to the bowl and toss to combine. 5. Put the chickpeas on the prepared baking sheet and cook for 30 minutes, or until the chickpeas turn golden brown. At 15 minutes, move the chickpeas around on the baking sheet to avoid burning. Check every 10 minutes in case the chickpeas begin to crisp up before the full cooking time has elapsed. 6. Remove from the oven and set them aside to cool.

Per Serving:
½ cup: calories: 308 | fat: 13g | protein: 11g | carbs: 40g | fiber: 11g | sodium: 292mg

Red Lentils with Sumac

Prep time: 5 minutes | Cook time: 20 minutes | Serves 6 to 8

1 cup red lentils, picked through and rinsed

1 teaspoon ground sumac

½ teaspoon salt

Pita chips, warm pita bread, or raw vegetables, for serving

1. In a medium saucepan, combine the lentils, sumac, and 2 cups water. Bring the water to a boil. Reduce the heat to maintain a simmer and cook for 15 minutes, or until the lentils are softened and most of the water has been absorbed. Stir in the salt and cook until the lentils have absorbed all the water, about 5 minutes more. 2. Serve with pita chips, warm pita bread, or as a dip for raw vegetables.

Per Serving:
1 cup: calories: 162 | fat: 1g | protein: 11g | carbs: 30g | fiber: 9g | sodium: 219mg

Taste of the Mediterranean Fat Bombs

Prep time: 15 minutes | Cook time: 0 minutes | Makes 6 fat bombs

1 cup crumbled goat cheese

4 tablespoons jarred pesto

12 pitted Kalamata olives, finely chopped

½ cup finely chopped walnuts

1 tablespoon chopped fresh rosemary

1. In a medium bowl, combine the goat cheese, pesto, and olives and mix well using a fork. Place in the refrigerator for at least 4 hours to harden. 2. Using your hands, form the mixture into 6 balls, about ¾-inch diameter. The mixture will be sticky. 3. In a small bowl, place the walnuts and rosemary and roll the goat cheese balls in the nut mixture to coat. 4. Store the fat bombs in the refrigerator for up to 1 week or in the freezer for up to 1 month.

Per Serving:
1 fat bomb: calories: 235 | fat: 22g | protein: 10g | carbs: 2g | fiber: 1g | sodium: 365mg

Red Pepper Tapenade

Prep time: 5 minutes | Cook time: 5 minutes | Serves 4

1 large red bell pepper

2 tablespoons plus 1 teaspoon olive oil, divided

½ cup Kalamata olives, pitted

and roughly chopped

1 garlic clove, minced

½ teaspoon dried oregano

1 tablespoon lemon juice

1. Preheat the air fryer to 380°F(193°C). 2. Brush the outside of a whole red pepper with 1 teaspoon olive oil and place it inside the air fryer basket. Roast for 5 minutes. 3. Meanwhile, in a medium bowl combine the remaining 2 tablespoons of olive oil with the olives, garlic, oregano, and lemon juice. 4. Remove the red pepper from the air fryer, then gently slice off the stem and remove the seeds. Roughly chop the roasted pepper into small pieces. 5. Add the red pepper to the olive mixture and stir all together until combined. 6. Serve with pita chips, crackers, or crusty bread.

Per Serving:
calories: 94 | fat: 9g | protein: 1g | carbs: 4g | fiber: 2g | sodium: 125mg

Garlic-Lemon Hummus

Prep time: 15 minutes | Cook time: 0 minutes | Serves 6

1 (15 ounces / 425 g) can chickpeas, drained and rinsed

4 to 5 tablespoons tahini (sesame seed paste)

4 tablespoons extra-virgin olive oil, divided

2 lemons, juice

1 lemon, zested, divided

1 tablespoon minced garlic

Pinch salt

1. In a food processor, combine the chickpeas, tahini, 2 tablespoons of olive oil, lemon juice, half of the lemon zest, and garlic and blend for up to 1 minute. After 30 seconds of blending, stop and scrape the sides down with a spatula, before blending for another 30 seconds. At this point, you've made hummus! Taste and add salt as desired. Feel free to add 1 teaspoon of water at a time to help thin the hummus to a better consistency. 2. Scoop the hummus into a bowl, then drizzle with the remaining 2 tablespoons of olive oil and remaining lemon zest.

Per Serving:

calories: 216 | fat: 15g | protein: 5g | carbs: 17g | fiber: 5g | sodium: 12mg

Goat Cheese and Garlic Crostini

Prep time: 3 minutes | Cook time: 5 minutes | Serves 4

1 whole wheat baguette

¼ cup olive oil

2 garlic cloves, minced

4 ounces (113 g) goat cheese

2 tablespoons fresh basil, minced

1. Preheat the air fryer to 380°F(193°C). 2. Cut the baguette into ½-inch-thick slices. 3. In a small bowl, mix together the olive oil and garlic, then brush it over one side of each slice of bread. 4. Place the olive-oil-coated bread in a single layer in the air fryer basket and bake for 5 minutes. 5. Meanwhile, in a small bowl, mix together the goat cheese and basil. 6. Remove the toast from the air fryer, then spread a thin layer of the goat cheese mixture over the top of each piece and serve.

Per Serving:

calories: 315 | fat: 24g | protein: 11g | carbs: 14g | fiber: 1g | sodium: 265mg

Chapter 7 Vegetables and Sides

Crispy Roasted Red Potatoes with Garlic, Rosemary, and Parmesan

Prep time: 10 minutes | Cook time: 55 minutes | Serves 2

12 ounces (340 g) red potatoes (3 to 4 small potatoes)
1 tablespoon olive oil
½ teaspoon garlic powder
¼ teaspoon salt

1 tablespoon grated Parmesan cheese
1 teaspoon minced fresh rosemary (from 1 sprig)

1. Preheat the oven to 425°F(220ºC) and set the rack to the bottom position. Line a baking sheet with parchment paper. (Do not use foil, as the potatoes will stick.) 2. Scrub the potatoes and dry them well. Dice into 1-inch pieces. 3. In a mixing bowl, combine the potatoes, olive oil, garlic powder, and salt. Toss well to coat. 4. Lay the potatoes on the parchment paper and roast for 10 minutes. Flip the potatoes over and return to the oven for 10 more minutes. 5. Check the potatoes to make sure they are golden brown on the top and bottom. Toss them again, turn the heat down to 350°F(180ºC), and roast for 30 minutes more. 6. When the potatoes are golden, crispy, and cooked through, sprinkle the Parmesan cheese over them and toss again. Return to the oven for 3 minutes to let the cheese melt a bit. 7. Remove from the oven and sprinkle with the fresh rosemary.

Per Serving:
calories: 193 | fat: 8g | protein: 5g | carbs: 28g | fiber: 3g | sodium: 334mg

Sweet-and-Sour Brussels Sprouts

Prep time: 10 minutes | Cook time: 20 minutes | Serves 2

¼ cup Thai sweet chili sauce
2 tablespoons black vinegar or balsamic vinegar
½ teaspoon hot sauce, such as Tabasco
8 ounces (227 g) Brussels sprouts, trimmed (large sprouts

halved)
2 small shallots, cut into ¼-inch-thick slices
Kosher salt and freshly ground black pepper, to taste
2 teaspoons lightly packed fresh cilantro leaves

1. In a large bowl, whisk together the chili sauce, vinegar, and hot sauce. Add the Brussels sprouts and shallots, season with salt and

pepper, and toss to combine. Scrape the Brussels sprouts and sauce into a cake pan. 2. Place the pan in the air fryer and roast at 375ºF (191ºC), stirring every 5 minutes, until the Brussels sprouts are tender and the sauce is reduced to a sticky glaze, about 20 minutes. 3. Remove the pan from the air fryer and transfer the Brussels sprouts to plates. Sprinkle with the cilantro and serve warm.

Per Serving:
calories: 106 | fat: 0g | protein: 5g | carbs: 21g | fiber: 7g | sodium: 498mg

Glazed Sweet Potato Bites

Prep time: 10 minutes | Cook time: 25 minutes | Serves 4

Oil, for spraying
3 medium sweet potatoes, peeled and cut into 1-inch pieces

2 tablespoons honey
1 tablespoon olive oil
2 teaspoons ground cinnamon

1. Line the air fryer basket with parchment and spray lightly with oil. 2. In a large bowl, toss together the sweet potatoes, honey, olive oil, and cinnamon until evenly coated. 3. Place the potatoes in the prepared basket. 4. Air fry at 400ºF (204ºC) for 20 to 25 minutes, or until crispy and easily pierced with a fork.

Per Serving:
calories: 149 | fat: 3g | protein: 2g | carbs: 29g | fiber: 4g | sodium: 54mg

Roasted Fennel with Za'atar

Prep time: 10 minutes | Cook time: 30 minutes | Serves 4

4 fennel bulbs, quartered
1 tablespoon olive oil

1 tablespoon za'atar seasoning
¼ teaspoon salt

1. Preheat the oven to 425ºF (220ºC). 2. In a large bowl, toss the fennel bulbs with the olive oil, za'atar, and salt. Spread them on a large baking sheet and roast for 25 to 30 minutes, tossing once after 15 minutes, until softened and caramelized.

Per Serving:
calories: 109 | fat: 3g | protein: 3g | carbs: 18g | fiber: 7g | sodium: 422mg

Spiced Honey-Walnut Carrots

Prep time: 5 minutes | Cook time: 12 minutes | Serves 6

1 pound (454 g) baby carrots

2 tablespoons olive oil

¼ cup raw honey

¼ teaspoon ground cinnamon

¼ cup black walnuts, chopped

1. Preheat the air fryer to 360°F(182°C). 2. In a large bowl, toss the baby carrots with olive oil, honey, and cinnamon until well coated. 3. Pour into the air fryer and roast for 6 minutes. Shake the basket, sprinkle the walnuts on top, and roast for 6 minutes more. 4. Remove the carrots from the air fryer and serve.

Per Serving:

calories: 142 | fat: 8g | protein: 2g | carbs: 18g | fiber: 3g | sodium: 60mg

Grilled Vegetables

Prep time: 15 minutes | Cook time: 8 minutes | Serves 4

4 carrots, peeled and cut in half

2 onions, quartered

1 zucchini, cut into ½-inch rounds

1 red bell pepper, seeded and

cut into cubes

¼ cup olive oil

Sea salt and freshly ground pepper, to taste

Balsamic vinegar

1. Heat the grill to medium-high. 2. Brush the vegetables lightly with olive oil, and season with sea salt and freshly ground pepper. 3. Place the carrots and onions on the grill first because they take the longest. Cook the vegetables for 3–4 minutes on each side. 4. Transfer to a serving dish, and drizzle with olive oil and balsamic vinegar.

Per Serving:

calories: 209 | fat: 14g | protein: 3g | carbs: 20g | fiber: 6g | sodium: 92mg

Caramelized Root Vegetables

Prep time: 20 minutes | Cook time: 40 minutes | Serves 6

2 medium carrots, peeled and cut into chunks

2 medium red or gold beets, cut into chunks

2 turnips, peeled and cut into chunks

2 tablespoons olive oil

1 teaspoon cumin

1 teaspoon sweet paprika

Sea salt and freshly ground pepper, to taste

Juice of 1 lemon

1 small bunch flat-leaf parsley, chopped

1. Preheat oven to 400°F (205°C). 2. Toss the vegetables with the olive oil and seasonings. 3. Lay in a single layer on a sheet pan, cover with lemon juice, and roast for 30–40 minutes, until veggies are slightly browned and crisp. 4. Serve warm, topped with the chopped parsley.

Per Serving:

calories: 79 | fat: 5g | protein: 1g | carbs: 9g | fiber: 3g | sodium: 69mg

Savory Butternut Squash and Apples

Prep time: 20 minutes | Cook time: 4 hours | Serves 10

1 (3-pound / 1.4-kg) butternut squash, peeled, seeded, and cubed

4 cooking apples (granny smith or honeycrisp work well), peeled, cored, and chopped

¾ cup dried currants

½ sweet yellow onion such as vidalia, sliced thin

1 tablespoon ground cinnamon

1½ teaspoons ground nutmeg

1. Combine the squash, apples, currants, and onion in the slow cooker. Sprinkle with the cinnamon and nutmeg. 2. Cook on high for 4 hours, or until the squash is tender and cooked through. Stir occasionally while cooking.

Per Serving:

calories: 114 | fat: 0g | protein: 2g | carbs: 28g | fiber: 6g | sodium: 8mg

Fried Zucchini Salad

Prep time: 10 minutes | Cook time: 5 to 7 minutes | Serves 4

2 medium zucchini, thinly sliced

5 tablespoons olive oil, divided

¼ cup chopped fresh parsley

2 tablespoons chopped fresh mint

Zest and juice of ½ lemon

1 clove garlic, minced

¼ cup crumbled feta cheese

Freshly ground black pepper, to taste

1. Preheat the air fryer to 400°F (204°C). 2. In a large bowl, toss the zucchini slices with 1 tablespoon of the olive oil. 3. Working in batches if necessary, arrange the zucchini slices in an even layer in the air fryer basket. Pausing halfway through the cooking time to shake the basket, air fry for 5 to 7 minutes until soft and lightly browned on each side. 4. Meanwhile, in a small bowl, combine the remaining 4 tablespoons olive oil, parsley, mint, lemon zest, lemon juice, and garlic. 5. Arrange the zucchini on a plate and drizzle with the dressing. Sprinkle the feta and black pepper on top. Serve warm or at room temperature.

Per Serving:

calories: 194 | fat: 19g | protein: 3g | carbs: 4g | fiber: 1g | sodium: 96mg

Roasted Brussels Sprouts with Delicata Squash and Balsamic Glaze

Prep time: 10 minutes | Cook time: 30 minutes |
Serves 2

½ pound (227 g) Brussels sprouts, ends trimmed and outer leaves removed

1 medium delicata squash, halved lengthwise, seeded, and cut into 1-inch pieces

1 cup fresh cranberries

2 teaspoons olive oil

Salt

Freshly ground black pepper

½ cup balsamic vinegar

2 tablespoons roasted pumpkin seeds

2 tablespoons fresh pomegranate arils (seeds)

1. Preheat oven to 400°F (205ºC) and set the rack to the middle position. Line a sheet pan with parchment paper. 2. Combine the Brussels sprouts, squash, and cranberries in a large bowl. Drizzle with olive oil, and season liberally with salt and pepper. Toss well to coat and arrange in a single layer on the sheet pan. 3. Roast for 30 minutes, turning vegetables halfway through, or until Brussels sprouts turn brown and crisp in spots and squash has golden-brown spots. 4. While vegetables are roasting, prepare the balsamic glaze by simmering the vinegar for 10 to 12 minutes, or until mixture has reduced to about ¼ cup and turns a syrupy consistency. 5. Remove the vegetables from the oven, drizzle with balsamic syrup, and sprinkle with pumpkin seeds and pomegranate arils before serving.

Per Serving:

calories: 201 | fat: 7g | protein: 6g | carbs: 21g | fiber: 8g | sodium: 34mg

Grits Casserole

Prep time: 5 minutes | Cook time: 28 to 30 minutes |
Serves 4

10 fresh asparagus spears, cut into 1-inch pieces

2 cups cooked grits, cooled to room temperature

1 egg, beaten

2 teaspoons Worcestershire

sauce

½ teaspoon garlic powder

¼ teaspoon salt

2 slices provolone cheese (about 1½ ounces / 43 g)

Oil for misting or cooking spray

1. Mist asparagus spears with oil and air fry at 390ºF (199°C) for 5 minutes, until crisp-tender. 2. In a medium bowl, mix together the grits, egg, Worcestershire, garlic powder, and salt. 3. Spoon half of grits mixture into a baking pan and top with asparagus. 4. Tear cheese slices into pieces and layer evenly on top of asparagus. 5. Top with remaining grits. 6. Bake at 360ºF (182ºC) for 23 to 25 minutes. The casserole will rise a little as it cooks. When done, the top will have browned lightly with just a hint of crispiness.

Per Serving:

calories: 161 | fat: 6g | protein: 8g | carbs: 20g | fiber: 2g | sodium: 704mg

Easy Greek Briami (Ratatouille)

Prep time: 15 minutes | Cook time: 40 minutes |
Serves 6

2 russet potatoes, cubed

½ cup Roma tomatoes, cubed

1 eggplant, cubed

1 zucchini, cubed

1 red onion, chopped

1 red bell pepper, chopped

2 garlic cloves, minced

1 teaspoon dried mint

1 teaspoon dried parsley

1 teaspoon dried oregano

½ teaspoon salt

½ teaspoon black pepper

¼ teaspoon red pepper flakes

⅓ cup olive oil

1 (8 ounces / 227 g) can tomato paste

¼ cup vegetable broth

¼ cup water

1. Preheat the air fryer to 320°F(160ºC). 2. In a large bowl, combine the potatoes, tomatoes, eggplant, zucchini, onion, bell pepper, garlic, mint, parsley, oregano, salt, black pepper, and red pepper flakes. 3. In a small bowl, mix together the olive oil, tomato paste, broth, and water. 4. Pour the oil-and-tomato-paste mixture over the vegetables and toss until everything is coated. 5. Pour the coated vegetables into the air fryer basket in an even layer and roast for 20 minutes. After 20 minutes, stir well and spread out again. Roast for an additional 10 minutes, then repeat the process and cook for another 10 minutes.

Per Serving:

calories: 239 | fat: 13g | protein: 5g | carbs: 31g | fiber: 7g | sodium: 250mg

Crispy Garlic Oven Potatoes

Prep time: 30 minutes | Cook time: 30 minutes |
Serves 2

10 ounces (283 g) golden mini potatoes, halved

4 tablespoons extra-virgin olive oil

2 teaspoons dried, minced garlic

1 teaspoon onion salt

½ teaspoon paprika

¼ teaspoon freshly ground black pepper

¼ teaspoon red pepper flakes

¼ teaspoon dried dill

1. Preheat the oven to 400°F(205ºC). 2. Soak the potatoes and put in a bowl of ice water for 30 minutes. Change the water if you return and the water is milky. 3. Rinse and dry the potatoes, then put them on a baking sheet. 4. Drizzle the potatoes with oil and sprinkle with the garlic, onion salt, paprika, pepper, red pepper flakes, and dill. Using tongs or your hands, toss well to coat. 5. Lower the heat to 375°F(190ºC), add potatoes to the oven, and bake for 20 minutes. 6. At 20 minutes, check and flip potatoes. Bake for another 10 minutes, or until the potatoes are fork-tender.

Per Serving:

½ cup: calories: 344 | fat: 28g | protein: 3g | carbs: 24g | fiber: 4g | sodium: 723mg

Corn on the Cob

Prep time: 5 minutes | Cook time: 12 to 15 minutes | Serves 4

2 large ears fresh corn
Olive oil for misting

Salt, to taste (optional)

1. Shuck corn, remove silks, and wash. 2. Cut or break each ear in half crosswise. 3. Spray corn with olive oil. 4. Air fry at 390°F (199°C) for 12 to 15 minutes or until browned as much as you like. 5. Serve plain or with coarsely ground salt.

Per Serving:

calories: 67 | fat: 1g | protein: 2g | carbs: 14g | fiber: 2g | sodium: 156mg

Roasted Grape Tomatoes and Asparagus

Prep time: 5 minutes | Cook time: 12 minutes | Serves 6

2 cups grape tomatoes
1 bunch asparagus, trimmed
2 tablespoons olive oil

3 garlic cloves, minced
½ teaspoon kosher salt

1. Preheat the air fryer to 380°F(193°C). 2. In a large bowl, combine all of the ingredients, tossing until the vegetables are well coated with oil. 3. Pour the vegetable mixture into the air fryer basket and spread into a single layer, then roast for 12 minutes.

Per Serving:

calories: 56 | fat: 5g | protein: 1g | carbs: 3g | fiber: 1g | sodium: 197mg

Green Beans with Tomatoes and Potatoes

Prep time: 15 minutes | Cook time: 5 minutes | Serves 8

1 pound (454 g) small new potatoes
1 cup water
1 teaspoon salt
2 pounds (907 g) fresh green beans, trimmed
2 medium tomatoes, seeded and diced

2 tablespoons olive oil
1 tablespoon red wine vinegar
1 clove garlic, peeled and minced
½ teaspoon dry mustard powder
¼ teaspoon smoked paprika
¼ teaspoon ground black pepper

1. Place potatoes in a steamer basket. Place the rack in the Instant Pot®, add water, and then top with the steamer basket. Close lid, set steam release to Sealing, press the Manual button, and set time to 4 minutes. When the timer beeps, quick-release the pressure until the float valve drops. Press the Cancel button and open lid. 2. Add salt, green beans, and tomatoes to the Instant Pot®. Close lid, set steam release to Sealing, press the Manual button, and set time to 1 minute. When the timer beeps, quick-release the pressure until the float valve drops, press the Cancel button, and open lid. Transfer mixture to a serving platter or large bowl. 3. In a small bowl, whisk oil, vinegar, garlic, mustard, paprika, and pepper. Pour dressing over vegetables and gently toss to coat. Serve hot.

Per Serving:

calories: 112 | fat: 4g | protein: 2g | carbs: 20g | fiber: 5g | sodium: 368mg

Garlic Zucchini and Red Peppers

Prep time: 5 minutes | Cook time: 15 minutes | Serves 6

2 medium zucchini, cubed
1 red bell pepper, diced
2 garlic cloves, sliced

2 tablespoons olive oil
½ teaspoon salt

1. Preheat the air fryer to 380°F(193°C). 2. In a large bowl, mix together the zucchini, bell pepper, and garlic with the olive oil and salt. 3. Pour the mixture into the air fryer basket, and roast for 7 minutes. Shake or stir, then roast for 7 to 8 minutes more.

Per Serving:

calories: 59 | fat: 5g | protein: 1g | carbs: 4g | fiber: 1g | sodium: 200mg

Mushrooms with Goat Cheese

Prep time: 10 minutes | Cook time: 10 minutes | Serves 4

3 tablespoons vegetable oil
1 pound (454 g) mixed mushrooms, trimmed and sliced
1 clove garlic, minced
¼ teaspoon dried thyme

½ teaspoon black pepper
4 ounces (113 g) goat cheese, diced
2 teaspoons chopped fresh thyme leaves (optional)

1. In a baking pan, combine the oil, mushrooms, garlic, dried thyme, and pepper. Stir in the goat cheese. Place the pan in the air fryer basket. Set the air fryer to 400°F (204°C) for 10 minutes, stirring halfway through the cooking time. 2. Sprinkle with fresh thyme, if desired.

Per Serving:

calories: 218 | fat: 19g | protein: 10g | carbs: 4g | fiber: 1g | sodium: 124mg

Sesame-Ginger Broccoli

Prep time: 10 minutes | Cook time: 15 minutes | Serves 4

3 tablespoons toasted sesame oil	½ teaspoon kosher salt
2 teaspoons sesame seeds	½ teaspoon black pepper
1 tablespoon chili-garlic sauce	1 (16 ounces / 454 g) package frozen broccoli florets (do not thaw)
2 teaspoons minced fresh ginger	

1. In a large bowl, combine the sesame oil, sesame seeds, chili-garlic sauce, ginger, salt, and pepper. Stir until well combined. Add the broccoli and toss until well coated. 2. Arrange the broccoli in the air fryer basket. Set the air fryer to 325ºF (163ºC) for 15 minutes, or until the broccoli is crisp, tender, and the edges are lightly browned, gently tossing halfway through the cooking time.

Per Serving:

calories: 143 | fat: 11g | protein: 4g | carbs: 9g | fiber: 4g | sodium: 385mg

Rosemary New Potatoes

Prep time: 10 minutes | Cook time: 5 to 6 minutes | Serves 4

3 large red potatoes (enough to make 3 cups sliced)	⅛ teaspoon salt
¼ teaspoon ground rosemary	⅛ teaspoon ground black pepper
¼ teaspoon ground thyme	2 teaspoons extra-light olive oil

1. Preheat the air fryer to 330ºF (166ºC). 2. Place potatoes in large bowl and sprinkle with rosemary, thyme, salt, and pepper. 3. Stir with a spoon to distribute seasonings evenly. 4. Add oil to potatoes and stir again to coat well. 5. Air fry at 330ºF (166ºC) for 4 minutes. Stir and break apart any that have stuck together. 6. Cook an additional 1 to 2 minutes or until fork-tender.

Per Serving:

calories: 214 | fat: 3g | protein: 5g | carbs: 44g | fiber: 5g | sodium: 127mg

Roasted Garlic

Prep time: 5 minutes | Cook time: 20 minutes | Makes 12 cloves

1 medium head garlic	2 teaspoons avocado oil

1. Remove any hanging excess peel from the garlic but leave the cloves covered. Cut off ¼ of the head of garlic, exposing the tips of the cloves. 2. Drizzle with avocado oil. Place the garlic head into a small sheet of aluminum foil, completely enclosing it. Place it into the air fryer basket. 3. Adjust the temperature to 400ºF (204ºC) and air fry for 20 minutes. If your garlic head is a bit smaller, check it after 15 minutes. 4. When done, garlic should be golden brown and very soft. 5. To serve, cloves should pop out and easily be spread or sliced. Store in an airtight container in the refrigerator up to 5 days. You may also freeze individual cloves on a baking sheet, then store together in a freezer-safe storage bag once frozen.

Per Serving:

calories: 8 | fat: 1g | protein: 0g | carbs: 0g | fiber: 0g | sodium: 0mg

Swiss Chard with White Beans and Bell Peppers

Prep time: 15 minutes | Cook time: 15 minutes | Serves 4

2 tablespoons olive oil	tough stems removed, cut into bite-size pieces
1 medium onion, chopped	
1 bell pepper, diced	2 cups white beans, cooked
2 cloves garlic, minced	Sea salt and freshly ground pepper, to taste
1 large bunch of Swiss chard,	

1. Heat the oil in a large skillet over medium-high heat. Add the onion and pepper and cook for 5 minutes until soft. 2. Add the garlic, stir, and add the Swiss chard. Cook for 10 minutes until greens are tender. 3. Add the beans, stir until heated through, and season with sea salt and freshly ground pepper. 4. Serve immediately.

Per Serving:

calories: 212 | fat: 7g | protein: 10g | carbs: 28g | fiber: 7g | sodium: 66mg

Corn Croquettes

Prep time: 10 minutes | Cook time: 12 to 14 minutes | Serves 4

½ cup leftover mashed potatoes	pepper
2 cups corn kernels (if frozen, thawed, and well drained)	¼ teaspoon salt
¼ teaspoon onion powder	½ cup panko bread crumbs
⅛ teaspoon ground black	Oil for misting or cooking spray

1. Place the potatoes and half the corn in food processor and pulse until corn is well chopped. 2. Transfer mixture to large bowl and stir in remaining corn, onion powder, pepper and salt. 3. Shape mixture into 16 balls. 4. Roll balls in panko crumbs, mist with oil or cooking spray, and place in air fryer basket. 5. Air fry at 360ºF (182ºC) for 12 to 14 minutes, until golden brown and crispy.

Per Serving:

calories: 149 | fat: 1g | protein: 5g | carbs: 33g | fiber: 3g | sodium: 250mg

Garlicky Sautéed Zucchini with Mint

Prep time: 5 minutes | Cook time: 10 minutes |
Serves 4

3 large green zucchini

3 tablespoons extra-virgin olive oil

1 large onion, chopped

3 cloves garlic, minced

1 teaspoon salt

1 teaspoon dried mint

1. Cut the zucchini into ½-inch cubes. 2. In a large skillet over medium heat, cook the olive oil, onions, and garlic for 3 minutes, stirring constantly. 3. Add the zucchini and salt to the skillet and toss to combine with the onions and garlic, cooking for 5 minutes. 4. Add the mint to the skillet, tossing to combine. Cook for another 2 minutes. Serve warm.

Per Serving:
calories: 147 | fat: 11g | protein: 4g | carbs: 12g | fiber: 3g | sodium: 607mg

Citrus-Roasted Broccoli Florets

Prep time: 5 minutes | Cook time: 12 minutes |
Serves 6

4 cups broccoli florets (approximately 1 large head)

2 tablespoons olive oil

½ teaspoon salt

½ cup orange juice

1 tablespoon raw honey

Orange wedges, for serving (optional)

1. Preheat the air fryer to 360°F(182ºC). 2. In a large bowl, combine the broccoli, olive oil, salt, orange juice, and honey. Toss the broccoli in the liquid until well coated. 3. Pour the broccoli mixture into the air fryer basket and roast for 6 minutes. Stir and roast for 6 minutes more. 4. Serve alone or with orange wedges for additional citrus flavor, if desired.

Per Serving:
calories: 73 | fat: 5g | protein: 2g | carbs: 8g | fiber: 0g | sodium: 207mg

Vibrant Green Beans

Prep time: 10 minutes | Cook time: 15 minutes |
Serves 6

2 tablespoons olive oil

2 leeks, white parts only, sliced

Sea salt and freshly ground pepper, to taste

1 pound (454 g) fresh green

string beans, trimmed

1 tablespoon Italian seasoning

2 tablespoons white wine

Zest of 1 lemon

1. Heat the olive oil over medium heat in a large skillet. 2. Add leeks and cook, stirring often, until they start to brown and become lightly caramelized. 3. Season with sea salt and freshly ground pepper. 4. Add green beans and Italian seasoning, cooking for a few minutes until beans are tender but still crisp to the bite. 5. Add the wine and continue cooking until beans are done to your liking and leeks are crispy and browned. 6. Sprinkle with lemon zest before serving.

Per Serving:
calories: 87 | fat: 5g | protein: 2g | carbs: 11g | fiber: 3g | sodium: 114mg

Tahini-Lemon Kale

Prep time: 5 minutes | Cook time: 15 minutes |
Serves 2 to 4

¼ cup tahini

¼ cup fresh lemon juice

2 tablespoons olive oil

1 teaspoon sesame seeds

½ teaspoon garlic powder

¼ teaspoon cayenne pepper

4 cups packed torn kale leaves (stems and ribs removed and leaves torn into palm-size pieces; about 4 ounces / 113 g)

Kosher salt and freshly ground black pepper, to taste

1. In a large bowl, whisk together the tahini, lemon juice, olive oil, sesame seeds, garlic powder, and cayenne until smooth. Add the kale leaves, season with salt and black pepper, and toss in the dressing until completely coated. Transfer the kale leaves to a cake pan. 2. Place the pan in the air fryer and roast at 350ºF (177ºC), stirring every 5 minutes, until the kale is wilted and the top is lightly browned, about 15 minutes. Remove the pan from the air fryer and serve warm.

Per Serving:
calories: 221 | fat: 21g | protein: 5g | carbs: 8g | fiber: 3g | sodium: 32mg

Parmesan-Rosemary Radishes

Prep time: 5 minutes | Cook time: 15 to 20 minutes |
Serves 4

1 bunch radishes, stemmed, trimmed, and quartered

1 tablespoon avocado oil

2 tablespoons finely grated fresh Parmesan cheese

1 tablespoon chopped fresh rosemary

Sea salt and freshly ground black pepper, to taste

1. Place the radishes in a medium bowl and toss them with the avocado oil, Parmesan cheese, rosemary, salt, and pepper. 2. Set the air fryer to 375ºF (191ºC). Arrange the radishes in a single layer in the air fryer basket. Roast for 15 to 20 minutes, until golden brown and tender. Let cool for 5 minutes before serving.

Per Serving:
calories: 58 | fat: 4g | protein: 1g | carbs: 4g | fiber: 2g | sodium: 63mg

Dill-and-Garlic Beets

Prep time: 10 minutes | Cook time: 30 minutes | Serves 4

4 beets, cleaned, peeled, and sliced	dill
1 garlic clove, minced	¼ teaspoon salt
2 tablespoons chopped fresh	¼ teaspoon black pepper
	3 tablespoons olive oil

1. Preheat the air fryer to 380°F(193ºC). 2. In a large bowl, mix together all of the ingredients so the beets are well coated with the oil. 3. Pour the beet mixture into the air fryer basket, and roast for 15 minutes before stirring, then continue roasting for 15 minutes more.

Per Serving:

calories: 136 | fat: 2g | protein: 2g | carbs: 10g | fiber: 3g | sodium: 210mg

Brown Rice and Vegetable Pilaf

Prep time: 20 minutes | Cook time: 5 hours | Makes 9 (¾-cup) servings

1 onion, minced	½ teaspoon salt
1 cup sliced cremini mushrooms	½ teaspoon dried marjoram leaves
2 carrots, sliced	
2 garlic cloves, minced	⅛ teaspoon freshly ground black pepper
1½ cups long-grain brown rice	
2½ cups vegetable broth	⅓ cup grated Parmesan cheese

1. In the slow cooker, combine the onion, mushrooms, carrots, garlic, and rice. 2. Add the broth, salt, marjoram, and pepper, and stir. 3. Cover and cook on low for 5 hours, or until the rice is tender and the liquid is absorbed. 4. Stir in the cheese and serve.

Per Serving:

calories: 68 | fat: 1g | protein: 2g | carbs: 12g | fiber: 1g | sodium: 207mg

Stewed Okra

Prep time: 5 minutes | Cook time: 25 minutes | Serves 4

¼ cup extra-virgin olive oil	tomato sauce
1 large onion, chopped	2 cups water
4 cloves garlic, finely chopped	½ cup fresh cilantro, finely chopped
1 teaspoon salt	
1 pound (454 g) fresh or frozen okra, cleaned	½ teaspoon freshly ground black pepper
1 (15 ounces / 425 g) can plain	

1. In a large pot over medium heat, stir and cook the olive oil, onion, garlic, and salt for 1 minute. 2. Stir in the okra and cook for 3 minutes. 3. Add the tomato sauce, water, cilantro, and black pepper; stir, cover, and let cook for 15 minutes, stirring occasionally. 4. Serve warm.

Per Serving:

calories: 202 | fat: 14g | protein: 4g | carbs: 19g | fiber: 6g | sodium: 607mg

Mashed Sweet Potato Tots

Prep time: 10 minutes | Cook time: 12 to 13 minutes per batch | Makes 18 to 24 tots

1 cup cooked mashed sweet potatoes	2 tablespoons chopped pecans
	1½ teaspoons honey
1 egg white, beaten	Salt, to taste
⅛ teaspoon ground cinnamon	½ cup panko bread crumbs
1 dash nutmeg	Oil for misting or cooking spray

1. Preheat the air fryer to 390ºF (199ºC). 2. In a large bowl, mix together the potatoes, egg white, cinnamon, nutmeg, pecans, honey, and salt to taste. 3. Place panko crumbs on a sheet of wax paper. 4. For each tot, use about 2 teaspoons of sweet potato mixture. To shape, drop the measure of potato mixture onto panko crumbs and push crumbs up and around potatoes to coat edges. Then turn tot over to coat other side with crumbs. 5. Mist tots with oil or cooking spray and place in air fryer basket in single layer. 6. Air fry at 390ºF (199ºC) for 12 to 13 minutes, until browned and crispy. 7. Repeat steps 5 and 6 to cook remaining tots.

Per Serving:

calories: 51 | fat: 1g | protein: 1g | carbs: 9g | fiber: 1g | sodium: 45mg

Sautéed Kale with Tomato and Garlic

Prep time: 5 minutes | Cook time: 10 minutes | Serves 4

1 tablespoon extra-virgin olive oil	chopped or torn into pieces
	1 (14½ ounces / 411 g) can no-salt-added diced tomatoes
4 garlic cloves, sliced	
¼ teaspoon red pepper flakes	½ teaspoon kosher salt
2 bunches kale, stemmed and	

1. Heat the olive oil in a wok or large skillet over medium-high heat. Add the garlic and red pepper flakes, and sauté until fragrant, about 30 seconds. Add the kale and sauté, about 3 to 5 minutes, until the kale shrinks down a bit. 2. Add the tomatoes and the salt, stir together, and cook for 3 to 5 minutes, or until the liquid reduces and the kale cooks down further and becomes tender.

Per Serving:

calories: 110 | fat: 5g | protein: 6g | carbs: 15g | fiber: 6g | sodium: 222mg

Curry Roasted Cauliflower

Prep time: 10 minutes | Cook time: 20 minutes |
Serves 4

¼ cup olive oil

2 teaspoons curry powder

½ teaspoon salt

¼ teaspoon freshly ground black pepper

1 head cauliflower, cut into bite-size florets

½ red onion, sliced

2 tablespoons freshly chopped parsley, for garnish (optional)

1. Preheat the air fryer to 400°F (204°C). 2. In a large bowl, combine the olive oil, curry powder, salt, and pepper. Add the cauliflower and onion. Toss gently until the vegetables are completely coated with the oil mixture. Transfer the vegetables to the basket of the air fryer. 3. Pausing about halfway through the cooking time to shake the basket, air fry for 20 minutes until the cauliflower is tender and beginning to brown. Top with the parsley, if desired, before serving.

Per Serving:

calories: 141 | fat: 14g | protein: 2g | carbs: 4g | fiber: 2g | sodium: 312mg

Heirloom Tomato Basil Soup

Prep time: 15 minutes | Cook time: 15 minutes |
Serves 4

1 tablespoon olive oil

1 small onion, peeled and diced

1 stalk celery, sliced

8 medium heirloom tomatoes, seeded and quartered

¼ cup julienned fresh basil

½ teaspoon salt

3 cups low-sodium chicken broth

1 cup heavy cream

1 teaspoon ground black pepper

1. Press the Sauté button on the Instant Pot® and heat oil. Add onion and celery and cook until translucent, about 5 minutes. Add tomatoes and cook for 3 minutes, or until tomatoes are tender and start to break down. Add basil, salt, and broth. Press the Cancel button. 2. Close lid, set steam release to Sealing, press the Manual button, and set time to 7 minutes. When the timer beeps, quick-release the pressure until the float valve drops and then open lid. 3. Add cream and pepper. Purée soup with an immersion blender, or purée in batches in a blender. Ladle into bowls and serve warm.

Per Serving:

calories: 282 | fat: 24g | protein: 4g | carbs: 9g | fiber: 1g | sodium: 466mg

Lebanese Baba Ghanoush

Prep time: 15 minutes | Cook time: 20 minutes |
Serves 4

1 medium eggplant

2 tablespoons vegetable oil

2 tablespoons tahini (sesame paste)

2 tablespoons fresh lemon juice

½ teaspoon kosher salt

1 tablespoon extra-virgin olive oil

½ teaspoon smoked paprika

2 tablespoons chopped fresh parsley

1. Rub the eggplant all over with the vegetable oil. Place the eggplant in the air fryer basket. Set the air fryer to 400°F (204°C) for 20 minutes, or until the eggplant skin is blistered and charred. 2. Transfer the eggplant to a resealable plastic bag, seal, and set aside for 15 minutes (the eggplant will finish cooking in the residual heat trapped in the bag). 3. Transfer the eggplant to a large bowl. Peel off and discard the charred skin. Roughly mash the eggplant flesh. Add the tahini, lemon juice, and salt. Stir to combine. 4. Transfer the mixture to a serving bowl. Drizzle with the olive oil. Sprinkle with the paprika and parsley and serve.

Per Serving:

calories: 171 | fat: 15g | protein: 3g | carbs: 10g | fiber: 5g | sodium: 303mg

Air-Fried Okra

Prep time: 10 minutes | Cook time: 10 minutes |
Serves 4

1 egg

½ cup almond milk

½ cup crushed pork rinds

¼ cup grated Parmesan cheese

¼ cup almond flour

1 teaspoon garlic powder

¼ teaspoon freshly ground black pepper

½ pound (227 g) fresh okra, stems removed and chopped into 1-inch slices

1. Preheat the air fryer to 400°F (204°C). 2. In a shallow bowl, whisk together the egg and milk. 3. In a second shallow bowl, combine the pork rinds, Parmesan, almond flour, garlic powder, and black pepper. 4. Working with a few slices at a time, dip the okra into the egg mixture followed by the crumb mixture. Press lightly to ensure an even coating. 5. Working in batches if necessary, arrange the okra in a single layer in the air fryer basket and spray lightly with olive oil. Pausing halfway through the cooking time to turn the okra, air fry for 10 minutes until tender and golden brown. Serve warm.

Per Serving:

calories: 200 | fat: 16g | protein: 6g | carbs: 8g | fiber: 2g | sodium: 228mg

Green Beans and Potatoes

Nonstick cooking spray

1 onion, chopped

2 garlic cloves, minced

1 leek, white part only, sliced thin

2 cups whole fresh green string beans

3 cups small creamer potatoes

½ cup vegetable broth

2 tablespoons freshly squeezed lemon juice

½ teaspoon salt

½ teaspoon dried thyme leaves

⅛ teaspoon freshly ground black pepper

1. Spray the slow cooker with the nonstick cooking spray. 2. In the slow cooker, combine all the ingredients. 3. Cover and cook on low for 5 to 6 hours, or until the potatoes and beans are tender, and serve.

Per Serving:

calories: 59 | fat: 0g | protein: 2g | carbs: 13g | fiber: 2g | sodium: 167mg

Mushroom-Stuffed Zucchini

2 tablespoons olive oil

2 cups button mushrooms, finely chopped

2 cloves garlic, finely chopped

2 tablespoons chicken broth

1 tablespoon flat-leaf parsley, finely chopped

1 tablespoon Italian seasoning

Sea salt and freshly ground pepper, to taste

2 medium zucchini, cut in half lengthwise

1. Preheat oven to 350ºF (180ºC). 2. Heat a large skillet over medium heat, and add the olive oil. Add the mushrooms and cook until tender, about 4 minutes. Add the garlic and cook for 2 more minutes. 3. Add the chicken broth and cook another 3–4 minutes. 4. Add the parsley and Italian seasoning, and season with sea salt and freshly ground pepper. 5. Stir and remove from heat. 6. Scoop out the insides of the halved zucchini and stuff with mushroom mixture. 7. Place zucchini in a casserole dish, and drizzle a tablespoon of water or broth in the bottom. 8. Cover with foil and bake for 30–40 minutes until zucchini are tender. Serve immediately.

Per Serving:

calories: 189 | fat: 14g | protein: 5g | carbs: 12g | fiber: 3g | sodium: 335mg

Caramelized Eggplant with Harissa Yogurt

1 medium eggplant (about ¾ pound / 340 g), cut crosswise into ½-inch-thick slices and quartered

2 tablespoons vegetable oil

Kosher salt and freshly ground black pepper, to taste

½ cup plain yogurt (not Greek)

2 tablespoons harissa paste

1 garlic clove, grated

2 teaspoons honey

1. In a bowl, toss together the eggplant and oil, season with salt and pepper, and toss to coat evenly. Transfer to the air fryer and air fry at 400ºF (204ºC), shaking the basket every 5 minutes, until the eggplant is caramelized and tender, about 15 minutes. 2. Meanwhile, in a small bowl, whisk together the yogurt, harissa, and garlic, then spread onto a serving plate. 3. Pile the warm eggplant over the yogurt and drizzle with the honey just before serving.

Per Serving:

calories: 247 | fat: 16g | protein: 5g | carbs: 25g | fiber: 8g | sodium: 34mg

Chapter 8 Vegetarian Mains

Eggplants Stuffed with Walnuts and Feta

Prep time: 10 minutes | Cook time: 55 minutes |

Serves 6

3 medium eggplants, halved lengthwise	pieces
2 teaspoons salt, divided	2¼ teaspoons ground cinnamon
¼ cup olive oil, plus 2 tablespoons, divided	1½ teaspoons dried oregano
2 medium onions, diced	½ teaspoon freshly ground black pepper
1½ pints cherry or grape tomatoes, halved	¼ cup whole-wheat breadcrumbs
¾ cup roughly chopped walnut	⅔ cup (about 3 ounces / 85 g) crumbled feta cheese

1. Scoop out the flesh of the eggplants, leaving a ½-inch thick border of flesh in the skins. Dice the flesh that you removed and place it in a colander set over the sink. Sprinkle 1½ teaspoons of salt over the diced eggplant and inside the eggplant shells and let stand for 30 minutes. Rinse the shells and the pieces and pat dry with paper towels. 2. Heat ¼ cup of olive oil in a large skillet over medium heat. Add the eggplant shells, skin-side down, and cook for about 4 minutes, until browned and softened. Turn over and cook on the cut side until golden brown and soft, about 4 minutes more. Transfer to a plate lined with paper towel to drain. 3. Drain off all but about 1 to 2 tablespoons of the oil in the skillet and heat over medium-high heat. Add the onions and cook, stirring, until beginning to soften, about 3 minutes. Add the diced eggplant, tomatoes, walnuts, cinnamon, oregano, ¼ cup water, the remaining ½ teaspoon of salt, and the pepper. Cook, stirring occasionally, until the vegetables are golden brown and softened, about 8 minutes. 4. Preheat the broiler to high. 5. In a small bowl, toss together the breadcrumbs and 1 tablespoon olive oil. 6. Arrange the eggplant shells cut-side up on a large, rimmed baking sheet. Brush each shell with about ½ teaspoon of olive oil. Cook under the broiler until tender and just starting to turn golden brown, about 5 minutes. Remove the eggplants from the broiler and reduce the heat of the oven to 375ºF (190ºC). 7. Spoon the sautéed vegetable mixture into the eggplant shells, dividing equally. Sprinkle the breadcrumbs over the tops of the filled eggplants, dividing equally. Sprinkle the cheese on top, again dividing equally. Bake in the oven until the filling and shells are heated through and the topping is nicely browned and crisp, about 35 minutes.

Per Serving:

calories: 274 | fat: 15g | protein: 7g | carbs: 34g | fiber: 13g | sodium: 973mg

Cauliflower Rice-Stuffed Peppers

Prep time: 10 minutes | Cook time: 15 minutes |

Serves 4

2 cups uncooked cauliflower rice	¼ teaspoon salt
¾ cup drained canned petite diced tomatoes	¼ teaspoon ground black pepper
2 tablespoons olive oil	4 medium green bell peppers, tops removed, seeded
1 cup shredded Mozzarella cheese	

1. In a large bowl, mix all ingredients except bell peppers. Scoop mixture evenly into peppers. 2. Place peppers into ungreased air fryer basket. Adjust the temperature to 350ºF (177ºC) and air fry for 15 minutes. Peppers will be tender and cheese will be melted when done. Serve warm.

Per Serving:

calories: 144 | fat: 7g | protein: 11g | carbs: 11g | fiber: 5g | sodium: 380mg

Caprese Eggplant Stacks

Prep time: 5 minutes | Cook time: 12 minutes |

Serves 4

1 medium eggplant, cut into ¼-inch slices	Mozzarella, cut into ½-ounce / 14-g slices
2 large tomatoes, cut into ¼-inch slices	2 tablespoons olive oil
4 ounces (113 g) fresh	¼ cup fresh basil, sliced

1. In a baking dish, place four slices of eggplant on the bottom. Place a slice of tomato on top of each eggplant round, then Mozzarella, then eggplant. Repeat as necessary. 2. Drizzle with olive oil. Cover dish with foil and place dish into the air fryer basket. 3. Adjust the temperature to 350ºF (177ºC) and bake for 12 minutes. 4. When done, eggplant will be tender. Garnish with fresh basil to serve.

Per Serving:

calories: 97 | fat: 7g | protein: 2g | carbs: 8g | fiber: 4g | sodium: 11mg

Tangy Asparagus and Broccoli

Prep time: 25 minutes | Cook time: 22 minutes | Serves 4

½ pound (227 g) asparagus, cut into 1½-inch pieces
½ pound (227 g) broccoli, cut into 1½-inch pieces
2 tablespoons olive oil

Salt and white pepper, to taste
½ cup vegetable broth
2 tablespoons apple cider vinegar

1. Place the vegetables in a single layer in the lightly greased air fryer basket. Drizzle the olive oil over the vegetables. 2. Sprinkle with salt and white pepper. 3. Cook at 380ºF (193ºC) for 15 minutes, shaking the basket halfway through the cooking time. 4. Add ½ cup of vegetable broth to a saucepan; bring to a rapid boil and add the vinegar. Cook for 5 to 7 minutes or until the sauce has reduced by half. 5. Spoon the sauce over the warm vegetables and serve immediately. Bon appétit!

Per Serving:

calories: 93 | fat: 7g | protein: 3g | carbs: 6g | fiber: 3g | sodium: 89mg

Crustless Spanakopita

Prep time: 15 minutes | Cook time: 45 minutes | Serves 6

12 tablespoons extra-virgin olive oil, divided
1 small yellow onion, diced
1 (32-ounce / 907-g) bag frozen chopped spinach, thawed, fully drained, and patted dry (about 4 cups)
4 garlic cloves, minced

½ teaspoon salt
½ teaspoon freshly ground black pepper
1 cup whole-milk ricotta cheese
4 large eggs
¾ cup crumbled traditional feta cheese
¼ cup pine nuts

1. Preheat the oven to 375ºF (190ºC). 2. In a large skillet, heat 4 tablespoons olive oil over medium-high heat. Add the onion and sauté until softened, 6 to 8 minutes. 3. Add the spinach, garlic, salt, and pepper and sauté another 5 minutes. Remove from the heat and allow to cool slightly. 4. In a medium bowl, whisk together the ricotta and eggs. Add to the cooled spinach and stir to combine. 5. Pour 4 tablespoons olive oil in the bottom of a 9-by-13-inch glass baking dish and swirl to coat the bottom and sides. Add the spinach-ricotta mixture and spread into an even layer. 6. Bake for 20 minutes or until the mixture begins to set. Remove from the oven and crumble the feta evenly across the top of the spinach. Add the pine nuts and drizzle with the remaining 4 tablespoons olive oil. Return to the oven and bake for an additional 15 to 20 minutes, or until the spinach is fully set and the top is starting to turn golden brown. Allow to cool slightly before cutting to serve.

Per Serving:

calories: 497 | fat: 44g | protein: 18g | carbs: 11g | fiber: 5g | sodium: 561mg

Cauliflower Steaks with Olive Citrus Sauce

Prep time: 15 minutes | Cook time: 30 minutes | Serves 4

1 or 2 large heads cauliflower (at least 2 pounds / 907 g, enough for 4 portions)
⅓ cup extra-virgin olive oil
¼ teaspoon kosher salt
⅛ teaspoon ground black pepper
Juice of 1 orange

Zest of 1 orange
¼ cup black olives, pitted and chopped
1 tablespoon Dijon or grainy mustard
1 tablespoon red wine vinegar
½ teaspoon ground coriander

1. Preheat the oven to 400ºF (205ºC). Line a baking sheet with parchment paper or foil. 2. Cut off the stem of the cauliflower so it will sit upright. Slice it vertically into four thick slabs. Place the cauliflower on the prepared baking sheet. Drizzle with the olive oil, salt, and black pepper. Bake for about 30 minutes, turning over once, until tender and golden brown. 3. In a medium bowl, combine the orange juice, orange zest, olives, mustard, vinegar, and coriander; mix well. 4. Serve the cauliflower warm or at room temperature with the sauce.

Per Serving:

calories: 265 | fat: 21g | protein: 5g | carbs: 19g | fiber: 4g | sodium: 310mg

Cheese Stuffed Zucchini

Prep time: 20 minutes | Cook time: 8 minutes | Serves 4

1 large zucchini, cut into four pieces
2 tablespoons olive oil
1 cup Ricotta cheese, room temperature
2 tablespoons scallions, chopped
1 heaping tablespoon fresh

parsley, roughly chopped
1 heaping tablespoon coriander, minced
2 ounces (57 g) Cheddar cheese, preferably freshly grated
1 teaspoon celery seeds
½ teaspoon salt
½ teaspoon garlic pepper

1. Cook your zucchini in the air fryer basket for approximately 10 minutes at 350ºF (177ºC). Check for doneness and cook for 2-3 minutes longer if needed. 2. Meanwhile, make the stuffing by mixing the other items. 3. When your zucchini is thoroughly cooked, open them up. Divide the stuffing among all zucchini pieces and bake an additional 5 minutes.

Per Serving:

calories: 242 | fat: 20g | protein: 12g | carbs: 5g | fiber: 1g | sodium: 443mg

Root Vegetable Soup with Garlic Aioli

Prep time: 10 minutes | Cook time 25 minutes |
Serves 4

For the Soup:
8 cups vegetable broth
½ teaspoon salt
1 medium leek, cut into thick rounds
1 pound (454 g) carrots, peeled and diced
1 pound (454 g) potatoes, peeled and diced

1 pound (454 g) turnips, peeled and cut into 1-inch cubes
1 red bell pepper, cut into strips
2 tablespoons fresh oregano
For the Aioli:
5 garlic cloves, minced
¼ teaspoon salt
⅔ cup olive oil
1 drop lemon juice

1. Bring the broth and salt to a boil and add the vegetables one at a time, letting the water return to a boil after each addition. Add the carrots first, then the leeks, potatoes, turnips, and finally the red bell peppers. Let the vegetables cook for about 3 minutes after adding the green beans and bringing to a boil. The process will take about 20 minutes in total. 2. Meanwhile, make the aioli. In a mortar and pestle, grind the garlic to a paste with the salt. Using a whisk and whisking constantly, add the olive oil in a thin stream. Continue whisking until the mixture thickens to the consistency of mayonnaise. Add the lemon juice. 3. Serve the vegetables in the broth, dolloped with the aioli and garnished with the fresh oregano.

Per Serving:
calories: 538 | fat: 37g | protein: 5g | carbs: 50g | fiber: 9g | sodium: 773mg

Mediterranean Baked Chickpeas

Prep time: 15 minutes | Cook time: 15 minutes |
Serves 4

1 tablespoon extra-virgin olive oil
½ medium onion, chopped
3 garlic cloves, chopped
2 teaspoons smoked paprika
¼ teaspoon ground cumin

4 cups halved cherry tomatoes
2 (15 ounces / 425 g) cans chickpeas, drained and rinsed
½ cup plain, unsweetened, full-fat Greek yogurt, for serving
1 cup crumbled feta, for serving

1. Preheat the oven to 425ºF (220ºC). 2. In an oven-safe sauté pan or skillet, heat the oil over medium heat and sauté the onion and garlic. Cook for about 5 minutes, until softened and fragrant. Stir in the paprika and cumin and cook for 2 minutes. Stir in the tomatoes and chickpeas. 3. Bring to a simmer for 5 to 10 minutes before placing in the oven. 4. Roast in oven for 25 to 30 minutes, until bubbling and thickened. To serve, top with Greek yogurt and feta.

Per Serving:
calories: 412 | fat: 15g | protein: 20g | carbs: 51g | fiber: 13g | sodium: 444mg

Stuffed Portobellos

Prep time: 10 minutes | Cook time: 8 minutes |
Serves 4

3 ounces (85 g) cream cheese, softened
½ medium zucchini, trimmed and chopped
¼ cup seeded and chopped red bell pepper
1½ cups chopped fresh spinach

leaves
4 large portobello mushrooms, stems removed
2 tablespoons coconut oil, melted
½ teaspoon salt

1. In a medium bowl, mix cream cheese, zucchini, pepper, and spinach. 2. Drizzle mushrooms with coconut oil and sprinkle with salt. Scoop ¼ zucchini mixture into each mushroom. 3. Place mushrooms into ungreased air fryer basket. Adjust the temperature to 400ºF (204ºC) and air fry for 8 minutes. Portobellos will be tender and tops will be browned when done. Serve warm.

Per Serving:
calories: 151 | fat: 13g | protein: 4g | carbs: 6g | fiber: 2g | sodium: 427mg

Linguine and Brussels Sprouts

Prep time: 10 minutes | Cook time: 25 minutes |
Serves 4

8 ounces (227 g) whole-wheat linguine
⅓ cup, plus 2 tablespoons extra-virgin olive oil, divided
1 medium sweet onion, diced
2 to 3 garlic cloves, smashed
8 ounces (227 g) Brussels

sprouts, chopped
½ cup chicken stock, as needed
⅓ cup dry white wine
½ cup shredded Parmesan cheese
1 lemon, cut in quarters

1. Bring a large pot of water to a boil and cook the pasta according to package directions. Drain, reserving 1 cup of the pasta water. Mix the cooked pasta with 2 tablespoons of olive oil, then set aside. 2. In a large sauté pan or skillet, heat the remaining ⅓ cup of olive oil on medium heat. Add the onion to the pan and cook for about 5 minutes, until softened. Add the smashed garlic cloves and cook for 1 minute, until fragrant. 3. Add the Brussels sprouts and cook covered for 15 minutes. Add chicken stock as needed to prevent burning. Once Brussels sprouts have wilted and are fork-tender, add white wine and cook down for about 7 minutes, until reduced. 4. Add the pasta to the skillet and add the pasta water as needed. 5. Serve with the Parmesan cheese and lemon for squeezing over the dish right before eating.

Per Serving:
calories: 502 | fat: 31g | protein: 15g | carbs: 50g | fiber: 9g | sodium: 246mg

Quinoa with Almonds and Cranberries

Prep time: 15 minutes | Cook time: 0 minutes |
Serves 4

2 cups cooked quinoa
⅓ teaspoon cranberries or currants
¼ cup sliced almonds
2 garlic cloves, minced
1¼ teaspoons salt
½ teaspoon ground cumin
½ teaspoon turmeric
¼ teaspoon ground cinnamon
¼ teaspoon freshly ground black pepper

1. In a large bowl, toss the quinoa, cranberries, almonds, garlic, salt, cumin, turmeric, cinnamon, and pepper and stir to combine. Enjoy alone or with roasted cauliflower.

Per Serving:

calories: 194 | fat: 6g | protein: 7g | carbs: 31g | fiber: 4g | sodium: 727mg

Parmesan Artichokes

Prep time: 10 minutes | Cook time: 10 minutes |
Serves 4

2 medium artichokes, trimmed and quartered, center removed
2 tablespoons coconut oil
1 large egg, beaten
½ cup grated vegetarian
Parmesan cheese
¼ cup blanched finely ground almond flour
½ teaspoon crushed red pepper flakes

1. In a large bowl, toss artichokes in coconut oil and then dip each piece into the egg. 2. Mix the Parmesan and almond flour in a large bowl. Add artichoke pieces and toss to cover as completely as possible, sprinkle with pepper flakes. Place into the air fryer basket. 3. Adjust the temperature to 400ºF (204ºC) and air fry for 10 minutes. 4. Toss the basket two times during cooking. Serve warm.

Per Serving:

calories: 207 | fat: 13g | protein: 10g | carbs: 15g | fiber: 5g | sodium: 211mg

Mushroom Ragù with Parmesan Polenta

Prep time: 20 minutes | Cook time: 30 minutes |
Serves 2

½ ounce (14 g) dried porcini mushrooms (optional but recommended)
2 tablespoons olive oil
1 pound (454 g) baby bella
(cremini) mushrooms, quartered
1 large shallot, minced (about ⅓ cup)
1 garlic clove, minced
1 tablespoon flour
2 teaspoons tomato paste
½ cup red wine
1 cup mushroom stock (or reserved liquid from soaking the porcini mushrooms, if using)
½ teaspoon dried thyme
1 fresh rosemary sprig
1½ cups water
½ teaspoon salt
⅓ cup instant polenta
2 tablespoons grated Parmesan cheese

1. If using the dried porcini mushrooms, soak them in 1 cup of hot water for about 15 minutes to soften them. When they're softened, scoop them out of the water, reserving the soaking liquid. (I strain it through a coffee filter to remove any possible grit.) Mince the porcini mushrooms. 2. Heat the olive oil in a large sauté pan over medium-high heat. Add the mushrooms, shallot, and garlic, and sauté for 10 minutes, or until the vegetables are wilted and starting to caramelize. 3. Add the flour and tomato paste, and cook for another 30 seconds. Add the red wine, mushroom stock or porcini soaking liquid, thyme, and rosemary. Bring the mixture to a boil, stirring constantly until it thickens. Reduce the heat and let it simmer for 10 minutes. 4. While the mushrooms are simmering, bring the water to a boil in a saucepan and add salt. 5. Add the instant polenta and stir quickly while it thickens. Stir in the Parmesan cheese. Taste and add additional salt if needed.

Per Serving:

calories: 451 | fat: 16g | protein: 14g | carbs: 58g | fiber: 5g | sodium: 165mg

Moroccan Red Lentil and Pumpkin Stew

Prep time: 10 minutes | Cook time: 30 minutes |
Serves 4

2 tablespoons olive oil
1 teaspoon ground cumin
1 teaspoon ground turmeric
1 tablespoon curry powder
1 large onion, diced
1 teaspoon salt
2 tablespoons minced fresh ginger
4 cloves garlic, minced
1 pound (454 g) pumpkin, peeled, seeded, and cut into 1-inch dice
1 red bell pepper, seeded and diced
1½ cups red lentils, rinsed
6 cups vegetable broth
¼ cup chopped cilantro, for garnish

1. Heat the olive oil in a stockpot over medium heat. Add the cumin, turmeric, and curry powder and cook, stirring, for 1 minute, until fragrant. Add the onion and salt and cook, stirring frequently, until softened, about 5 minutes. Add the ginger and garlic and cook, stirring frequently, for 2 more minutes. Stir in the pumpkin and bell pepper, and then the lentils and broth and bring to a boil. 2. Reduce the heat to low and simmer, uncovered, for about 20 minutes, until the lentils are very tender. Serve hot, garnished with cilantro.

Per Serving:

calories: 405 | fat: 9g | protein: 20g | carbs: 66g | fiber: 11g | sodium: 594mg

Grilled Eggplant Stacks

1 medium eggplant, cut crosswise into 8 slices	2 tablespoons olive oil
¼ teaspoon salt	1 large tomato, cut into 4 slices
1 teaspoon Italian herb seasoning mix	4 (1 ounce / 28 g) slices of buffalo mozzarella
	Fresh basil, for garnish

1. Place the eggplant slices in a colander set in the sink or over a bowl. Sprinkle both sides with the salt. Let the eggplant sit for 15 minutes. 2. While the eggplant is resting, heat the grill to medium-high heat (about 350ºF / 180ºC). 3. Pat the eggplant dry with paper towels and place it in a mixing bowl. Sprinkle it with the Italian herb seasoning mix and olive oil. Toss well to coat. 4. Grill the eggplant for 5 minutes, or until it has grill marks and is lightly charred. Flip each eggplant slice over, and grill on the second side for another 5 minutes. 5. Flip the eggplant slices back over and top four of the slices with a slice of tomato and a slice of mozzarella. Top each stack with one of the remaining four slices of eggplant. 6. Turn the grill down to low and cover it to let the cheese melt. Check after 30 seconds and remove when the cheese is soft and mostly melted. 7. Sprinkle with fresh basil slices.

Per Serving:

calories: 354 | fat: 29g | protein: 13g | carbs: 19g | fiber: 9g | sodium: 340mg

Spinach-Artichoke Stuffed Mushrooms

2 tablespoons olive oil	crumbled
4 large portobello mushrooms, stems removed and gills scraped out	½ cup chopped marinated artichoke hearts
½ teaspoon salt	1 cup frozen spinach, thawed and squeezed dry
¼ teaspoon freshly ground pepper	½ cup grated Parmesan cheese
4 ounces (113 g) goat cheese,	2 tablespoons chopped fresh parsley

1. Preheat the air fryer to 400ºF (204ºC). 2. Rub the olive oil over the portobello mushrooms until thoroughly coated. Sprinkle both sides with the salt and black pepper. Place top-side down on a clean work surface. 3. In a small bowl, combine the goat cheese, artichoke hearts, and spinach. Mash with the back of a fork until thoroughly combined. Divide the cheese mixture among the mushrooms and sprinkle with the Parmesan cheese. 4. Air fry for 10 to 14 minutes until the mushrooms are tender and the cheese has begun to brown. Top with the fresh parsley just before serving.

Per Serving:

calories: 284 | fat: 21g | protein: 16g | carbs: 10g | fiber: 4g | sodium: 686mg

Crispy Eggplant Rounds

1 large eggplant, ends trimmed, cut into ½-inch slices	cheese crisps, finely ground
½ teaspoon salt	½ teaspoon paprika
2 ounces (57 g) Parmesan 100%	¼ teaspoon garlic powder
	1 large egg

1. Sprinkle eggplant rounds with salt. Place rounds on a kitchen towel for 30 minutes to draw out excess water. Pat rounds dry. 2. In a medium bowl, mix cheese crisps, paprika, and garlic powder. In a separate medium bowl, whisk egg. Dip each eggplant round in egg, then gently press into cheese crisps to coat both sides. 3. Place eggplant rounds into ungreased air fryer basket. Adjust the temperature to 400ºF (204ºC) and air fry for 10 minutes, turning rounds halfway through cooking. Eggplant will be golden and crispy when done. Serve warm.

Per Serving:

calories: 113 | fat: 5g | protein: 7g | carbs: 10g | fiber: 4g | sodium: 567mg

Turkish Red Lentil and Bulgur Kofte

⅓ cup olive oil, plus 2 tablespoons, divided, plus more for brushing	2 tablespoons tomato paste
1 cup red lentils	1 teaspoon ground cumin
½ cup bulgur	¼ cup finely chopped flat-leaf parsley
1 teaspoon salt	3 scallions, thinly sliced
1 medium onion, finely diced	Juice of ½ lemon

1. Preheat the oven to 400°F(205ºC). 2. Brush a large, rimmed baking sheet with olive oil. 3. In a medium saucepan, combine the lentils with 2 cups water and bring to a boil. Reduce the heat to low and cook, stirring occasionally, for about 15 minutes, until the lentils are tender and have soaked up most of the liquid. Remove from the heat, stir in the bulgur and salt, cover, and let sit for 15 minutes or so, until the bulgur is tender. 4. Meanwhile, heat ⅓ cup olive oil in a medium skillet over medium-high heat. Add the onion and cook, stirring frequently, until softened, about 5 minutes. Stir in the tomato paste and cook for 2 minutes more. Remove from the heat and stir in the cumin. 5. Add the cooked onion mixture to the lentil-bulgur mixture and stir to combine. Add the parsley, scallions, and lemon juice and stir to mix well. 6. Shape the mixture into walnut-sized balls and place them on the prepared baking sheet. Brush the balls with the remaining 2 tablespoons of olive oil and bake for 15 to 20 minutes, until golden brown. Serve hot.

Per Serving:

calories: 460 | fat: 25g | protein: 16g | carbs: 48g | fiber: 19g | sodium: 604mg

Three-Cheese Zucchini Boats

Prep time: 15 minutes | Cook time: 20 minutes | Serves 2

2 medium zucchini	cheese
1 tablespoon avocado oil	¼ teaspoon dried oregano
¼ cup low-carb, no-sugar-added pasta sauce	¼ teaspoon garlic powder
¼ cup full-fat ricotta cheese	½ teaspoon dried parsley
¼ cup shredded Mozzarella	2 tablespoons grated vegetarian Parmesan cheese

1. Cut off 1 inch from the top and bottom of each zucchini. Slice zucchini in half lengthwise and use a spoon to scoop out a bit of the inside, making room for filling. Brush with oil and spoon 2 tablespoons pasta sauce into each shell. 2. In a medium bowl, mix ricotta, Mozzarella, oregano, garlic powder, and parsley. Spoon the mixture into each zucchini shell. Place stuffed zucchini shells into the air fryer basket. 3. Adjust the temperature to 350ºF (177ºC) and air fry for 20 minutes. 4. To remove from the basket, use tongs or a spatula and carefully lift out. Top with Parmesan. Serve immediately.

Per Serving:

calories: 208 | fat: 14g | protein: 12g | carbs: 11g | fiber: 3g | sodium: 247mg

One-Pan Mushroom Pasta with Mascarpone

Prep time: 10 minutes | Cook time: 20 minutes | Serves 2

2 tablespoons olive oil	stock
1 large shallot, minced	6 ounces (170 g) dry
8 ounces (227 g) baby bella (cremini) mushrooms, sliced	pappardelle pasta
¼ cup dry sherry	2 tablespoons mascarpone cheese
1 teaspoon dried thyme	Salt
2 cups low-sodium vegetable	Freshly ground black pepper

1. Heat olive oil in a large sauté pan over medium-high heat. Add the shallot and mushrooms and sauté for 10 minutes, or until the mushrooms have given up much of their liquid. 2. Add the sherry, thyme, and vegetable stock. Bring the mixture to a boil. 3. Add the pasta, breaking it up as needed so it fits into the pan and is covered by the liquid. Return the mixture to a boil. Cover, and reduce the heat to medium-low. Let the pasta cook for 10 minutes, or until al dente. Stir it occasionally so it doesn't stick. If the sauce gets too dry, add some water or additional chicken stock. 4. When the pasta is tender, stir in the mascarpone cheese and season with salt and pepper. 5. The sauce will thicken up a bit when it's off the heat.

Per Serving:

calories: 517 | fat: 18g | protein: 16g | carbs: 69g | fiber: 3g | sodium: 141mg

Stuffed Pepper Stew

Prep time: 20 minutes | Cook time: 50 minutes | Serves 2

2 tablespoons olive oil	vegetarian Worcestershire sauce
2 sweet peppers, diced (about 2 cups)	1 cup low-sodium vegetable stock
½ large onion, minced	1 cup low-sodium tomato juice
1 garlic clove, minced	¼ cup brown lentils
1 teaspoon oregano	¼ cup brown rice
1 tablespoon gluten-free	Salt

1. Heat olive oil in a Dutch oven over medium-high heat. Add the sweet peppers and onion and sauté for 10 minutes, or until the peppers are wilted and the onion starts to turn golden. 2. Add the garlic, oregano, and Worcestershire sauce, and cook for another 30 seconds. Add the vegetable stock, tomato juice, lentils, and rice. 3. Bring the mixture to a boil. Cover, and reduce the heat to medium-low. Simmer for 45 minutes, or until the rice is cooked and the lentils are softened. Season with salt.

Per Serving:

calories: 379 | fat: 16g | protein: 11g | carbs: 53g | fiber: 7g | sodium: 392mg

Ricotta, Basil, and Pistachio-Stuffed Zucchini

Prep time: 15 minutes | Cook time: 25 minutes | Serves 4

2 medium zucchini, halved lengthwise	¾ cup ricotta cheese
1 tablespoon extra-virgin olive oil	¼ cup unsalted pistachios, shelled and chopped
1 onion, diced	¼ cup fresh basil, chopped
1 teaspoon kosher salt	1 large egg, beaten
2 garlic cloves, minced	¼ teaspoon freshly ground black pepper

1. Preheat the oven to 425ºF (220ºC). Line a baking sheet with parchment paper or foil. 2. Scoop out the seeds/pulp from the zucchini, leaving ¼-inch flesh around the edges. Transfer the pulp to a cutting board and chop the pulp. 3. Heat the olive oil in a large skillet or sauté pan over medium heat. Add the onion, pulp, and salt and sauté about 5 minutes. Add the garlic and sauté 30 seconds. 4. In a medium bowl, combine the ricotta cheese, pistachios, basil, egg, and black pepper. Add the onion mixture and mix together well. 5. Place the 4 zucchini halves on the prepared baking sheet. Fill the zucchini halves with the ricotta mixture. Bake for 20 minutes, or until golden brown.

Per Serving:

calories: 200 | fat: 12g | protein: 11g | carbs: 14g | fiber: 3g | sodium: 360mg

Broccoli-Cheese Fritters

Prep time: 5 minutes | Cook time: 20 to 25 minutes |
Serves 4

1 cup broccoli florets
1 cup shredded Mozzarella cheese
¾ cup almond flour
½ cup flaxseed meal, divided
2 teaspoons baking powder
1 teaspoon garlic powder
Salt and freshly ground black pepper, to taste
2 eggs, lightly beaten
½ cup ranch dressing

1. Preheat the air fryer to 400°F (204°C). 2. In a food processor fitted with a metal blade, pulse the broccoli until very finely chopped. 3. Transfer the broccoli to a large bowl and add the Mozzarella, almond flour, ¼ cup of the flaxseed meal, baking powder, and garlic powder. Stir until thoroughly combined. Season to taste with salt and black pepper. Add the eggs and stir again to form a sticky dough. Shape the dough into 1¼-inch fritters. 4. Place the remaining ¼ cup flaxseed meal in a shallow bowl and roll the fritters in the meal to form an even coating. 5. Working in batches if necessary, arrange the fritters in a single layer in the basket of the air fryer and spray generously with olive oil. Pausing halfway through the cooking time to shake the basket, air fry for 20 to 25 minutes until the fritters are golden brown and crispy. Serve with the ranch dressing for dipping.

Per Serving:

calories: 388 | fat: 30g | protein: 19g | carbs: 14g | fiber: 7g | sodium: 526mg

Mozzarella and Sun-Dried Portobello Mushroom Pizza

Prep time: 10 minutes | Cook time: 10 minutes |
Serves 4

4 large portobello mushroom caps
3 tablespoons extra-virgin olive oil
Salt
Freshly ground black pepper
4 sun-dried tomatoes
1 cup mozzarella cheese, divided
½ to ¾ cup low-sodium tomato sauce

1. Preheat the broiler on high. 2. On a baking sheet, drizzle the mushroom caps with the olive oil and season with salt and pepper. Broil the portobello mushrooms for 5 minutes on each side, flipping once, until tender. 3. Fill each mushroom cap with 1 sun-dried tomato, 2 tablespoons of cheese, and 2 to 3 tablespoons of sauce. Top each with 2 tablespoons of cheese. Place the caps back under the broiler for a final 2 to 3 minutes, then quarter the mushrooms and serve.

Per Serving:

calories: 218| fat: 16g | protein: 11g | carbs: 12g | fiber: 2g | sodium: 244mg

Pesto Spinach Flatbread

Prep time: 10 minutes | Cook time: 8 minutes |
Serves 4

1 cup blanched finely ground almond flour
2 ounces (57 g) cream cheese
2 cups shredded Mozzarella
cheese
1 cup chopped fresh spinach leaves
2 tablespoons basil pesto

1. Place flour, cream cheese, and Mozzarella in a large microwave-safe bowl and microwave on high 45 seconds, then stir. 2. Fold in spinach and microwave an additional 15 seconds. Stir until a soft dough ball forms. 3. Cut two pieces of parchment paper to fit air fryer basket. Separate dough into two sections and press each out on ungreased parchment to create 6-inch rounds. 4. Spread 1 tablespoon pesto over each flatbread and place rounds on parchment into ungreased air fryer basket. Adjust the temperature to 350°F (177°C) and air fry for 8 minutes, turning crusts halfway through cooking. Flatbread will be golden when done. 5. Let cool 5 minutes before slicing and serving.

Per Serving:

calories: 387 | fat: 28g | protein: 28g | carbs: 10g | fiber: 5g | sodium: 556mg

Rustic Vegetable and Brown Rice Bowl

Prep time: 15 minutes | Cook time: 20 minutes |
Serves 4

Nonstick cooking spray
2 cups broccoli florets
2 cups cauliflower florets
1 (15 ounces / 425 g) can chickpeas, drained and rinsed
1 cup carrots sliced 1 inch thick
2 to 3 tablespoons extra-virgin olive oil, divided
Salt
Freshly ground black pepper
2 to 3 tablespoons sesame seeds, for garnish
2 cups cooked brown rice
For the Dressing:
3 to 4 tablespoons tahini
2 tablespoons honey
1 lemon, juiced
1 garlic clove, minced
Salt
Freshly ground black pepper

1. Preheat the oven to 400°F (205°C). Spray two baking sheets with cooking spray. 2. Cover the first baking sheet with the broccoli and cauliflower and the second with the chickpeas and carrots. Toss each sheet with half of the oil and season with salt and pepper before placing in oven. 3. Cook the carrots and chickpeas for 10 minutes, leaving the carrots still just crisp, and the broccoli and cauliflower for 20 minutes, until tender. Stir each halfway through cooking. 4. To make the dressing, in a small bowl, mix the tahini, honey, lemon juice, and garlic. Season with salt and pepper and set aside. 5. Divide the rice into individual bowls, then layer with vegetables and drizzle dressing over the dish.

Per Serving:

calories: 454 | fat: 18g | protein: 12g | carbs: 62g | fiber: 11g | sodium: 61mg

Broccoli Crust Pizza

Prep time: 15 minutes | Cook time: 12 minutes | Serves 4

3 cups riced broccoli, steamed and drained well
1 large egg
½ cup grated vegetarian Parmesan cheese

3 tablespoons low-carb Alfredo sauce
½ cup shredded Mozzarella cheese

1. In a large bowl, mix broccoli, egg, and Parmesan. 2. Cut a piece of parchment to fit your air fryer basket. Press out the pizza mixture to fit on the parchment, working in two batches if necessary. Place into the air fryer basket. 3. Adjust the temperature to 370ºF (188ºC) and air fry for 5 minutes. 4. The crust should be firm enough to flip. If not, add 2 additional minutes. Flip crust. 5. Top with Alfredo sauce and Mozzarella. Return to the air fryer basket and cook an additional 7 minutes or until cheese is golden and bubbling. Serve warm.

Per Serving:

calories: 87 | fat: 2g | protein: 11g | carbs: 5g | fiber: 1g | sodium: 253mg

Cauliflower Steak with Gremolata

Prep time: 15 minutes | Cook time: 25 minutes | Serves 4

2 tablespoons olive oil
1 tablespoon Italian seasoning
1 large head cauliflower, outer leaves removed and sliced lengthwise through the core into thick "steaks"
Salt and freshly ground black pepper, to taste
¼ cup Parmesan cheese

Gremolata:
1 bunch Italian parsley (about 1 cup packed)
2 cloves garlic
Zest of 1 small lemon, plus 1 to 2 teaspoons lemon juice
½ cup olive oil
Salt and pepper, to taste

1. Preheat the air fryer to 400ºF (204ºC). 2. In a small bowl, combine the olive oil and Italian seasoning. Brush both sides of each cauliflower "steak" generously with the oil. Season to taste with salt and black pepper. 3. Working in batches if necessary, arrange the cauliflower in a single layer in the air fryer basket. Pausing halfway through the cooking time to turn the "steaks," air fry for 15 to 20 minutes until the cauliflower is tender and the edges begin to brown. Sprinkle with the Parmesan and air fry for 5 minutes longer. 4. To make the gremolata: In a food processor fitted with a metal blade, combine the parsley, garlic, and lemon zest and juice. With the motor running, add the olive oil in a steady stream until the mixture forms a bright green sauce. Season to taste with salt and black pepper. Serve the cauliflower steaks with the gremolata spooned over the top.

Per Serving:

calories: 336 | fat: 30g | protein: 7g | carbs: 15g | fiber: 5g | sodium: 340mg

Pesto Vegetable Skewers

Prep time: 30 minutes | Cook time: 8 minutes | Makes 8 skewers

1 medium zucchini, trimmed and cut into ½-inch slices
½ medium yellow onion, peeled and cut into 1-inch squares
1 medium red bell pepper, seeded and cut into 1-inch

squares
16 whole cremini mushrooms
⅓ cup basil pesto
½ teaspoon salt
¼ teaspoon ground black pepper

1. Divide zucchini slices, onion, and bell pepper into eight even portions. Place on 6-inch skewers for a total of eight kebabs. Add 2 mushrooms to each skewer and brush kebabs generously with pesto. 2. Sprinkle each kebab with salt and black pepper on all sides, then place into ungreased air fryer basket. Adjust the temperature to 375ºF (191ºC) and air fry for 8 minutes, turning kebabs halfway through cooking. Vegetables will be browned at the edges and tender-crisp when done. Serve warm.

Per Serving:

calories: 75 | fat: 6g | protein: 3g | carbs: 4g | fiber: 1g | sodium: 243mg

Vegetable Burgers

Prep time: 10 minutes | Cook time: 12 minutes | Serves 4

8 ounces (227 g) cremini mushrooms
2 large egg yolks
½ medium zucchini, trimmed and chopped
¼ cup peeled and chopped

yellow onion
1 clove garlic, peeled and finely minced
½ teaspoon salt
¼ teaspoon ground black pepper

1. Place all ingredients into a food processor and pulse twenty times until finely chopped and combined. 2. Separate mixture into four equal sections and press each into a burger shape. Place burgers into ungreased air fryer basket. Adjust the temperature to 375ºF (191ºC) and air fry for 12 minutes, turning burgers halfway through cooking. Burgers will be browned and firm when done. 3. Place burgers on a large plate and let cool 5 minutes before serving.

Per Serving:

calories: 50 | fat: 3g | protein: 3g | carbs: 4g | fiber: 1g | sodium: 299mg

Chapter 9 Desserts

Crunchy Sesame Cookies

Prep time: 10 minutes | Cook time: 15 minutes | Yield 14 to 16

1 cup sesame seeds, hulled	butter, softened
1 cup sugar	2 large eggs
8 tablespoons (1 stick) salted	1¼ cups flour

1. Preheat the oven to 350°F(180ºC). Toast the sesame seeds on a baking sheet for 3 minutes. Set aside and let cool. 2. Using a mixer, cream together the sugar and butter. 3. Add the eggs one at a time until well-blended. 4. Add the flour and toasted sesame seeds and mix until well-blended. 5. Drop spoonfuls of cookie dough onto a baking sheet and form them into round balls, about 1-inch in diameter, similar to a walnut. 6. Put in the oven and bake for 5 to 7 minutes or until golden brown. 7. Let the cookies cool and enjoy.

Per Serving:

calories: 218 | fat: 12g | protein: 4g | carbs: 25g | fiber: 2g | sodium: 58mg

Date and Nut Balls

Prep time: 10 minutes | Cook time: 10 minutes | Serves 6 to 8

1 cup walnuts or pistachios	14 medjool dates, pits removed
1 cup unsweetened shredded coconut	8 tablespoons (1 stick) butter, melted

1. Preheat the oven to 350°F. 2. Put the nuts on a baking sheet. Toast the nuts for 5 minutes. 3. Put the shredded coconut on a clean baking sheet; toast just until it turns golden brown, about 3 to 5 minutes (coconut burns fast so keep an eye on it). Once done, remove it from the oven and put it in a shallow bowl. 4. In a food processor fitted with a chopping blade, process the nuts until they have a medium chop. Put the chopped nuts into a medium bowl. 5. Add the dates and melted butter to the food processor and blend until the dates become a thick paste. Pour the chopped nuts into the food processor with the dates and pulse just until the mixture is combined, about 5 to 7 pulses. 6. Remove the mixture from the food processor and scrape it into a large bowl. 7. To make the balls, spoon 1 to 2 tablespoons of the date mixture into the palm of your hand and roll around between your hands until you form a ball. Put the ball on a clean, lined baking sheet. Repeat until all the mixture is formed into balls. 8. Roll each ball in the toasted coconut until the outside of the ball is coated, put the ball back on the baking sheet, and repeat. 9. Put all the balls into the fridge for 20 minutes before serving so that they firm up. You can also store any leftovers in the fridge in an airtight container.

Per Serving:

calories: 489 | fat: 35g | protein: 5g | carbs: 48g | fiber: 7g | sodium: 114mg

Cocoa and Coconut Banana Slices

Prep time: 10 minutes | Cook time: 0 minutes | Serves 1

1 banana, peeled and sliced	1 tablespoon unsweetened
2 tablespoons unsweetened,	cocoa powder
shredded coconut	1 teaspoon honey

1. Lay the banana slices on a parchment-lined baking sheet in a single layer. Put in the freezer for about 10 minutes, until firm but not frozen solid. Mix the coconut with the cocoa powder in a small bowl. 2. Roll the banana slices in honey, followed by the coconut mixture. 3. You can either eat immediately or put back in the freezer for a frozen, sweet treat.

Per Serving:

calories: 187 | fat: 4g | protein: 3g | carbs: 41g | fiber: 6g | sodium: 33mg

S'mores

Prep time: 5 minutes | Cook time: 30 seconds | Makes 8 s'mores

Oil, for spraying	bars
8 graham cracker squares	4 large marshmallows
2 (1½ ounces / 43 g) chocolate	

1. Line the air fryer basket with parchment and spray lightly with oil. 2. Place 4 graham cracker squares in the prepared basket. 3. Break the chocolate bars in half and place 1 piece on top of each graham cracker. Top with 1 marshmallow. 4. Air fry at 370ºF (188ºC) for 30 seconds, or until the marshmallows are puffed and golden brown and slightly melted. 5. Top with the remaining graham cracker squares and serve.

Per Serving:

calories: 154 | fat: 7g | protein: 2g | carbs: 22g | fiber: 2g | sodium: 75mg

Pumpkin-Ricotta Cheesecake

Prep time: 25 minutes | Cook time: 45 minutes |
Serves 10 to 12

1 cup almond flour
½ cup butter, melted
1 (14½ ounces / 411 g) can pumpkin purée
8 ounces (227 g) cream cheese, at room temperature
½ cup whole-milk ricotta

cheese
½ to ¾ cup sugar-free sweetener
4 large eggs
2 teaspoons vanilla extract
2 teaspoons pumpkin pie spice
Whipped cream, for garnish (optional)

1. Preheat the oven to 350°F(180°C). Line the bottom of a 9-inch springform pan with parchment paper. 2. In a small bowl, combine the almond flour and melted butter with a fork until well combined. Using your fingers, press the mixture into the bottom of the prepared pan. 3. In a large bowl, beat together the pumpkin purée, cream cheese, ricotta, and sweetener using an electric mixer on medium. 4. Add the eggs, one at a time, beating after each addition. Stir in the vanilla and pumpkin pie spice until just combined. 5. Pour the mixture over the crust and bake until set, 40 to 45 minutes. 6. Allow to cool to room temperature. Refrigerate for at least 6 hours before serving. 7. Serve chilled, garnishing with whipped cream, if desired.

Per Serving:

calories: 230 | fat: 21g | protein: 6g | carbs: 5g | fiber: 1g | sodium: 103mg

Almond Rice Pudding

Prep time: 5 minutes | Cook time: 45 minutes |
Serves 8

1 cup Arborio rice
¼ teaspoon kosher salt
5 cups unsweetened almond milk
2 tablespoons chopped preserved lemon or dried

lemons
½ cup sugar
2 teaspoons vanilla extract
2 tablespoons slivered almonds, toasted (optional)

1. In a medium saucepan, combine the rice, salt, and 2 cups water. Bring to a boil. Reduce the heat to low-medium, cover the pan with the lid ajar, and cook until the water has been almost completely absorbed, 6 to 8 minutes, stirring occasionally. 2. Stir in the almond milk, sugar, dried or preserved lemon, and vanilla. Bring the mixture to a simmer, stirring occasionally, and cook until the rice is tender and the mixture has thickened, 30 to 35 minutes. Let cool slightly before serving. 3. Serve warm, topped with toasted almonds, if desired.

Per Serving:

calories: 203 | fat: 10g | protein: 9g | carbs: 23g | fiber: 4g | sodium: 146mg

Chocolate Pudding

Prep time: 10 minutes | Cook time: 0 minutes |
Serves 4

2 ripe avocados, halved and pitted
¼ cup unsweetened cocoa powder
¼ cup heavy whipping cream, plus more if needed
2 teaspoons vanilla extract

1 to 2 teaspoons liquid stevia or monk fruit extract (optional)
½ teaspoon ground cinnamon (optional)
¼ teaspoon salt
Whipped cream, for serving (optional)

1. Using a spoon, scoop out the ripe avocado into a blender or large bowl, if using an immersion blender. Mash well with a fork. 2. Add the cocoa powder, heavy whipping cream, vanilla, sweetener (if using), cinnamon (if using), and salt. Blend well until smooth and creamy, adding additional cream, 1 tablespoon at a time, if the mixture is too thick. 3. Cover and refrigerate for at least 1 hour before serving. Serve chilled with additional whipped cream, if desired.

Per Serving:

calories: 205 | fat: 18g | protein: 3g | carbs: 12g | fiber: 9g | sodium: 156mg

Chocolate Turtle Hummus

Prep time: 15 minutes | Cook time: 0 minutes |
Serves 2

For the Caramel:
2 tablespoons coconut oil
1 tablespoon maple syrup
1 tablespoon almond butter
Pinch salt
For the Hummus:
½ cup chickpeas, drained and rinsed

2 tablespoons unsweetened cocoa powder
1 tablespoon maple syrup, plus more to taste
2 tablespoons almond milk, or more as needed, to thin
Pinch salt
2 tablespoons pecans

Make the caramel 1. put the coconut oil in a small microwave-safe bowl. If it's solid, microwave it for about 15 seconds to melt it. 2. Stir in the maple syrup, almond butter, and salt. 3. Place the caramel in the refrigerator for 5 to 10 minutes to thicken. Make the hummus 1. In a food processor, combine the chickpeas, cocoa powder, maple syrup, almond milk, and pinch of salt, and process until smooth. Scrape down the sides to make sure everything is incorporated. 2. If the hummus seems too thick, add another tablespoon of almond milk. 3. Add the pecans and pulse 6 times to roughly chop them. 4. Transfer the hummus to a serving bowl and when the caramel is thickened, swirl it into the hummus. Gently fold it in, but don't mix it in completely. 5. Serve with fresh fruit or pretzels.

Per Serving:

calories: 321 | fat: 22g | protein: 7g | carbs: 30g | fiber: 6g | sodium: 100mg

Roasted Plums with Nut Crumble

Prep time: 5 minutes | Cook time: 25 minutes | Serves 4

¼ cup honey

¼ cup freshly squeezed orange juice

4 large plums, halved and pitted

¼ cup whole-wheat pastry flour

1 tablespoon pure maple sugar

1 tablespoon nuts, coarsely chopped (your choice; I like almonds, pecans, and walnuts)

1½ teaspoons canola oil

½ cup plain Greek yogurt

1. Preheat the oven to 400°F (205°C). Combine the honey and orange juice in a square baking dish. Place the plums, cut-side down, in the dish. Roast about 15 minutes, and then turn the plums over and roast an additional 10 minutes, or until tender and juicy. 2. In a medium bowl, combine the flour, maple sugar, nuts, and canola oil and mix well. Spread on a small baking sheet and bake alongside the plums, tossing once, until golden brown, about 5 minutes. Set aside until the plums have finished cooking. 3. Serve the plums drizzled with pan juices and topped with the nut crumble and a dollop of yogurt.

Per Serving:

calories: 175 | fat: 3g | protein: 4g | carbs: 36g | fiber: 2g | sodium: 10mg

Lemon Coconut Cake

Prep time: 5 minutes | Cook time: 40 minutes | Serves 9

Base:

6 large eggs, separated

⅓ cup melted ghee or virgin coconut oil

1 tablespoon fresh lemon juice

Zest of 2 lemons

2 cups almond flour

½ cup coconut flour

¼ cup collagen powder

1 teaspoon baking soda

1 teaspoon vanilla powder or 1 tablespoon unsweetened vanilla extract

Optional: low-carb sweetener, to taste

Topping:

½ cup unsweetened large coconut flakes

1 cup heavy whipping cream or coconut cream

¼ cup mascarpone, more heavy whipping cream, or coconut cream

½ teaspoon vanilla powder or 1½ teaspoons unsweetened vanilla extract

1. Preheat the oven to 285°F (140°C) fan assisted or 320°F (160°C) conventional. Line a baking tray with parchment paper (or use a silicone tray). A square 8 × 8–inch (20 × 20 cm) or a rectangular tray of similar size will work best. 2. To make the base: Whisk the egg whites in a bowl until stiff peaks form. In a separate bowl, whisk the egg yolks, melted ghee, lemon juice, and lemon zest. In a third bowl, mix the almond flour, coconut flour, collagen, baking soda, vanilla and optional sweetener. 3. Add the whisked egg yolk–ghee mixture into the dry mixture and combine well. Gently fold in the egg whites, trying not to deflate them. 4. Pour into the baking tray. Bake for 35 to 40 minutes, until lightly golden on top and set inside. Remove from the oven and let cool completely before adding the topping. 5. To make the topping: Preheat the oven to 350°F (175°C) fan assisted or 380°F (195°C) conventional. Place the coconut flakes on a baking tray and bake for 2 to 3 minutes. Remove from the oven and set aside to cool. 6. Once the cake is cool, place the cream, mascarpone, and vanilla in a bowl. Whip until soft peaks form. Spread on top of the cooled cake and top with the toasted coconut flakes. 7. To store, refrigerate for up to 5 days or freeze for up to 3 months. Coconut flakes will soften in the fridge. If you want to keep them crunchy, sprinkle on top of each slice before serving.

Per Serving:

calories: 342 | fat: 31g | protein: 9g | carbs: 10g | fiber: 4g | sodium: 208mg

Cherry-Stuffed Apples

Prep time: 15 minutes | Cook time: 4 hours | Serves 2

3 apples

1 tablespoon freshly squeezed lemon juice

⅓ cup dried cherries

2 tablespoons apple cider

2 tablespoons honey

¼ cup water

1. Cut about half an inch off the top of each of the apples, and peel a small strip of the skin away around the top. 2. Using a small serrated spoon or melon baller, core the apples, making sure not to go through the bottom. Drizzle with the lemon juice. 3. Fill the apples with the dried cherries. Carefully spoon the cider and honey into the apples. 4. Place the apples in the slow cooker. Pour the water around the apples. 5. Cover and cook on low for 4 hours, or until the apples are soft, and serve.

Per Serving:

calories: 227 | fat: 1g | protein: 1g | carbs: 60g | fiber: 7g | sodium: 6mg

Minty Watermelon Salad

Prep time: 10 minutes | Cook time: 0 minutes | Serves 6 to 8

1 medium watermelon

1 cup fresh blueberries

2 tablespoons fresh mint leaves

2 tablespoons lemon juice

⅓ cup honey

1. Cut the watermelon into 1-inch cubes. Put them in a bowl. 2. Evenly distribute the blueberries over the watermelon. 3. Finely chop the mint leaves and put them into a separate bowl. 4. Add the lemon juice and honey to the mint and whisk together. 5. Drizzle the mint dressing over the watermelon and blueberries. Serve cold.

Per Serving:

calories: 238 | fat: 1g | protein: 4g | carbs: 61g | fiber: 3g | sodium: 11mg

Strawberry-Pomegranate Molasses Sauce

Prep time: 10 minutes | Cook time: 5 minutes | Serves 6

3 tablespoons olive oil
¼ cup honey
2 pints strawberries, hulled and halved
1 to 2 tablespoons pomegranate molasses
2 tablespoons chopped fresh mint
Greek yogurt, for serving

1. In a medium saucepan, heat the olive oil over medium heat. Add the strawberries; cook until their juices are released. Stir in the honey and cook for 1 to 2 minutes. Stir in the molasses and mint. Serve warm over Greek yogurt.

Per Serving:

calories: 189 | fat: 7g | protein: 4g | carbs: 24g | fiber: 3g | sodium: 12mg

Figs with Mascarpone and Honey

Prep time: 5 minutes | Cook time: 5 minutes | Serves 4

⅓ cup walnuts, chopped
8 fresh figs, halved
¼ cup mascarpone cheese
1 tablespoon honey
¼ teaspoon flaked sea salt

1. In a skillet over medium heat, toast the walnuts, stirring often, 3 to 5 minutes. 2. Arrange the figs cut-side up on a plate or platter. Using your finger, make a small depression in the cut side of each fig and fill with mascarpone cheese. Sprinkle with a bit of the walnuts, drizzle with the honey, and add a tiny pinch of sea salt.

Per Serving:

calories: 200 | fat: 13g | protein: 3g | carbs: 24g | fiber: 3g | sodium: 105mg

Red Grapefruit Granita

Prep time: 5 minutes | Cook time: 0 minutes | Serves 4 to 6

3 cups red grapefruit sections
1 cup freshly squeezed red grapefruit juice
¼ cup honey
1 tablespoon freshly squeezed lime juice
Fresh basil leaves for garnish

1. Remove as much pith (white part) and membrane as possible from the grapefruit segments. 2. Combine all ingredients except the basil in a blender or food processor and pulse just until smooth. 3. Pour the mixture into a shallow glass baking dish and place in the freezer for 1 hour. Stir with a fork and freeze for another 30 minutes, then repeat. To serve, scoop into small dessert glasses and garnish with fresh basil leaves.

Per Serving:

calories: 94 | fat: 0g | protein: 1g | carbs: 24g | fiber: 1g | sodium: 1mg

Cinnamon-Stewed Dried Plums with Greek Yogurt

Prep time: 5 minutes | Cook time: 3 minutes | Serves 6

3 cups dried plums
2 cups water
2 tablespoons sugar
2 cinnamon sticks
3 cups low-fat plain Greek yogurt

1. Add dried plums, water, sugar, and cinnamon to the Instant Pot®. Close lid, set steam release to Sealing, press the Manual button, and set time to 3 minutes. 2. When the timer beeps, quick-release the pressure until the float valve drops. Press the Cancel button and open lid. Remove and discard cinnamon sticks. Serve warm over Greek yogurt.

Per Serving:

calories: 301 | fat: 2g | protein: 14g | carbs: 61g | fiber: 4g | sodium: 50mg

Grilled Fruit Kebabs with Honey Labneh

Prep time: 15 minutes | Cook time: 10 minutes | Serves 2

⅔ cup prepared labneh, or, if making your own, ⅔ cup full-fat plain Greek yogurt
2 tablespoons honey
1 teaspoon vanilla extract
Pinch salt
3 cups fresh fruit cut into 2-inch chunks (pineapple, cantaloupe, nectarines, strawberries, plums, or mango)

1. If making your own labneh, place a colander over a bowl and line it with cheesecloth. Place the Greek yogurt in the cheesecloth and wrap it up. Put the bowl in the refrigerator and let sit for at least 12 to 24 hours, until it's thick like soft cheese. 2. Mix honey, vanilla, and salt into labneh. Stir well to combine and set it aside. 3. Heat the grill to medium (about 300°F/ 150ºC) and oil the grill grate. Alternatively, you can cook these on the stovetop in a heavy grill pan (cast iron works well). 4. Thread the fruit onto skewers and grill for 4 minutes on each side, or until fruit is softened and has grill marks on each side. 5. Serve the fruit with labneh to dip.

Per Serving:

calories: 292 | fat: 6g | protein: 5g | carbs: 60g | fiber: 4g | sodium: 131mg

Greek Island Almond Cocoa Bites

Prep time: 5 minutes | Cook time: 0 minutes | Serves 6

½ cup roasted, unsalted whole almonds (with skins)

3 tablespoons granulated sugar, divided

1½ teaspoons unsweetened

cocoa powder

1¼ tablespoons unseasoned breadcrumbs

¾ teaspoon pure vanilla extract

1½ teaspoons orange juice

1. Place the almonds in a food processor and process until you have a coarse ground texture. 2. In a medium bowl, combine the ground almonds, 2 tablespoons sugar, the cocoa powder, and the breadcrumbs. Mix well. 3. In a small bowl, combine the vanilla extract and orange juice. Stir and then add the mixture to the almond mixture. Mix well. 4. Measure out a teaspoon of the mixture. Squeeze the mixture with your hand to make the dough stick together, then mold the dough into a small ball. 5. Add the remaining tablespoon of the sugar to a shallow bowl. Roll the balls in the sugar until covered, then transfer the bites to an airtight container. Store covered at room temperature for up to 1 week.

Per Serving:

calories: 102 | fat: 6g | protein: 3g | carbs: 10g | fiber: 2g | sodium: 11mg

Almond Pistachio Biscotti

Prep time: 5 minutes | Cook time: 1 hour 20 minutes | Serves 12

2 cups almond flour or hazelnut flour

½ packed cup flax meal

½ teaspoon baking soda

½ teaspoon ground nutmeg

½ teaspoon vanilla powder or 1½ teaspoons unsweetened vanilla extract

¼ teaspoon salt

1 tablespoon fresh lemon zest

2 large eggs

2 tablespoons extra-virgin olive oil

1 tablespoon unsweetened almond extract

1 teaspoon apple cider vinegar or fresh lemon juice

Optional: low-carb sweetener, to taste

⅔ cup unsalted pistachio nuts

1. Preheat the oven to 285°F (140°C) fan assisted or 320°F (160°C) conventional. Line one or two baking trays with parchment paper. 2. In a bowl, mix the almond flour, flax meal, baking soda, nutmeg, vanilla, salt, and lemon zest. Add the eggs, olive oil, almond extract, vinegar, and optional sweetener. Mix well until a dough forms, then mix in the pistachio nuts. 3. Form the dough into a low, wide log shape, about 8 × 5 inches (20 × 13 cm). Place in the oven and bake for about 45 minutes. Remove from oven and let cool for 15 to 20 minutes. Using a sharp knife, cut into 12 slices. 4. Reduce the oven temperature to 250°F (120°C) fan assisted or 285°F (140°C) conventional. Lay the slices very carefully in a flat layer on the lined trays. Bake for 15 to 20 minutes, flip over, and bake for 15 to 20 minutes. 5. Remove from the oven and let the biscotti cool down completely to fully crisp up. Store in a sealed jar for up to 2 weeks.

Per Serving:

calories: 196 | fat: 17g | protein: 7g | carbs: 7g | fiber: 4g | sodium: 138mg

Peaches Poached in Rose Water

Prep time: 15 minutes | Cook time: 1 minute | Serves 6

1 cup water

1 cup rose water

¼ cup wildflower honey

8 green cardamom pods, lightly crushed

1 teaspoon vanilla bean paste

6 large yellow peaches, pitted and quartered

½ cup chopped unsalted roasted pistachio meats

1. Add water, rose water, honey, cardamom, and vanilla to the Instant Pot®. Whisk well, then add peaches. Close lid, set steam release to Sealing, press the Manual button, and set time to 1 minute. 2. When the timer beeps, quick-release the pressure until the float valve drops. Press the Cancel button and open lid. Allow peaches to stand for 10 minutes. Carefully remove peaches from poaching liquid with a slotted spoon. 3. Slip skins from peach slices. Arrange slices on a plate and garnish with pistachios. Serve warm or at room temperature.

Per Serving:

calories: 145 | fat: 3g | protein: 2g | carbs: 28g | fiber: 2g | sodium: 8mg

Dark Chocolate Lava Cake

Prep time: 5 minutes | Cook time: 10 minutes | Serves 4

Olive oil cooking spray

¼ cup whole wheat flour

1 tablespoon unsweetened dark chocolate cocoa powder

⅛ teaspoon salt

½ teaspoon baking powder

¼ cup raw honey

1 egg

2 tablespoons olive oil

1. Preheat the air fryer to 380°F(193°C). Lightly coat the insides of four ramekins with olive oil cooking spray. 2. In a medium bowl, combine the flour, cocoa powder, salt, baking powder, honey, egg, and olive oil. 3. Divide the batter evenly among the ramekins. 4. Place the filled ramekins inside the air fryer and bake for 10 minutes. 5. Remove the lava cakes from the air fryer and slide a knife around the outside edge of each cake. Turn each ramekin upside down on a saucer and serve.

Per Serving:

calories: 179 | fat: 8g | protein: 3g | carbs: 26g | fiber: 1g | sodium: 95mg

Grilled Stone Fruit with Whipped Ricotta

Prep time: 10 minutes |Cook time: 10 minutes|

Serves: 4

Nonstick cooking spray

4 peaches or nectarines (or 8 apricots or plums), halved and pitted

2 teaspoons extra-virgin olive oil

¾ cup whole-milk ricotta

cheese

1 tablespoon honey

¼ teaspoon freshly grated nutmeg

4 sprigs mint, for garnish (optional)

1. Spray the cold grill or a grill pan with nonstick cooking spray. Heat the grill or grill pan to medium heat. 2. Place a large, empty bowl in the refrigerator to chill. 3. Brush the fruit all over with the oil. Place the fruit cut-side down on the grill or pan and cook for 3 to 5 minutes, or until grill marks appear. (If you're using a grill pan, cook in two batches.) Using tongs, turn the fruit over. Cover the grill (or the grill pan with aluminum foil) and cook for 4 to 6 minutes, until the fruit is easily pierced with a sharp knife. Set aside to cool. 4. Remove the bowl from the refrigerator and add the ricotta. Using an electric beater, beat the ricotta on high for 2 minutes. Add the honey and nutmeg and beat for 1 more minute. Divide the warm (or room temperature) fruit among 4 serving bowls, top with the ricotta mixture, and a sprig of mint (if using) and serve.

Per Serving:

calories: 180 | fat: 9g | protein: 7g | carbs: 21g | fiber: 3g | sodium: 39mg

Tortilla Fried Pies

Prep time: 10 minutes | Cook time: 5 minutes per batch | Makes 12 pies

12 small flour tortillas (4-inch diameter)

½ cup fig preserves

¼ cup sliced almonds

2 tablespoons shredded, unsweetened coconut

Oil for misting or cooking spray

1. Wrap refrigerated tortillas in damp paper towels and heat in microwave 30 seconds to warm. 2. Working with one tortilla at a time, place 2 teaspoons fig preserves, 1 teaspoon sliced almonds, and ½ teaspoon coconut in the center of each. 3. Moisten outer edges of tortilla all around. 4. Fold one side of tortilla over filling to make a half-moon shape and press down lightly on center. Using the tines of a fork, press down firmly on edges of tortilla to seal in filling. 5. Mist both sides with oil or cooking spray. 6. Place hand pies in air fryer basket close but not overlapping. It's fine to lean some against the sides and corners of the basket. You may need to cook in 2 batches. 7. Air fry at 390ºF (199ºC) for 5 minutes or until lightly browned. Serve hot. 8. Refrigerate any leftover pies in a closed container. To serve later, toss them back in the air fryer basket and cook for 2 or 3 minutes to reheat.

Per Serving:

1 pie: calories: 137 | fat: 4g | protein: 4g | carbs: 22g | fiber: 2g | sodium: 279mg

Fruit Compote

Prep time: 15 minutes | Cook time: 11 minutes |

Serves 6

1 cup apple juice

1 cup dry white wine

2 tablespoons honey

1 cinnamon stick

¼ teaspoon ground nutmeg

1 tablespoon grated lemon zest

1½ tablespoons grated orange

zest

3 large apples, peeled, cored, and chopped

3 large pears, peeled, cored, and chopped

½ cup dried cherries

1. Place all ingredients in the Instant Pot® and stir well. Close lid, set steam release to Sealing, press the Manual button, and set time to 1 minute. When the timer beeps, quick-release the pressure until the float valve drops. Press the Cancel button and open lid. 2. Use a slotted spoon to transfer fruit to a serving bowl. Remove and discard cinnamon stick. Press the Sauté button and bring juice in the pot to a boil. Cook, stirring constantly, until reduced to a syrup that will coat the back of a spoon, about 10 minutes. 3. Stir syrup into fruit mixture. Allow to cool slightly, then cover with plastic wrap and refrigerate overnight.

Per Serving:

calories: 211 | fat: 1g | protein: 2g | carbs: 44g | fiber: 5g | sodium: 7mg

Creamy Spiced Almond Milk

Prep time: 5 minutes | Cook time: 1 minute | Serves 6

1 cup raw almonds

5 cups filtered water, divided

1 teaspoon vanilla bean paste

½ teaspoon pumpkin pie spice

1. Add almonds and 1 cup water to the Instant Pot®. Close lid, set steam release to Sealing, press the Manual button, and set time to 1 minute. 2. When the timer beeps, quick-release the pressure until the float valve drops. Press the Cancel button and open lid. Strain almonds and rinse under cool water. Transfer to a high-powered blender with remaining 3.cups water. Purée for 2 minutes on high speed. 4. Pour mixture into a nut milk bag set over a large bowl. Squeeze bag to extract all liquid. Stir in vanilla and pumpkin pie spice. Transfer to a Mason jar or sealed jug and refrigerate for 8 hours. Stir or shake gently before serving.

Per Serving:

calories: 86 | fat: 8g | protein: 3g | carbs: 3g | fiber: 2g | sodium: 0mg

Fresh Figs with Chocolate Sauce

Prep time: 5 minutes | Cook time: 0 minutes | Serves 4

¼ cup honey
2 tablespoons cocoa powder

8 fresh figs

1. Combine the honey and cocoa powder in a small bowl, and mix well to form a syrup. 2. Cut the figs in half and place cut side up. Drizzle with the syrup and serve.

Per Serving:

calories: 112 | fat: 1g | protein: 1g | carbs: 30g | fiber: 3g | sodium: 3mg

Minty Cantaloupe Granita

Prep time: 10 minutes | Cook time: 5 minutes |
Serves 4

½ cup plus 2 tablespoons honey
¼ cup water
2 tablespoons fresh mint leaves, plus more for garnish

1 medium cantaloupe (about 4 pounds/ 1.8 kg) peeled, seeded, and cut into 1-inch chunks

1. In a small saucepan set over low heat, combine the honey and water and cook, stirring, until the honey has fully dissolved. Stir in the mint and remove from the heat. Set aside to cool. 2. In a food processor, process the cantaloupe until very smooth. Transfer to a medium bowl. Remove the mint leaves from the syrup and discard them. Pour the syrup into the cantaloupe purée and stir to mix. 3. Transfer the mixture into a 7-by-12-inch glass baking dish and freeze, stirring with a fork every 30 minutes, for 3 to 4 hours, until it is frozen, but still grainy. Serve chilled, scooped into glasses and garnished with mint leaves.

Per Serving:

calories: 174 | fat: 0g | protein: 1g | carbs: 47g | fiber: 1g | sodium: 9mg

Apricot and Mint No-Bake Parfait

Prep time: 10 minutes | Cook time: 0 minutes |
Serves 6

4 ounces (113 g) Neufchâtel or other light cream cheese
1 (7 ounces / 198 g) container 2% Greek yogurt
½ cup plus 2 tablespoons sugar
2 teaspoons vanilla extract
1 tablespoon fresh lemon juice

1 pound (454 g) apricots, rinsed, pitted, and cut into bite-size pieces
2 tablespoons finely chopped fresh mint, plus whole leaves for garnish if desired

1. In the bowl of a stand mixer fitted with the paddle attachment, beat the Neufchâtel cheese and yogurt on low speed until well combined, about 2 minutes, scraping down the bowl as needed. Add ½ cup of the sugar, the vanilla, and the lemon juice. Mix until smooth and free of lumps, 2 to 3 minutes; set aside. 2. In a medium bowl, combine the apricots, mint, and remaining 2 tablespoons sugar. Stir occasionally, waiting to serve until after the apricots have released their juices and have softened. 3. Line up six 6-to 8-ounces (170 to 227 g) glasses. Using an ice cream scoop, spoon 3 to 4 tablespoons of the cheesecake mixture evenly into the bottom of each glass. (Alternatively, transfer the cheesecake mixture to a piping bag or a small zip-top bag with one corner snipped and pipe the mixture into the glasses.) Add a layer of the same amount of apricots to each glass. Repeat so you have two layers of cheesecake mixture and two layers of the apricots, ending with the apricots.) Garnish with the mint, if desired, and serve.

Per Serving:

calories: 132 | fat: 2g | protein: 5g | carbs: 23g | fiber: 2g | sodium: 35mg

Pomegranate-Quinoa Dark Chocolate Bark

Prep time: 10 minutes |Cook time: 10 minutes|
Serves: 6

Nonstick cooking spray
½ cup uncooked tricolor or regular quinoa
½ teaspoon kosher or sea salt

8 ounces (227 g) dark chocolate or 1 cup dark chocolate chips
½ cup fresh pomegranate seeds

1. In a medium saucepan coated with nonstick cooking spray over medium heat, toast the uncooked quinoa for 2 to 3 minutes, stirring frequently. Do not let the quinoa burn. Remove the pan from the stove, and mix in the salt. Set aside 2 tablespoons of the toasted quinoa to use for the topping. 2. Break the chocolate into large pieces, and put it in a gallon-size zip-top plastic bag. Using a metal ladle or a meat pounder, pound the chocolate until broken into smaller pieces. (If using chocolate chips, you can skip this step.) Dump the chocolate out of the bag into a medium, microwave-safe bowl and heat for 1 minute on high in the microwave. Stir until the chocolate is completely melted. Mix the toasted quinoa (except the topping you set aside) into the melted chocolate. 3. Line a large, rimmed baking sheet with parchment paper. Pour the chocolate mixture onto the sheet and spread it evenly until the entire pan is covered. Sprinkle the remaining 2 tablespoons of quinoa and the pomegranate seeds on top. Using a spatula or the back of a spoon, press the quinoa and the pomegranate seeds into the chocolate. 4. Freeze the mixture for 10 to 15 minutes, or until set. Remove the bark from the freezer, and break it into about 2-inch jagged pieces. Store in a sealed container or zip-top plastic bag in the refrigerator until ready to serve.

Per Serving:

calories: 290 | fat: 17g | protein: 5g | carbs: 29g | fiber: 6g | sodium: 202mg

Grilled Stone Fruit

Prep time: 15 minutes | Cook time: 6 minutes | Serves 2

2 peaches, halved and pitted

2 plums, halved and pitted

3 apricots, halved and pitted

½ cup low-fat ricotta cheese

2 tablespoons honey

1. Heat grill to medium heat. 2. Oil the grates or spray with cooking spray. 3. Place the fruit cut side down on the grill, and grill for 2–3 minutes per side, until lightly charred and soft. 4. Serve warm with the ricotta and drizzle with honey.

Per Serving:

calories: 263 | fat: 6g | protein: 10g | carbs: 48g | fiber: 4g | sodium: 63mg

Cucumber-Lime Popsicles

Prep time: 5 minutes | Cook time: 0 minutes | Serves 4 to 6

2 cups cold water

1 cucumber, peeled

¼ cup honey

Juice of 1 lime

1. In a blender, purée the water, cucumber, honey, and lime juice. Pour into popsicle molds, freeze, and enjoy on a hot summer day!

Per Serving:

calories: 49 | fat: 0g | protein: 0g | carbs: 13g | fiber: 0g | sodium: 3mg

Chapter 10 Salads

Easy Greek Salad

Prep time: 10 minutes | Cook time: 0 minutes |

Serves 4 to 6

1 head iceberg lettuce	1 teaspoon salt
1 pint (2 cups) cherry tomatoes	1 clove garlic, minced
1 large cucumber	1 cup Kalamata olives, pitted
1 medium onion	1 (6 ounces / 170 g) package
½ cup extra-virgin olive oil	feta cheese, crumbled
¼ cup lemon juice	

1. Cut the lettuce into 1-inch pieces and put them in a large salad bowl. 2. Cut the tomatoes in half and add them to the salad bowl. 3. Slice the cucumber into bite-size pieces and add them to the salad bowl. 4. Thinly slice the onion and add it to the salad bowl. 5. In another small bowl, whisk together the olive oil, lemon juice, salt, and garlic. Pour the dressing over the salad and gently toss to evenly coat. 6. Top the salad with the Kalamata olives and feta cheese and serve.

Per Serving:

calories: 297 | fat: 27g | protein: 6g | carbs: 11g | fiber: 3g | sodium: 661mg

Caprese Salad with Fresh Mozzarella

Prep time: 10 minutes | Cook time: 0 minutes |

Serves 6 to 8

For the Pesto:	Freshly ground black pepper
2 cups (packed) fresh basil leaves, plus more for garnish	For the Salad:
⅓ cup pine nuts	4 to 6 large, ripe tomatoes, cut into thick slices
3 garlic cloves, minced	1 pound (454 g) fresh
½ cup (about 2 ounces / 57 g) freshly grated Parmesan cheese	mozzarella, cut into thick slices
½ cup extra-virgin olive oil	3 tablespoons balsamic vinegar
Salt	Salt
	Freshly ground black pepper

1. To make the pesto, in a food processor combine the basil, pine nuts, and garlic and pulse several times to chop. Add the Parmesan cheese and pulse again until well combined. With the food processor running, add the olive oil in a slow, steady stream. Transfer to a small bowl, taste, and add salt and pepper as needed.

Slice, quarter, or halve the tomatoes, based on your preferred salad presentation. 2. To make the salad, on a large serving platter arrange the tomato slices and cheese slices, stacking them like fallen dominoes. 3. Dollop the pesto decoratively on top of the tomato and cheese slices. (You will likely have extra pesto. Refrigerate the extra in a tightly sealed container and use within 3 days, or freeze it for up to 3 months.) 4. Drizzle the balsamic vinegar over the top, garnish with basil leaves, sprinkle with salt and pepper to taste, and serve immediately.

Per Serving:

calories: 398 | fat: 32g | protein: 23g | carbs: 8g | fiber: 1g | sodium: 474mg

Spinach Salad with Pomegranate, Lentils, and Pistachios

Prep time: 10 minutes | Cook time: 30 minutes |

Serves 4

1 tablespoon extra-virgin olive oil	rinsed
1 shallot, finely chopped	3 cups water
1 small red chile pepper, such as a Fresno, finely chopped (wear plastic gloves when handling)	6 cups baby spinach
	½ cup pomegranate seeds
	¼ cup chopped fresh cilantro
½ teaspoon ground cumin	¼ cup chopped fresh flat-leaf parsley
¼ teaspoon ground coriander seeds	¼ cup chopped pistachi os
¼ teaspoon ground cinnamon	2 tablespoons fresh lemon juice
Pinch of kosher salt	1 teaspoon finely grated lemon peel
1 cup French green lentils,	Ground black pepper, to taste

1. In a medium saucepan over medium heat, warm the oil until shimmering. Cook the shallot and chile pepper, stirring, until the shallot is translucent, about 8 minutes. Stir in the cumin, coriander, cinnamon, and salt until fragrant, about 1 minute. Add the lentils and water and bring to a boil. Cover and reduce the heat to a simmer. Cook, stirring occasionally, until the lentils are completely tender and the liquid has been absorbed, about 30 minutes. 2. In a large bowl, toss the lentils with the spinach, pomegranate seeds, cilantro, parsley, pistachios, lemon juice, lemon peel, and pepper to taste.

Per Serving:

calories: 279 | fat: 7g | protein: 15g | carbs: 39g | fiber: 10g | sodium: 198mg

Bacalhau and Black-Eyed Pea Salad

Prep time: 10 minutes | Cook time: 10 minutes | Serves 4

1 pound (454 g) bacalhau (salt cod) fillets
¼ cup olive oil, plus 1 tablespoon, divided
3 tablespoons white wine vinegar
1 teaspoon salt
¼ teaspoon freshly ground black pepper
1 (15 ounces / 425 g) can black-eyed peas, drained and rinsed
1 small yellow onion, halved and thinly sliced crosswise
1 small clove garlic, minced
¼ cup chopped fresh flat-leaf parsley leaves, divided

1. Rinse the cod under cold running water to remove any surface salt. Place the fish pieces in a large nonreactive pot, cover with water and refrigerate (covered) for 24 hours, changing the water several times. 2. Pour off the water, refill the pot with clean water and gently boil the cod until it flakes easily with a fork, about 7 to 10 minutes (or longer), depending on the thickness. Drain and set aside to cool. 3. To make the dressing, whisk together the oil, vinegar, salt, and pepper in a small bowl. 4. In a large bowl, combine the beans, onion, garlic, and ¾ of the parsley. Add the dressing and mix to coat well. Stir in the salt cod, cover, and chill in the refrigerator for at least 2 hours to let the flavors meld. Let sit on the countertop for 30 minutes before serving. 5. Serve garnished with the remaining parsley.

Per Serving:

calories: 349 | fat: 18g | protein: 32g | carbs: 16g | fiber: 4g | sodium: 8mg

Endive with Shrimp

Prep time: 15 minutes | Cook time: 2 minutes | Serves 4

¼ cup olive oil
1 small shallot, minced
1 tablespoon Dijon mustard
Juice and zest of 1 lemon
Sea salt and freshly ground pepper, to taste
2 cups salted water
14 shrimp, peeled and deveined
1 head endive
½ cup tart green apple, diced
2 tablespoons toasted walnuts

1. For the vinaigrette, whisk together the first five ingredients in a small bowl until creamy and emulsified. 2. Refrigerate for at least 2 hours for best flavor. 3. In a small pan, boil salted water. Add the shrimp and cook 1–2 minutes, or until the shrimp turns pink. Drain and cool under cold water. 4. To assemble the salad, wash and break the endive. Place on serving plates and top with the shrimp, green apple, and toasted walnuts. 5. Drizzle with the vinaigrette before serving.

Per Serving:

calories: 194 | fat: 16g | protein: 6g | carbs: 8g | fiber: 5g | sodium: 191mg

Taverna-Style Greek Salad

Prep time: 20 minutes | Cook time: 0 minutes | Serves 4

4 to 5 medium tomatoes, roughly chopped
1 large cucumber, peeled and roughly chopped
1 medium green bell pepper, sliced
1 small red onion, sliced
16 pitted Kalamata olives
¼ cup capers, or more olives
1 teaspoon dried oregano or fresh herbs of your choice, such as parsley, cilantro, chives, or basil, divided
½ cup extra-virgin olive oil, divided
1 pack feta cheese
Optional: salt, pepper, and fresh oregano, for garnish

1. Place the vegetables in a large serving bowl. Add the olives, capers, feta, half of the dried oregano and half of the olive oil. Mix to combine. Place the whole piece of feta cheese on top, sprinkle with the remaining dried oregano, and drizzle with the remaining olive oil. Season to taste and serve immediately, or store in the fridge for up to 1 day.

Per Serving:

calories: 320 | fat: 31g | protein: 3g | carbs: 11g | fiber: 4g | sodium: 445mg

Arugula Salad with Grapes, Goat Cheese, and Za'atar Croutons

Prep time: 10 minutes | Cook time: 10 minutes | Serves 4

Croutons:
2 slices whole wheat bread, cubed
2 teaspoons olive oil, divided
1 teaspoon za'atar
Vinaigrette:
2 tablespoons olive oil
1 tablespoon red wine vinegar
½ teaspoon chopped fresh rosemary
¼ teaspoon kosher salt
⅛ teaspoon ground black pepper
Salad:
4 cups baby arugula
1 cup grapes, halved
½ red onion, thinly sliced
2 ounces (57 g) goat cheese, crumbled

1. Make the Croutons: Toss the bread cubes with 1 teaspoon of the oil and the za'atar. In a medium skillet over medium heat, warm the remaining 1 teaspoon oil. Cook the bread cubes, stirring frequently, until browned and crispy, 8 to 10 minutes. 2. Make the Vinaigrette: In a small bowl, whisk together the oil, vinegar, rosemary, salt, and pepper. 3. Make the Salad: In a large bowl, toss the arugula, grapes, and onion with the vinaigrette. Top with the cheese and croutons.

Per Serving:

calories: 204 | fat: 14g | protein: 6g | carbs: 15g | fiber: 2g | sodium: 283mg

Greek Village Salad

Prep time: 10 minutes | Cook time: 0 minutes |
Serves 4

5 large tomatoes, cut into medium chunks
2 red onions, cut into medium chunks or sliced
1 English cucumber, peeled and cut into medium chunks
2 green bell peppers, cut into medium chunks
¼ cup extra-virgin olive oil,

plus extra for drizzling
1 cup kalamata olives, for topping
¼ teaspoon dried oregano, plus extra for garnish
¼ lemon
4 ounces (113 g) Greek feta cheese, sliced

1. In a large bowl, mix the tomatoes, onions, cucumber, bell peppers, olive oil, olives, and oregano. 2. Divide the vegetable mixture evenly among four bowls and top each with a squirt of lemon juice and 1 slice of feta. Drizzle with olive oil, garnish with oregano, and serve.

Per Serving:
calories: 315 | fat: 24g | protein: 8g | carbs: 21g | fiber: 6g | sodium: 524mg

Greek Salad with Lemon-Oregano Vinaigrette

Prep time: 15 minutes | Cook time: 15 minutes |
Serves 8

½ red onion, thinly sliced
¼ cup extra-virgin olive oil
3 tablespoons fresh lemon juice or red wine vinegar
1 clove garlic, minced
1 teaspoon chopped fresh oregano or ½ teaspoon dried
½ teaspoon ground black pepper
¼ teaspoon kosher salt
4 tomatoes, cut into large chunks

1 large English cucumber, peeled, seeded (if desired), and diced
1 large yellow or red bell pepper, chopped
½ cup pitted kalamata or Niçoise olives, halved
¼ cup chopped fresh flat-leaf parsley
4 ounces (113 g) Halloumi or feta cheese, cut into ½' cubes

1. In a medium bowl, soak the onion in enough water to cover for 10 minutes. 2. In a small bowl, combine the oil, lemon juice or vinegar, garlic, oregano, black pepper, and salt. 3. Drain the onion and add to a large bowl with the tomatoes, cucumber, bell pepper, olives, and parsley. Gently toss to mix the vegetables. 4. Pour the vinaigrette over the salad. Add the cheese and toss again to distribute. 5. Serve immediately, or chill for up to 30 minutes.

Per Serving:
calories: 190 | fat: 16g | protein: 5g | carbs: 8g | fiber: 2g | sodium: 554mg

Simple Insalata Mista (Mixed Salad) with Honey Balsamic Dressing

Prep time: 15 minutes | Cook time: 0 minutes |
Serves 2

For the Dressing:
¼ cup balsamic vinegar
¼ cup olive oil
1 tablespoon honey
1 teaspoon Dijon mustard
¼ teaspoon salt, plus more to taste
¼ teaspoon garlic powder
Pinch freshly ground black pepper
For the Salad:

4 cups chopped red leaf lettuce
½ cup cherry or grape tomatoes, halved
½ English cucumber, sliced in quarters lengthwise and then cut into bite-size pieces
Any combination fresh, torn herbs (parsley, oregano, basil, chives, etc.)
1 tablespoon roasted sunflower seeds

Make the Dressing: Combine the vinegar, olive oil, honey, mustard, salt, garlic powder, and pepper in a jar with a lid. Shake well. Make the Salad: 1. In a large bowl, combine the lettuce, tomatoes, cucumber, and herbs. 2. Toss well to combine. 3. Pour all or as much dressing as desired over the tossed salad and toss again to coat the salad with dressing. 4. Top with the sunflower seeds.

Per Serving:
calories: 339 | fat: 26g | protein: 4g | carbs: 24g | fiber: 3g | sodium: 171mg

Yellow and White Hearts of Palm Salad

Prep time: 10 minutes | Cook time: 0 minutes |
Serves 4

2 (14 ounces / 397 g) cans hearts of palm, drained and cut into ½-inch-thick slices
1 avocado, cut into ½-inch pieces
1 cup halved yellow cherry tomatoes
½ small shallot, thinly sliced
¼ cup coarsely chopped flat-

leaf parsley
2 tablespoons low-fat mayonnaise
2 tablespoons extra-virgin olive oil
¼ teaspoon salt
⅛ teaspoon freshly ground black pepper

1. In a large bowl, toss the hearts of palm, avocado, tomatoes, shallot, and parsley. 2. In a small bowl, whisk the mayonnaise, olive oil, salt, and pepper, then mix into the large bowl.

Per Serving:
calories: 192 | fat: 15g | protein: 5g | carbs: 14g | fiber: 7g | sodium: 841mg

Italian Tuna and Olive Salad

Prep time : 5 minutes | Cook time: 0 minutes |
Serves 4

¼ cup olive oil	seeded and diced
3 tablespoons white wine vinegar	1 small clove garlic, minced
1 teaspoon salt	2 (6 ounces / 170 g) cans or jars tuna in olive oil, well drained
1 cup pitted green olives	Several leaves curly green or
1 medium red bell pepper,	red lettuce

1. In a large bowl, whisk together the olive oil, vinegar, and salt. 2. Add the olives, bell pepper, and garlic to the dressing and toss to coat. Stir in the tuna, cover, and chill in the refrigerator for at least 1 hour to let the flavors meld. 3. To serve, line a serving bowl with the lettuce leaves and spoon the salad on top. Serve chilled.

Per Serving:

calories: 339 | fat: 24g | protein: 25g | carbs: 4g | fiber: 2g | sodium: 626mg

Asparagus Salad

Prep time: 10 minutes | Cook time: 0 minutes |
Serves 4

1 pound (454 g) asparagus	4 tablespoons olive oil
Sea salt and freshly ground pepper, to taste	1 tablespoon balsamic vinegar
	1 tablespoon lemon zest

1. Either roast the asparagus or, with a vegetable peeler, shave it into thin strips. 2. Season to taste. 3. Toss with the olive oil and vinegar, garnish with a sprinkle of lemon zest, and serve.

Per Serving:

calories: 146 | fat: 14g | protein: 3g | carbs: 5g | fiber: 3g | sodium: 4mg

Fruited Chicken Salad

Prep time: 10 minutes | Cook time: 0 minutes |
Serves 2

2 cups chopped cooked chicken breast	2 tablespoons honey Dijon mustard
2 Granny Smith apples, peeled, cored, and diced	1 tablespoon olive oil mayonnaise
½ cup dried cranberries	½ teaspoon salt
¼ cup diced red onion	¼ teaspoon freshly ground black pepper
¼ cup diced celery	

1. In a medium bowl, combine the chicken, apples, cranberries, onion, and celery and mix well. 2. In a small bowl, combine the mustard, mayonnaise, salt, and pepper and whisk together until well blended. 3. Stir the dressing into the chicken mixture until thoroughly combined.

Per Serving:

calories: 384 | fat: 9g | protein: 45g | carbs: 28g | fiber: 7g | sodium: 638mg

Wilted Kale Salad

Prep time: 10 minutes | Cook time: 5 minutes |
Serves 4

2 heads kale	1 cup cherry tomatoes, sliced
1 tablespoon olive oil, plus 1 teaspoon	Sea salt and freshly ground pepper, to taste
2 cloves garlic, minced	Juice of 1 lemon

1. Rinse and dry kale. 2. Tear the kale into bite-sized pieces. 3. Heat 1 tablespoon of the olive oil in a large skillet, and add the garlic. Cook for 1 minute and then add the kale. 4. Cook just until wilted, then add the tomatoes. 5. Cook until tomatoes are softened, then remove from heat. 6. Place tomatoes and kale in a bowl, and season with sea salt and freshly ground pepper. 7. Drizzle with remaining olive oil and lemon juice, serve, and enjoy.

Per Serving:

calories: 153 | fat: 6g | protein: 10g | carbs: 23g | fiber: 9g | sodium: 88mg

Arugula and Fennel Salad with Fresh Basil

Prep time: 5 minutes | Cook time: 0 minutes | Serves 4

3 tablespoons olive oil	sliced
3 tablespoons lemon juice	2 cups arugula
1 teaspoon honey	¼ cup toasted pine nuts
½ teaspoon salt	½ cup crumbled feta cheese
1 medium bulb fennel, very thinly sliced	¼ cup julienned fresh basil leaves
1 small cucumber, very thinly	

1. In a medium bowl, whisk together the olive oil, lemon juice, honey, and salt. Add the fennel and cucumber and toss to coat and let sit for 10 minutes or so. 2. Put the arugula in a large salad bowl. Add the marinated cucumber and fennel, along with the dressing, to the bowl and toss well. Serve immediately, sprinkled with pine nuts, feta cheese, and basil.

Per Serving:

calories: 237 | fat: 21g | protein: 6g | carbs: 11g | fiber: 3g | sodium: 537mg

Italian Coleslaw

Prep time: 10 minutes | Cook time: 0 minutes |

Serves 6

1 cup shredded green cabbage	¼ cup sliced red onion or
½ cup shredded red cabbage	shallot
½ cup shredded carrot	2 tablespoons olive oil
1 small yellow bell pepper,	3 tablespoons red wine vinegar
seeded and cut into thin strips	¼ teaspoon celery seeds

1. In a large bowl, mix all the ingredients. Refrigerate until chilled before serving.

Per Serving:

calories: 62 | fat: 4g | protein: 1g | carbs: 5g | fiber: 1g | sodium: 14mg

Watermelon Burrata Salad

Prep time: 10 minutes | Cook time: 0 minutes |

Serves 4

2 cups cubes or chunks	4 fresh basil leaves, sliced
watermelon	chiffonade-style (roll up leaves
1½ cups small burrata cheese	of basil, and slice into thin
balls, cut into medium chunks	strips)
1 small red onion or 2 shallots,	1 tablespoon lemon zest
thinly sliced into half-moons	Salt and freshly ground black
¼ cup olive oil	pepper, to taste
¼ cup balsamic vinegar	

1. In a large bowl, mix all the ingredients. Refrigerate until chilled before serving.

Per Serving:

1 cup: calories: 224 | fat: 14g | protein: 14g | carbs: 12g | fiber: 1g | sodium: 560mg

Cauliflower Tabbouleh Salad

Prep time: 15 minutes | Cook time: 0 minutes |

Serves 4

¼ cup extra-virgin olive oil	⅛ teaspoon ground cinnamon
¼ cup lemon juice	1 pound (454 g) riced
Zest of 1 lemon	cauliflower
¾ teaspoon kosher salt	1 English cucumber, diced
½ teaspoon ground turmeric	12 cherry tomatoes, halved
¼ teaspoon ground coriander	1 cup fresh parsley, chopped
¼ teaspoon ground cumin	½ cup fresh mint, chopped
¼ teaspoon black pepper	

1. In a large bowl, whisk together the olive oil, lemon juice, lemon zest, salt, turmeric, coriander, cumin, black pepper, and cinnamon. 2. Add the riced cauliflower to the bowl and mix well. Add in the cucumber, tomatoes, parsley, and mint and gently mix together.

Per Serving:

calories: 180 | fat: 15g | protein: 4g | carbs: 12g | fiber: 5g | sodium:260 mg

Pistachio-Parmesan Kale-Arugula Salad

Prep time: 20 minutes |Cook time: 0 minutes|

Serves: 6

6 cups raw kale, center ribs	½ teaspoon smoked paprika
removed and discarded, leaves	2 cups arugula
coarsely chopped	⅓ cup unsalted shelled
¼ cup extra-virgin olive oil	pistachios
2 tablespoons freshly squeezed	6 tablespoons grated Parmesan
lemon juice (from about 1 small	or Pecorino Romano cheese
lemon)	

1. In a large salad bowl, combine the kale, oil, lemon juice, and smoked paprika. With your hands, gently massage the leaves for about 15 seconds or so, until all are thoroughly coated. Let the kale sit for 10 minutes. 2. When you're ready to serve, gently mix in the arugula and pistachios. Divide the salad among six serving bowls, sprinkle 1 tablespoon of grated cheese over each, and serve.

Per Serving:

calories: 150 | fat: 14g | protein: 4g | carbs: 5g | fiber: 1g | sodium: 99mg

Spinach-Arugula Salad with Nectarines and Lemon Dressing

Prep time: 15 minutes | Cook time: 0 minutes |

Serves 6

1 (7 ounces / 198 g) package	taste
baby spinach and arugula blend	½ red onion, thinly sliced
3 tablespoons fresh lemon juice	3 ripe nectarines, pitted and
5 tablespoons olive oil	sliced into wedges
⅛ teaspoon salt	1 cucumber, peeled, seeded,
Pinch (teaspoon) sugar	and sliced
Freshly ground black pepper, to	½ cup crumbled feta cheese

1. Place the spinach-arugula blend in a large bowl. 2. In a small bowl, whisk together the lemon juice, olive oil, salt, and sugar and season with pepper. Taste and adjust the seasonings. 3. Add the dressing to the greens and toss. Top with the onion, nectarines, cucumber, and feta. 4. Serve immediately.

Per Serving:

1 cup: calories: 178 | fat: 14g | protein: 4g | carbs: 11g | fiber: 2g | sodium: 193mg

Greek Black-Eyed Pea Salad

Prep time: 10 minutes | Cook time: 0 minutes |
Serves 4

2 tablespoons olive oil

Juice of 1 lemon (about 2 tablespoons)

1 garlic clove, minced

1 teaspoon ground cumin

1 (15½ ounces / 439 g) can no-salt-added black-eyed peas, drained and rinsed

1 red bell pepper, seeded and chopped

1 shallot, finely chopped

2 scallions (green onions), chopped

2 tablespoons chopped fresh dill

¼ cup chopped fresh parsley

½ cup pitted Kalamata olives, sliced

½ cup crumbled feta cheese (optional)

1. In a large bowl, whisk together the olive oil, lemon juice, garlic, and cumin. 2. Add the black-eyed peas, bell pepper, shallot, scallions, dill, parsley, olives, and feta (if using) and toss to combine. Serve.

Per Serving:

calories: 213 | fat: 14g | protein: 7g | carbs: 16g | fiber: 5g | sodium: 426mg

Grain-Free Kale Tabbouleh

Prep time: 15 minutes | Cook time: 0 minutes |
Serves 8

2 plum tomatoes, seeded and chopped

½ cup finely chopped fresh parsley

4 scallions (green onions), finely chopped

1 head kale, finely chopped (about 2 cups)

1 cup finely chopped fresh mint

1 small Persian cucumber, peeled, seeded, and diced

3 tablespoons extra-virgin olive oil

2 tablespoons fresh lemon juice

Coarsely ground black pepper (optional)

1. Place the tomatoes in a strainer set over a bowl and set aside to drain as much liquid as possible. 2. In a large bowl, stir to combine the parsley, scallions, kale, and mint. 3. Shake any remaining liquid from the tomatoes and add them to the kale mixture. Add the cucumber. 4. Add the olive oil and lemon juice and toss to combine. Season with pepper, if desired.

Per Serving:

1 cup: calories: 65 | fat: 5g | protein: 1g | carbs: 4g | fiber: 1g | sodium: 21mg

Riviera Tuna Salad

Prep time: 15 minutes | Cook time: 0 minutes |
Serves 4

¼ cup olive oil

¼ cup balsamic vinegar

½ teaspoon minced garlic

¼ teaspoon dried oregano

Sea salt and freshly ground pepper, to taste

2 tablespoons capers, drained

4 to 6 cups baby greens

1 (6 ounces / 170 g) can solid white albacore tuna, drained

1 cup canned garbanzo beans, rinsed and drained

¼ cup low-salt olives, pitted and quartered

2 Roma tomatoes, chopped

1. To make the vinaigrette, whisk together the olive oil, balsamic vinegar, garlic, oregano, sea salt, and pepper until emulsified. 2. Stir in the capers. Refrigerate for up to 6 hours before serving. 3. Place the baby greens in a salad bowl or on individual plates, and top with the tuna, beans, olives, and tomatoes. 4. Drizzle the vinaigrette over all, and serve immediately.

Per Serving:

calories: 300 | fat: 19g | protein: 16g | carbs: 17g | fiber: 5g | sodium: 438mg

Traditional Greek Salad

Prep time: 10 minutes | Cook time: 0 minutes |
Serves 4

2 large English cucumbers

4 Roma tomatoes, quartered

1 green bell pepper, cut into 1- to 1½-inch chunks

¼ small red onion, thinly sliced

4 ounces (113 g) pitted Kalamata olives

¼ cup extra-virgin olive oil

2 tablespoons freshly squeezed

lemon juice

1 tablespoon red wine vinegar

1 tablespoon chopped fresh oregano or 1 teaspoon dried oregano

¼ teaspoon freshly ground black pepper

4 ounces (113 g) crumbled traditional feta cheese

1. Cut the cucumbers in half lengthwise and then into ½-inch-thick half-moons. Place in a large bowl. 2. Add the quartered tomatoes, bell pepper, red onion, and olives. 3. In a small bowl, whisk together the olive oil, lemon juice, vinegar, oregano, and pepper. Drizzle over the vegetables and toss to coat. 4. Divide between salad plates and top each with 1 ounce (28 g) of feta.

Per Serving:

calories: 256 | fat: 22g | protein: 6g | carbs: 11g | fiber: 3g | sodium: 476mg

Chapter 11 Pizzas, Wraps, and Sandwiches

Greek Salad Pita

Prep time: 15 minutes | Cook time: 0 minutes | Serves 4

1 cup chopped romaine lettuce
1 tomato, chopped and seeded
½ cup baby spinach leaves
½ small red onion, thinly sliced
½ small cucumber, chopped and deseeded
2 tablespoons olive oil

1 tablespoon crumbled feta cheese
½ tablespoon red wine vinegar
1 teaspoon Dijon mustard
Sea salt and freshly ground pepper, to taste
1 whole-wheat pita

1. Combine everything except the sea salt, freshly ground pepper, and pita bread in a medium bowl. 2. Toss until the salad is well combined. 3. Season with sea salt and freshly ground pepper to taste. Fill the pita with the salad mixture, serve, and enjoy!

Per Serving:

calories: 123 | fat: 8g | protein: 3g | carbs: 12g | fiber: 2g | sodium: 125mg

Grilled Eggplant and Feta Sandwiches

Prep time: 10 minutes | Cook time: 8 minutes | Serves 2

1 medium eggplant, sliced into ½-inch-thick slices
2 tablespoons olive oil
Sea salt and freshly ground pepper, to taste
5 to 6 tablespoons hummus

4 slices whole-wheat bread, toasted
1 cup baby spinach leaves
2 ounces (57 g) feta cheese, softened

1. Preheat a gas or charcoal grill to medium-high heat. 2. Salt both sides of the sliced eggplant, and let sit for 20 minutes to draw out the bitter juices. 3. Rinse the eggplant and pat dry with a paper towel. 4. Brush the eggplant slices with olive oil and season with sea salt and freshly ground pepper. 5. Grill the eggplant until lightly charred on both sides but still slightly firm in the middle, about 3–4 minutes a side. 6. Spread the hummus on the bread and top with the spinach leaves, feta, and eggplant. Top with the other slice of bread and serve warm.

Per Serving:

calories: 516 | fat: 27g | protein: 14g | carbs: 59g | fiber: 14g | sodium: 597mg

Chicken and Goat Cheese Pizza

Prep time: 10 minutes | Cook time: 10 minutes | Serves 4

All-purpose flour, for dusting
1 pound (454 g) premade pizza dough
2 tablespoons olive oil
1 cup shredded cooked chicken

3 ounces (85 g) goat cheese, crumbled
Sea salt
Freshly ground black pepper

1. Preheat the oven to 475°F (245ºC) . 2. On a floured surface, roll out the dough to a 12-inch round and place it on a lightly floured pizza pan or baking sheet. Drizzle the dough with the olive oil and spread it out evenly. Top the dough with the chicken and goat cheese. 3. Bake the pizza for 8 to 10 minutes, until the crust is cooked through and golden. 4. Season with salt and pepper and serve.

Per Serving:

calories: 555 | fat: 23g | protein: 24g | carbs: 60g | fiber: 2g | sodium: 660mg

Barbecue Chicken Pita Pizza

Prep time: 5 minutes | Cook time: 5 to 7 minutes per batch | Makes 4 pizzas

1 cup barbecue sauce, divided
4 pita breads
2 cups shredded cooked chicken
2 cups shredded Mozzarella

cheese
½ small red onion, thinly sliced
2 tablespoons finely chopped fresh cilantro

1. Measure ½ cup of the barbecue sauce in a small measuring cup. Spread 2 tablespoons of the barbecue sauce on each pita. 2. In a medium bowl, mix together the remaining ½ cup of barbecue sauce and chicken. Place ½ cup of the chicken on each pita. Top each pizza with ½ cup of the Mozzarella cheese. Sprinkle the tops of the pizzas with the red onion. 3. Place one pizza in the air fryer. Air fry at 400°F (204ºC) for 5 to 7 minutes. Repeat this process with the remaining pizzas. 4. Top the pizzas with the cilantro.

Per Serving:

calories: 530 | fat: 19g | protein: 40g | carbs: 47g | fiber: 2g | sodium: 672mg

Turkish Pizza

4 ounces (113 g) ground lamb or 85% lean ground beef

¼ cup finely chopped green bell pepper

¼ cup chopped fresh parsley

1 small plum tomato, seeded and finely chopped

2 tablespoons finely chopped yellow onion

1 garlic clove, minced

2 teaspoons tomato paste

¼ teaspoon sweet paprika

¼ teaspoon ground cumin

⅛ to ¼ teaspoon red pepper flakes

⅛ teaspoon ground allspice

⅛ teaspoon kosher salt

⅛ teaspoon black pepper

4 (6-inch) flour tortillas

For Serving:

Chopped fresh mint

Extra-virgin olive oil

Lemon wedges

1. In a medium bowl, gently mix the ground lamb, bell pepper, parsley, chopped tomato, onion, garlic, tomato paste, paprika, cumin, red pepper flakes, allspice, salt, and black pepper until well combined. 2. Divide the meat mixture evenly among the tortillas, spreading it all the way to the edge of each tortilla. 3. Place 1 tortilla in the air fryer basket. Set the air fryer to 400ºF (204ºC) for 10 minutes, or until the meat topping has browned and the edge of the tortilla is golden. Transfer to a plate and repeat to cook the remaining tortillas. 4. Serve the pizzas warm, topped with chopped fresh mint and a drizzle of extra-virgin olive oil and with lemon wedges alongside.

Per Serving:

calories: 172 | fat: 8g | protein: 8g | carbs: 18g | fiber: 2g | sodium: 318mg

Grilled Eggplant and Chopped Greek Salad Wraps

15 small tomatoes, such as cherry or grape tomatoes, halved

10 pitted Kalamata olives, chopped

1 medium red onion, halved and thinly sliced

¾ cup crumbled feta cheese (about 4 ounces / 113 g)

2 tablespoons balsamic vinegar

1 tablespoon chopped fresh parsley

1 clove garlic, minced

2 tablespoons olive oil, plus 2 teaspoons, divided

¾ teaspoon salt, divided

1 medium cucumber, peeled, halved lengthwise, seeded, and diced

1 large eggplant, sliced ½-inch thick

½ teaspoon freshly ground black pepper

4 whole-wheat sandwich wraps

or whole-wheat flour tortillas

1. In a medium bowl, toss together the tomatoes, olives, onion, cheese, vinegar, parsley, garlic, 2 teaspoons olive oil, and ¼ teaspoon of salt. Let sit at room temperature for 20 minutes. Add the cucumber, toss to combine, and let sit another 10 minutes. 2. While the salad is resting, grill the eggplant. Heat a grill or grill pan to high heat. Brush the remaining 2 tablespoons olive oil onto both sides of the eggplant slices. Grill for about 8 to 10 minutes per side, until grill marks appear and the eggplant is tender and cooked through. Transfer to a plate and season with the remaining ½ teaspoon of salt and the pepper. 3. Heat the wraps in a large, dry skillet over medium heat just until warm and soft, about 1 minute on each side. Place 2 or 3 eggplant slices down the center of each wrap. Spoon some of the salad mixture on top of the eggplant, using a slotted spoon so that any excess liquid is drained off. Fold in the sides of the wrap and roll up like a burrito. Serve immediately.

Per Serving:

calories: 233 | fat: 10g | protein: 8g | carbs: 29g | fiber: 7g | sodium: 707mg

Roasted Vegetable Bocadillo with Romesco Sauce

2 small yellow squash, sliced lengthwise

2 small zucchini, sliced lengthwise

1 medium red onion, thinly sliced

4 large button mushrooms, sliced

2 tablespoons olive oil

1 teaspoon salt, divided

½ teaspoon freshly ground

black pepper, divided

2 roasted red peppers from a jar, drained

2 tablespoons blanched almonds

1 tablespoon sherry vinegar

1 small clove garlic

4 crusty multigrain rolls

4 ounces (113 g) goat cheese, at room temperature

1 tablespoon chopped fresh basil

1. Preheat the oven to 400°F(205ºC). 2. In a medium bowl, toss the yellow squash, zucchini, onion, and mushrooms with the olive oil, ½ teaspoon salt, and ¼ teaspoon pepper. Spread on a large baking sheet. Roast the vegetables in the oven for about 20 minutes, until softened. 3. Meanwhile, in a food processor, combine the roasted peppers, almonds, vinegar, garlic, the remaining ½ teaspoon salt, and the remaining ¼ teaspoon pepper and process until smooth. 4. Split the rolls and spread ¼ of the goat cheese on the bottom of each. Place the roasted vegetables on top of the cheese, dividing equally. Top with chopped basil. Spread the top halves of the rolls with the roasted red pepper sauce and serve immediately.

Per Serving:

calories: 379 | fat: 21g | protein: 17g | carbs: 32g | fiber: 4g | sodium: 592mg

Moroccan Lamb Wrap with Harissa

Prep time: 10 minutes | Cook time: 10 minutes |

Serves 4

1 clove garlic, minced

2 teaspoons ground cumin

2 teaspoons chopped fresh thyme

¼ cup olive oil, divided

1 lamb leg steak, about 12 ounces (340 g)

4 (8-inch) pocketless pita rounds or naan, preferably whole-wheat

1 medium eggplant, sliced ½-inch thick

1 medium zucchini, sliced lengthwise into 4 slices

1 bell pepper (any color), roasted and skinned

6 to 8 Kalamata olives, sliced

Juice of 1 lemon

2 to 4 tablespoons harissa

2 cups arugula

1. In a large bowl, combine the garlic, cumin, thyme, and 1 tablespoon of the olive oil. Add the lamb, turn to coat, cover, refrigerate, and marinate for at least an hour. 2. Preheat the oven to 400°F(205°C). 3. Heat a grill or grill pan to high heat. Remove the lamb from the marinade and grill for about 4 minutes per side, until medium-rare. Transfer to a plate and let rest for about 10 minutes before slicing thinly across the grain. 4. While the meat is resting, wrap the bread rounds in aluminum foil and heat in the oven for about 10 minutes. 5. Meanwhile, brush the eggplant and zucchini slices with the remaining olive oil and grill until tender, about 3 minutes. Dice them and the bell pepper. Toss in a large bowl with the olives and lemon juice. 6. Spread some of the harissa onto each warm flatbread round and top each evenly with roasted vegetables, a few slices of lamb, and a handful of the arugula. 7. Roll up the wraps, cut each in half crosswise, and serve immediately.

Per Serving:

calories: 553 | fat: 24g | protein: 33g | carbs: 53g | fiber: 11g | sodium: 531mg

Mediterranean Tuna Salad Sandwiches

Prep time: 10 minutes | Cook time: 5 minutes |

Serves 2

1 can white tuna, packed in water or olive oil, drained

1 roasted red pepper, diced

½ small red onion, diced

10 low-salt olives, pitted and finely chopped

¼ cup plain Greek yogurt

1 tablespoon flat-leaf parsley, chopped

Juice of 1 lemon

Sea salt and freshly ground pepper, to taste

4 whole-grain pieces of bread

1. In a small bowl, combine all of the ingredients except the bread, and mix well. 2. Season with sea salt and freshly ground pepper to taste. Toast the bread or warm in a pan. 3. Make the sandwich and serve immediately.

Per Serving:

calories: 307 | fat: 7g | protein: 30g | carbs: 31g | fiber: 5g | sodium: 564mg

Dill Salmon Salad Wraps

Prep time: 10 minutes |Cook time: 10 minutes|

Serves:6

1 pound (454 g) salmon filet, cooked and flaked, or 3 (5-ounce / 142-g) cans salmon

½ cup diced carrots (about 1 carrot)

½ cup diced celery (about 1 celery stalk)

3 tablespoons chopped fresh dill

3 tablespoons diced red onion (a little less than ⅛ onion)

2 tablespoons capers

1½ tablespoons extra-virgin olive oil

1 tablespoon aged balsamic vinegar

½ teaspoon freshly ground black pepper

¼ teaspoon kosher or sea salt

4 whole-wheat flatbread wraps or soft whole-wheat tortillas

1. In a large bowl, mix together the salmon, carrots, celery, dill, red onion, capers, oil, vinegar, pepper, and salt. 2. Divide the salmon salad among the flatbreads. Fold up the bottom of the flatbread, then roll up the wrap and serve.

Per Serving:

calories: 185 | fat: 8g | protein: 17g | carbs: 12g | fiber: 2g | sodium: 237mg

Sautéed Mushroom, Onion, and Pecorino Romano Panini

Prep time: 10 minutes | Cook time: 20 minutes |

Serves 4

3 tablespoons olive oil, divided

1 small onion, diced

10 ounces (283 g) button or cremini mushrooms, sliced

½ teaspoon salt

¼ teaspoon freshly ground black pepper

4 crusty Italian sandwich rolls

4 ounces (113 g) freshly grated Pecorino Romano

1. Heat 1 tablespoon of the olive oil in a skillet over medium-high heat. Add the onion and cook, stirring, until it begins to soften, about 3 minutes. Add the mushrooms, season with salt and pepper, and cook, stirring, until they soften and the liquid they release evaporates, about 7 minutes. 2. To make the panini, heat a skillet or grill pan over high heat and brush with 1 tablespoon olive oil. Brush the inside of the rolls with the remaining 1 tablespoon olive oil. Divide the mushroom mixture evenly among the rolls and top each with ¼ of the grated cheese. 3. Place the sandwiches in the hot pan and place another heavy pan, such as a cast-iron skillet, on top to weigh them down. Cook for about 3 to 4 minutes, until crisp and golden on the bottom, and then flip over and repeat on the second side, cooking for an additional 3 to 4 minutes until golden and crisp. Slice each sandwich in half and serve hot.

Per Serving:

calories: 348 | fat: 20g | protein: 14g | carbs: 30g | fiber: 2g | sodium: 506mg

Greek Salad Wraps

Prep time: 15 minutes |Cook time: 0 minutes|

Serves: 4

1½ cups seedless cucumber, peeled and chopped (about 1 large cucumber)
1 cup chopped tomato (about 1 large tomato)
½ cup finely chopped fresh mint
1 (2¼ ounces / 64 g) can sliced black olives (about ½ cup), drained
¼ cup diced red onion (about ¼ onion)
2 tablespoons extra-virgin olive oil
1 tablespoon red wine vinegar
¼ teaspoon freshly ground black pepper
¼ teaspoon kosher or sea salt
½ cup crumbled goat cheese (about 2 ounces / 57 g)
4 whole-wheat flatbread wraps or soft whole-wheat tortillas

1. In a large bowl, mix together the cucumber, tomato, mint, olives, and onion until well combined. 2. In a small bowl, whisk together the oil, vinegar, pepper, and salt. Drizzle the dressing over the salad, and mix gently. 3. With a knife, spread the goat cheese evenly over the four wraps. Spoon a quarter of the salad filling down the middle of each wrap. 4. Fold up each wrap: Start by folding up the bottom, then fold one side over and fold the other side over the top. Repeat with the remaining wraps and serve.

Per Serving:

calories: 217 | fat: 14g | protein: 7g | carbs: 17g | fiber: 3g | sodium: 329mg

Avocado and Asparagus Wraps

Prep time: 10 minutes | Cook time: 10 minutes |

Serves 6

12 spears asparagus
1 ripe avocado, mashed slightly
Juice of 1 lime
2 cloves garlic, minced
2 cups brown rice, cooked and chilled
3 tablespoons Greek yogurt
Sea salt and freshly ground pepper, to taste
3 (8-inch) whole-grain tortillas
½ cup cilantro, diced
2 tablespoons red onion, diced

1. Steam asparagus in microwave or stove top steamer until tender. Mash the avocado, lime juice, and garlic in a medium mixing bowl. In a separate bowl, mix the rice and yogurt. 2. Season both mixtures with sea salt and freshly ground pepper to taste. Heat the tortillas in a dry nonstick skillet. 3. Spread each tortilla with the avocado mixture, and top with the rice, cilantro, and onion, followed by the asparagus. 4. Fold up both sides of the tortilla, and roll tightly to close. Cut in half diagonally before serving.

Per Serving:

calories: 361 | fat: 9g | protein: 9g | carbs: 63g | fiber: 7g | sodium: 117mg

Jerk Chicken Wraps

Prep time: 30 minutes | Cook time: 15 minutes |

Serves 4

1 pound (454 g) boneless, skinless chicken tenderloins
1 cup jerk marinade
Olive oil
4 large low-carb tortillas
1 cup julienned carrots
1 cup peeled cucumber ribbons
1 cup shredded lettuce
1 cup mango or pineapple chunks

1. In a medium bowl, coat the chicken with the jerk marinade, cover, and refrigerate for 1 hour. 2. Spray the air fryer basket lightly with olive oil. 3. Place the chicken in the air fryer basket in a single layer and spray lightly with olive oil. You may need to cook the chicken in batches. Reserve any leftover marinade. 4. Air fry at 375°F (191°C) for 8 minutes. Turn the chicken over and brush with some of the remaining marinade. Cook until the chicken reaches an internal temperature of at least 165°F (74°C), an additional 5 to 7 minutes. 5. To assemble the wraps, fill each tortilla with ¼ cup carrots, ¼ cup cucumber, ¼ cup lettuce, and ¼ cup mango. Place one quarter of the chicken tenderloins on top and roll up the tortilla. These are great served warm or cold.

Per Serving:

calories: 241 | fat: 4g | protein: 28g | carbs: 23g | fiber: 4g | sodium: 85mg

Herbed Focaccia Panini with Anchovies and Burrata

Prep time: 5 minutes | Cook time: 8 minutes | Serves 4

8 ounces (227 g) burrata cheese, chilled and sliced
1 pound (454 g) whole-wheat herbed focaccia, cut crosswise into 4 rectangles and split horizontally
1 can anchovy fillets packed in oil, drained
8 slices tomato, sliced
2 cups arugula
1 tablespoon olive oil

1. Divide the cheese evenly among the bottom halves of the focaccia rectangles. Top each with 3 or 4 anchovy fillets, 2 slices of tomato, and ½ cup arugula. Place the top halves of the focaccia on top of the sandwiches. 2. To make the panini, heat a skillet or grill pan over high heat and brush with the olive oil. 3. Place the sandwiches in the hot pan and place another heavy pan, such as a cast-iron skillet, on top to weigh them down. Cook for about 3 to 4 minutes, until crisp and golden on the bottom, and then flip over and repeat on the second side, cooking for an additional 3 to 4 minutes until golden and crisp. Slice each sandwich in half and serve hot.

Per Serving:

calories: 596 | fat: 30g | protein: 27g | carbs: 58g | fiber: 5g | sodium: 626mg

Moroccan Lamb Flatbread with Pine Nuts, Mint, and Ras Al Hanout

Prep time: 10 minutes | Cook time: 20 minutes | Serves 4

1⅓ cups plain Greek yogurt
Juice of 1½ lemons, divided
1¼ teaspoons salt, divided
1 pound (454 g) ground lamb
1 medium red onion, diced
1 clove garlic, minced
1 tablespoon ras al hanout
¼ cup chopped fresh mint

leaves
Freshly ground black pepper
4 Middle Eastern-style flatbread rounds
2 tablespoons toasted pine nuts
16 cherry tomatoes, halved
2 tablespoons chopped cilantro

1. Preheat the oven to 450°F(235°C). 2. In a small bowl, stir together the yogurt, the juice of ½ lemon, and ¼ teaspoon salt. 3. Heat a large skillet over medium-high heat. Add the lamb and cook, stirring frequently, until browned, about 5 minutes. Drain any excess rendered fat from the pan and then stir in the onion and garlic and cook, stirring, until softened, about 3 minutes more. Stir in the ras al hanout, mint, the remaining teaspoon of salt, and pepper. 4. Place the flatbread rounds on a baking sheet (or two if necessary) and top with the lamb mixture, pine nuts, and tomatoes, dividing equally. Bake in the preheated oven until the crust is golden brown and the tomatoes have softened, about 10 minutes. Scatter the cilantro over the flatbreads and squeeze the remaining lemon juice over them. Cut into wedges and serve dolloped with the yogurt sauce.

Per Serving:

calories: 463 | fat: 22g | protein: 34g | carbs: 34g | fiber: 3g | sodium: 859mg

Mediterranean-Pita Wraps

Prep time: 5 minutes | Cook time: 14 minutes | Serves 4

1 pound (454 g) mackerel fish fillets
2 tablespoons olive oil
1 tablespoon Mediterranean seasoning mix
½ teaspoon chili powder

Sea salt and freshly ground black pepper, to taste
2 ounces (57 g) feta cheese, crumbled
4 tortillas

1. Toss the fish fillets with the olive oil; place them in the lightly oiled air fryer basket. 2. Air fry the fish fillets at 400°C (204°C) for about 14 minutes, turning them over halfway through the cooking time. 3. Assemble your pitas with the chopped fish and remaining ingredients and serve warm.

Per Serving:

calories: 275 | fat: 13g | protein: 27g | carbs: 13g | fiber: 2g | sodium: 322mg

Beans and Greens Pizza

Prep time: 11 minutes | Cook time: 14 to 19 minutes | Serves 4

¾ cup whole-wheat pastry flour
½ teaspoon low-sodium baking powder
1 tablespoon olive oil, divided
1 cup chopped kale
2 cups chopped fresh baby spinach

1 cup canned no-salt-added cannellini beans, rinsed and drained
½ teaspoon dried thyme
1 piece low-sodium string cheese, torn into pieces

1. In a small bowl, mix the pastry flour and baking powder until well combined. 2. Add ¼ cup of water and 2 teaspoons of olive oil. Mix until a dough forms. 3. On a floured surface, press or roll the dough into a 7-inch round. Set aside while you cook the greens. 4. In a baking pan, mix the kale, spinach, and remaining teaspoon of the olive oil. Air fry at 350ºF (177ºC) for 3 to 5 minutes, until the greens are wilted. Drain well. 5. Put the pizza dough into the air fryer basket. Top with the greens, cannellini beans, thyme, and string cheese. Air fry for 11 to 14 minutes, or until the crust is golden brown and the cheese is melted. Cut into quarters to serve.

Per Serving:

calories: 181 | fat: 6g | protein: 8g | carbs: 27g | fiber: 6g | sodium: 103mg

Open-Faced Eggplant Parmesan Sandwich

Prep time: 10 minutes | Cook time: 10 minutes | Serves 2

1 small eggplant, sliced into ¼-inch rounds
Pinch sea salt
2 tablespoons olive oil
Sea salt and freshly ground pepper, to taste

2 slices whole-grain bread, thickly cut and toasted
1 cup marinara sauce (no added sugar)
¼ cup freshly grated, low-fat Parmesan cheese

1. Preheat broiler to high heat. 2. Salt both sides of the sliced eggplant, and let sit for 20 minutes to draw out the bitter juices. 3. Rinse the eggplant and pat dry with a paper towel. 4. Brush the eggplant with the olive oil, and season with sea salt and freshly ground pepper. 5. Lay the eggplant on a sheet pan, and broil until crisp, about 4 minutes. Flip over and crisp the other side. 6. Lay the toasted bread on a sheet pan. Spoon some marinara sauce on each slice of bread, and layer the eggplant on top. 7. Sprinkle half of the cheese on top of the eggplant and top with more marinara sauce. 8. Sprinkle with remaining cheese. 9. Put the sandwiches under the broiler until the cheese has melted, about 2 minutes. 10. Using a spatula, transfer the sandwiches to plates and serve.

Per Serving:

calories: 355 | fat: 19g | protein: 10g | carbs: 38g | fiber: 13g | sodium: 334mg

Pesto Chicken Mini Pizzas

Prep time: 5 minutes | Cook time: 10 minutes | Serves 4

2 cups shredded cooked chicken

¾ cup pesto

4 English muffins, split

2 cups shredded Mozzarella cheese

1. In a medium bowl, toss the chicken with the pesto. Place one-eighth of the chicken on each English muffin half. Top each English muffin with ¼ cup of the Mozzarella cheese. 2. Put four pizzas at a time in the air fryer and air fry at 350°F (177°C) for 5 minutes. Repeat this process with the other four pizzas.

Per Serving:

calories: 617 | fat: 36g | protein: 45g | carbs: 29g | fiber: 3g | sodium: 544mg

Vegetable Pita Sandwiches

Prep time: 15 minutes | Cook time: 9 to 12 minutes | Serves 4

1 baby eggplant, peeled and chopped

1 red bell pepper, sliced

½ cup diced red onion

½ cup shredded carrot

1 teaspoon olive oil

⅓ cup low-fat Greek yogurt

½ teaspoon dried tarragon

2 low-sodium whole-wheat pita breads, halved crosswise

1. In a baking pan, stir together the eggplant, red bell pepper, red onion, carrot, and olive oil. Put the vegetable mixture into the air fryer basket and roast at 390°F (199°C) for 7 to 9 minutes, stirring once, until the vegetables are tender. Drain if necessary. 2. In a small bowl, thoroughly mix the yogurt and tarragon until well combined. 3. Stir the yogurt mixture into the vegetables. Stuff one-fourth of this mixture into each pita pocket. 4. Place the sandwiches in the air fryer and cook for 2 to 3 minutes, or until the bread is toasted. Serve immediately.

Per Serving:

calories: 115 | fat: 2g | protein: 4g | carbs: 22g | fiber: 6g | sodium: 90mg

Chapter 12 Pasta

Greek Chicken Pasta Casserole

Prep time: 15 minutes | Cook time: 4 to 6 hours |
Serves 4

2 pounds (907 g) boneless, skinless chicken thighs or breasts, cut into 1-inch pieces
8 ounces (227 g) dried rotini pasta
7 cups low-sodium chicken broth
½ red onion, diced
3 garlic cloves, minced
¼ cup whole Kalamata olives,

pitted
3 Roma tomatoes, diced
2 tablespoons red wine vinegar
1 teaspoon extra-virgin olive oil
2 teaspoons dried oregano
1 teaspoon sea salt
½ teaspoon freshly ground black pepper
¼ cup crumbled feta cheese

1. In a slow cooker, combine the chicken, pasta, chicken broth, onion, garlic, olives, tomatoes, vinegar, olive oil, oregano, salt, and pepper. Stir to mix well. 2. Cover the cooker and cook for 4 to 6 hours on Low heat. 3. Garnish with the feta cheese for serving.

Per Serving:
calories: 608 | fat: 17g | protein: 59g | carbs: 55g | fiber: 8g | sodium: 775mg

Toasted Orzo with Shrimp and Feta

Prep time: 10 minutes | Cook time: 15 minutes |
Serves 4 to 6

1 pound (454 g) large shrimp (26 to 30 per pound), peeled and deveined
1 tablespoon grated lemon zest plus 1 tablespoon juice
¼ teaspoon table salt
¼ teaspoon pepper
2 tablespoons extra-virgin olive oil, plus extra for serving
1 onion, chopped fine
2 garlic cloves, minced

2 cups orzo
2 cups chicken broth, plus extra as needed
1¼ cups water
½ cup pitted kalamata olives, chopped coarse
1 ounce (28 g) feta cheese, crumbled (¼ cup), plus extra for serving
1 tablespoon chopped fresh dill

1. Toss shrimp with lemon zest, salt, and pepper in bowl; refrigerate until ready to use. 2. Using highest sauté function, heat oil in Instant Pot until shimmering. Add onion and cook until softened, about 5 minutes. Stir in garlic and cook until fragrant, about 30

seconds. Add orzo and cook, stirring frequently, until orzo is coated with oil and lightly browned, about 5 minutes. Stir in broth and water, scraping up any browned bits. 3. Lock lid in place and close pressure release valve. Select high pressure cook function and cook for 2 minutes. Turn off Instant Pot and quick-release pressure. Carefully remove lid, allowing steam to escape away from you. 4. Stir shrimp, olives, and feta into orzo. Cover and let sit until shrimp are opaque throughout, 5 to 7 minutes. Adjust consistency with extra hot broth as needed. Stir in dill and lemon juice, and season with salt and pepper to taste. Sprinkle individual portions with extra feta and drizzle with extra oil before serving.

Per Serving:
calories: 320 | fat: 8g | protein: 18g | carbs: 46g | fiber: 2g | sodium: 670mg

Baked Ziti

Prep time: 10 minutes | Cook time: 55 minutes |
Serves 8

For the Marinara Sauce:
2 tablespoons olive oil
¼ medium onion, diced (about 3 tablespoons)
3 cloves garlic, chopped
1 (28 ounces / 794 g) can whole, peeled tomatoes, roughly chopped
Sprig of fresh thyme
½ bunch fresh basil
Sea salt and freshly ground

pepper, to taste
For the Ziti:
1 pound (454 g) whole-wheat ziti
3½ cups marinara sauce
1 cup low-fat cottage cheese
1 cup grated, low-fat mozzarella cheese, divided
¾ cup freshly grated, low-fat Parmesan cheese, divided

Make the marinara sauce: 1. Heat the olive oil in a medium saucepan over medium-high heat. 2. Sauté the onion and garlic, stirring until lightly browned, about 3 minutes. 3. Add the tomatoes and the herb sprigs, and bring to a boil. Lower the heat and simmer, covered, for 10 minutes. Remove and discard the herb sprigs. 4. Stir in sea salt and season with freshly ground pepper to taste. Make the ziti: 1. Preheat the oven to 375ºF (190ºC). 2. Prepare the pasta according to package directions. Drain pasta. Combine the pasta in a bowl with 2 cups marinara sauce, the cottage cheese, and half the mozzarella and Parmesan cheeses. 3. Spread the mixture in a baking dish, and top with the remaining marinara sauce and cheese. 4. Bake for 30–40 minutes, or until bubbly and golden brown.

Per Serving:
calories: 389 | fat: 12g | protein: 18g | carbs: 56g | fiber: 9g | sodium: 369mg

Spicy Broccoli Pasta Salad

8 ounces (227 g) whole-wheat
pasta
2 cups broccoli florets
1 cup carrots, peeled and
shredded

¼ cup plain Greek yogurt
Juice of 1 lemon
1 teaspoon red pepper flakes
Sea salt and freshly ground
pepper, to taste

1. Cook the pasta according to the package directions for al dente
and drain well. 2. When the pasta is cool, combine it with the
veggies, yogurt, lemon juice, and red pepper flakes in a large bowl,
and stir thoroughly to combine. 3. Taste for seasoning, and add sea
salt and freshly ground pepper as needed. 4. This dish can be served
at room temperature or chilled.

Per Serving:

calories: 473 | fat: 2g | protein: 22g | carbs: 101g | fiber: 13g |
sodium: 101mg

Neapolitan Pasta and Zucchini

⅓ cup extra virgin olive oil
1 large onion (any variety),
diced
1 teaspoon fine sea salt, divided
2 large zucchini, quartered
lengthwise and cut into ½-inch
pieces
10 ounces (283 g) uncooked
spaghetti, broken into 1-inch

pieces
2 tablespoons grated Parmesan
cheese
2 ounces (57 g) grated or
shaved Parmesan cheese for
serving
½ teaspoon freshly ground
black pepper

1. Add the olive oil to a medium pot over medium heat. When the
oil begins to shimmer, add the onions and ¼ teaspoon of the sea
salt. Sauté for 3 minutes, add the zucchini, and continue sautéing
for 3 more minutes. 2. Add 2 cups of hot water to the pot or enough
to just cover the zucchini (the amount of water may vary depending
on the size of the pot). Cover, reduce the heat to low, and simmer
for 10 minutes. 3. Add the pasta to the pot, stir, then add 2 more
cups of hot water. Continue simmering, stirring occasionally,
until the pasta is cooked and the mixture has thickened, about 12
minutes. (If the pasta appears to be dry or undercooked, add small
amounts of hot water to the pot to ensure the pasta is covered in
the water.). When the pasta is cooked, remove the pot from the
heat. Add 2 tablespoons of the grated Parmesan and stir. 4. Divide
the pasta into three servings and then top each with 1 ounce (28 g)
of the grated or shaved Parmesan. Sprinkle the remaining sea salt
and black pepper over the top of each serving. Store covered in the
refrigerator for up to 3 days.

Per Serving:

calories: 718 | fat: 33g | protein: 24g | carbs: 83g | fiber: 6g | sodium:
815mg

Couscous with Crab and Lemon

1 cup couscous
1 clove garlic, peeled and
minced
2 cups water
3 tablespoons extra-virgin olive
oil, divided
¼ cup minced fresh flat-leaf
parsley

1 tablespoon minced fresh dill
8 ounces (227 g) jumbo lump
crabmeat
3 tablespoons lemon juice
½ teaspoon ground black
pepper
¼ cup grated Parmesan cheese

1. Place couscous, garlic, water, and 1 tablespoon oil in the Instant
Pot® and stir well. Close lid, set steam release to Sealing, press the
Manual button, and set time to 7 minutes. When the timer beeps,
let pressure release naturally for 10 minutes, then quick-release
the remaining pressure and open lid. 2. Fluff couscous with a fork.
Add parsley, dill, crabmeat, lemon juice, pepper, and remaining 2
tablespoons oil, and stir until combined. Top with cheese and serve
immediately.

Per Serving:

calories: 360 | fat: 15g | protein: 22g | carbs: 34g | fiber: 2g | sodium:
388mg

Mediterranean Pasta Salad

4 cups dried farfalle (bow-tie)
pasta
1 cup canned chickpeas, drained
and rinsed
⅔ cup water-packed artichoke
hearts, drained and diced
½ red onion, thinly sliced
1 cup packed baby spinach
½ red bell pepper, diced

1 Roma (plum) tomato, diced
½ English cucumber, quartered
lengthwise and cut into ½-inch
pieces
⅓ cup extra-virgin olive oil
Juice of ½ lemon
Sea salt
Freshly ground black pepper
½ cup crumbled feta cheese

1. Fill a large saucepan three-quarters full with water and bring
to a boil over high heat. Add the pasta and cook according to the
package directions until al dente, about 15 minutes. Drain the pasta
and run it under cold water to stop the cooking process and cool.
2. While the pasta is cooking, in a large bowl, mix the chickpeas,
artichoke hearts, onion, spinach, bell pepper, tomato, and cucumber.
3. Add the pasta to the bowl with the vegetables. Add the olive oil
and lemon juice and season with salt and black pepper. Mix well. 4.
Top the salad with the feta and serve.

Per Serving:

calories: 702 | fat: 25g | protein: 22g | carbs: 99g | fiber: 10g |
sodium: 207mg

Quick Shrimp Fettuccine

Prep time: 10 minutes | Cook time: 10 minutes |
Serves 4 to 6

8 ounces (227 g) fettuccine pasta
¼ cup extra-virgin olive oil
3 tablespoons garlic, minced
1 pound (454 g) large shrimp (21-25), peeled and deveined

⅓ cup lemon juice
1 tablespoon lemon zest
½ teaspoon salt
½ teaspoon freshly ground black pepper

1. Bring a large pot of salted water to a boil. Add the fettuccine and cook for 8 minutes. 2. In a large saucepan over medium heat, cook the olive oil and garlic for 1 minute. 3. Add the shrimp to the saucepan and cook for 3 minutes on each side. Remove the shrimp from the pan and set aside. 4. Add the lemon juice and lemon zest to the saucepan, along with the salt and pepper. 5. Reserve ½ cup of the pasta water and drain the pasta. 6. Add the pasta water to the saucepan with the lemon juice and zest and stir everything together. Add the pasta and toss together to evenly coat the pasta. Transfer the pasta to a serving dish and top with the cooked shrimp. Serve warm.

Per Serving:

calories: 615 | fat: 17g | protein: 33g | carbs: 89g | fiber: 4g | sodium: 407mg

Couscous with Tomatoes and Olives

Prep time: 5 minutes | Cook time: 3 minutes | Serves 4

1 tablespoon tomato paste
2 cups vegetable broth
1 cup couscous
1 cup halved cherry tomatoes
½ cup halved mixed olives
¼ cup minced fresh flat-leaf parsley
2 tablespoons minced fresh

oregano
2 tablespoons minced fresh chives
1 tablespoon extra-virgin olive oil
1 tablespoon red wine vinegar
½ teaspoon ground black pepper

1. Pour tomato paste and broth into the Instant Pot® and stir until completely dissolved. Stir in couscous. Close lid, set steam release to Sealing, press the Manual button, and set time to 3 minutes. When the timer beeps, let pressure release naturally for 10 minutes, then quick-release the remaining pressure and open lid. 2. Fluff couscous with a fork. Add tomatoes, olives, parsley, oregano, chives, oil, vinegar, and pepper, and stir until combined. Serve warm or at room temperature.

Per Serving:

calories: 232 | fat: 5g | protein: 7g | carbs: 37g | fiber: 2g | sodium: 513mg

Tahini Soup

Prep time: 5 minutes | Cook time: 4 minutes | Serves 6

2 cups orzo
8 cups water
1 tablespoon olive oil
1 teaspoon salt

½ teaspoon ground black pepper
½ cup tahini
¼ cup lemon juice

1. Add pasta, water, oil, salt, and pepper to the Instant Pot®. Close lid, set steam release to Sealing, press the Manual button, and set time to 4 minutes. When the timer beeps, quick-release the pressure until the float valve drops, and open lid. Set aside. 2. Add tahini to a small mixing bowl and slowly add lemon juice while whisking constantly. Once lemon juice has been incorporated, take about ½ cup hot broth from the pot and slowly add to tahini mixture while whisking, until creamy smooth. 3. Pour mixture into the soup and mix well. Serve immediately.

Per Serving:

calories: 338 | fat: 13g | protein: 12g | carbs: 49g | fiber: 5g | sodium: 389mg

Mixed Vegetable Couscous

Prep time: 20 minutes | Cook time: 10 minutes |
Serves 8

1 tablespoon light olive oil
1 medium zucchini, trimmed and chopped
1 medium yellow squash, chopped
1 large red bell pepper, seeded and chopped
1 large orange bell pepper, seeded and chopped
2 tablespoons chopped fresh

oregano
2 cups Israeli couscous
3 cups vegetable broth
½ cup crumbled feta cheese
¼ cup red wine vinegar
¼ cup extra-virgin olive oil
½ teaspoon ground black pepper
¼ cup chopped fresh basil

1. Press the Sauté button on the Instant Pot® and heat light olive oil. Add zucchini, squash, bell peppers, and oregano, and sauté 8 minutes. Press the Cancel button. Transfer to a serving bowl and set aside to cool. 2. Add couscous and broth to the Instant Pot® and stir well. Close lid, set steam release to Sealing, press the Manual button, and set time to 2 minutes. When the timer beeps, let pressure release naturally for 5 minutes, then quick-release the remaining pressure and open lid. 3. Fluff with a fork and stir in cooked vegetables, cheese, vinegar, extra-virgin olive oil, black pepper, and basil. Serve warm.

Per Serving:

calories: 355 | fat: 9g | protein: 14g | carbs: 61g | fiber: 7g | sodium: 588mg

Linguine with Avocado Pesto

Prep time: 10 minutes | Cook time: 10 minutes |
Serves 4

1 pound (454 g) dried linguine	1 tablespoon packed sun-dried
2 avocados, coarsely chopped	tomatoes
½ cup olive oil	⅛ teaspoon Italian seasoning
½ cup packed fresh basil	⅛ teaspoon red pepper flakes
½ cup pine nuts	Sea salt
Juice of 1 lemon	Freshly ground black pepper
3 garlic cloves	

1. Fill a large stockpot three-quarters full with water and bring to a boil over high heat. Add the pasta and cook according to the package instructions until al dente, about 15 minutes. 2. While the pasta is cooking, in a food processor, combine the avocados, olive oil, basil, pine nuts, lemon juice, garlic, sun-dried tomatoes, Italian seasoning, and red pepper flakes and process until a paste forms. Taste and season with salt and black pepper. 3. When the pasta is done, drain it and return it to the pot. Add half the pesto and mix. Add more pesto as desired and serve.

Per Serving:

calories: 694 | fat: 29g | protein: 17g | carbs: 93g | fiber: 8g | sodium: 11mg

Pine Nut and Currant Couscous with Butternut Squash

Prep time: 10 minutes | Cook time: 50 minutes |
Serves 4

3 tablespoons olive oil	1 (16 ounces / 454 g) can
1 medium onion, chopped	chickpeas, drained and rinsed
3 cloves garlic, minced	4½ cups vegetable broth,
6 canned plum tomatoes,	divided
crushed	1-inch strip lemon zest
1 cinnamon stick	½ cup currants
1 teaspoon ground coriander	4 cups (about 5 ounces / 142 g)
1 teaspoon ground cumin	chopped spinach
1 teaspoon salt, divided	Juice of ½ lemon
¼ teaspoon red pepper flakes	¼ teaspoon pepper
1½ pounds (680 g) diced	1 cup whole-wheat couscous
butternut squash	¼ cup toasted pine nuts

1. Heat the olive oil in a medium saucepan set over medium heat. Add the onion and cook, stirring frequently, until softened and lightly browned, about 10 minutes. Stir in the garlic, tomatoes, cinnamon stick, coriander, cumin, ½ teaspoon of the salt, and the red pepper flakes and cook for about 3 minutes more, until the tomatoes begin to break down. Stir in the butternut squash,

chickpeas, 3 cups broth, lemon zest, and currants and bring to a simmer. 2. Partially cover the pan and cook for about 25 minutes, until the squash is tender. Add the spinach and cook, stirring, for 2 or 3 more minutes, until the spinach is wilted. Stir in the lemon juice. 3. While the vegetables are cooking, prepare the couscous. Combine the remaining 1½ cups broth, the remaining ½ teaspoon of salt, and the pepper in a small saucepan and bring to a boil. Remove the pan from the heat and stir in the couscous. Cover immediately and let sit for about 5 minutes, until the liquid has been fully absorbed. Fluff with a fork. 4. Spoon the couscous into serving bowls, top with the vegetable and chickpea mixture, and sprinkle some of the pine nuts over the top of each bowl. Serve immediately.

Per Serving:

calories: 549 | fat: 19g | protein: 16g | carbs: 84g | fiber: 14g | sodium: 774mg

Orzo with Feta and Marinated Peppers

Prep time:1 hour 25 minutes | Cook time: 37 minutes
| Serves 2

2 medium red bell peppers	pinch for the orzo
¼ cup extra virgin olive oil	1 cup uncooked orzo
1 tablespoon balsamic vinegar	3 ounces (85 g) crumbled feta
plus 1 teaspoon for serving	1 tablespoon chopped fresh
¼ teaspoon ground cumin	basil
Pinch of ground cinnamon	¼ teaspoon freshly ground
Pinch of ground cloves	black pepper
¼ teaspoon fine sea salt plus a	

1. Preheat the oven at 350°F (180°C). Place the peppers on a baking pan and roast in the oven for 25 minutes or until they're soft and can be pierced with a fork. Set aside to cool for 10 minutes. 2. While the peppers are roasting, combine the olive oil, 1 tablespoon of the balsamic vinegar, cumin, cinnamon, cloves, and ¼ teaspoon of the sea salt. Stir to combine, then set aside. 3. Peel the cooled peppers, remove the seeds, and then chop into large pieces. Place the peppers in the olive oil and vinegar mixture and then toss to coat, ensuring the peppers are covered in the marinade. Cover and place in the refrigerator to marinate for 20 minutes. 4. While the peppers are marinating, prepare the orzo by bringing 3 cups of water and a pinch of salt to a boil in a large pot over high heat. When the water is boiling, add the orzo, reduce the heat to medium, and cook, stirring occasionally, for 10–12 minutes or until soft, then drain and transfer to a serving bowl. 5. Add the peppers and marinade to the orzo, mixing well, then place in the refrigerator and to cool for at least 1 hour. 6. To serve, top with the feta, basil, black pepper, and 1 teaspoon of the balsamic vinegar. Mix well, and serve promptly. Store covered in the refrigerator for up to 3 days.

Per Serving:

calories: 600 | fat: 37g | protein: 15g | carbs: 51g | fiber: 4g | sodium: 690mg

Rotini with Walnut Pesto, Peas, and Cherry Tomatoes

Prep time: 10 minutes | Cook time: 4 minutes | Serves 8

1 cup packed fresh basil leaves
⅓ cup chopped walnuts
¼ cup grated Parmesan cheese
¼ cup plus 1 tablespoon extra-virgin olive oil, divided
1 clove garlic, peeled
1 tablespoon lemon juice
¼ teaspoon salt

1 pound (454 g) whole-wheat rotini pasta
4 cups water
1 pint cherry tomatoes
1 cup fresh or frozen green peas
½ teaspoon ground black pepper

1. In a food processor, add basil and walnuts. Pulse until finely chopped, about 12 pulses. Add cheese, ¼ cup oil, garlic, lemon juice, and salt, and pulse until a rough paste forms, about 10 pulses. Refrigerate until ready to use. 2. Add pasta, water, and remaining 1 tablespoon oil to the Instant Pot®. Close lid, set steam release to Sealing, press the Manual button, and set time to 4 minutes. 3. When the timer beeps, quick-release the pressure until the float valve drops and open lid. Drain off any excess liquid. Allow pasta to cool to room temperature, about 30 minutes. Stir in basil mixture until pasta is well coated. Add tomatoes, peas, and pepper and toss to coat. Refrigerate for 2 hours. Stir well before serving.

Per Serving:
calories: 371 | fat: 15g | protein: 12g | carbs: 47g | fiber: 7g | sodium: 205mg

Penne with Broccoli and Anchovies

Prep time: 10 minutes | Cook time: 10 minutes | Serves 4

¼ cup olive oil
1 pound (454 g) whole-wheat pasta
½ pound (227 g) broccoli or broccoli rabe cut into 1-inch florets
3 to 4 anchovy fillets, packed in

olive oil
2 cloves garlic, sliced
Pinch red pepper flakes
¼ cup freshly grated, lowfat Parmesan
Sea salt and freshly ground pepper, to taste

1. Heat the olive oil in a deep skillet on medium heat. 2. In the meantime, prepare the pasta al dente, according to the package directions. 3. Fry the broccoli, anchovies, and garlic in the oil until the broccoli is almost tender and the garlic is slightly browned, about 5 minutes or so. 4. Rinse and drain the pasta, and add it to the broccoli mixture. Stir to coat the pasta with the garlic oil. Transfer to a serving dish, toss with red pepper flakes and Parmesan, and season.

Per Serving:
calories: 568 | fat: 17g | protein: 21g | carbs: 89g | fiber: 11g | sodium: 203mg

Spaghetti with Fresh Mint Pesto and Ricotta Salata

Prep time: 5 minutes | Cook time: 15 minutes | Serves 4

1 pound (454 g) spaghetti
¼ cup slivered almonds
2 cups packed fresh mint leaves, plus more for garnish
3 medium garlic cloves
1 tablespoon lemon juice and ½ teaspoon lemon zest from 1

lemon
⅓ cup olive oil
¼ teaspoon freshly ground black pepper
½ cup freshly grated ricotta salata, plus more for garnish

1. Set a large pot of salted water over high heat to boil for the pasta. 2. In a food processor, combine the almonds, mint leaves, garlic, lemon juice and zest, olive oil, and pepper and pulse to a smooth paste. Add the cheese and pulse to combine. 3. When the water is boiling, add the pasta and cook according to the package instructions. Drain the pasta and return it to the pot. Add the pesto to the pasta and toss until the pasta is well coated. Serve hot, garnished with additional mint leaves and cheese, if desired.

Per Serving:
calories: 619 | fat: 31g | protein: 21g | carbs: 70g | fiber: 4g | sodium: 113mg

Meaty Baked Penne

Prep time: 10 minutes | Cook time: 40 minutes | Serves 8

1 pound (454 g) penne pasta
1 pound (454 g) ground beef
1 teaspoon salt
1 (25 ounces / 709 g) jar marinara sauce

1 (1 pounds / 454 g) bag baby spinach, washed
3 cups shredded mozzarella cheese, divided

1. Bring a large pot of salted water to a boil, add the penne, and cook for 7 minutes. Reserve 2 cups of the pasta water and drain the pasta. 2. Preheat the oven to 350°F(180°C). 3. In a large saucepan over medium heat, cook the ground beef and salt. Brown the ground beef for about 5 minutes. 4. Stir in marinara sauce, and 2 cups of pasta water. Let simmer for 5 minutes. 5. Add a handful of spinach at a time into the sauce, and cook for another 3 minutes. 6. To assemble, in a 9-by-13-inch baking dish, add the pasta and pour the pasta sauce over it. Stir in 1½ cups of the mozzarella cheese. Cover the dish with foil and bake for 20 minutes. 7. After 20 minutes, remove the foil, top with the rest of the mozzarella, and bake for another 10 minutes. Serve warm.

Per Serving:
calories: 454 | fat: 13g | protein: 31g | carbs: 55g | fiber: 9g | sodium: 408mg

Chilled Pearl Couscous Salad

Prep time: 15 minutes | Cook time: 10 minutes | Serves 6

3 tablespoons olive oil, divided	¼ cup slivered almonds
1 cup pearl couscous	¼ cup chopped fresh mint leaves
1 cup water	
1 cup orange juice	2 tablespoons lemon juice
1 small cucumber, seeded and diced	1 teaspoon grated lemon zest
	¼ cup crumbled feta cheese
1 small yellow bell pepper, seeded and diced	¼ teaspoon fine sea salt
	1 teaspoon smoked paprika
2 small Roma tomatoes, seeded and diced	1 teaspoon garlic powder

1. Press the Sauté button and heat 1 tablespoon oil. Add couscous and cook for 2–4 minutes until couscous is slightly browned. Add water and orange juice. Press the Cancel button. 2. Close lid, set steam release to Sealing, press the Manual button, and set time to 5 minutes. When the timer beeps, let pressure release naturally for 5 minutes. Quick-release any remaining pressure until the float valve drops and open lid. Drain any liquid and set aside to cool for 20 minutes. 3. Combine remaining 2 tablespoons oil, cucumber, bell pepper, tomatoes, almonds, mint, lemon juice, lemon zest, cheese, salt, paprika, and garlic powder in a medium bowl. Add couscous and toss ingredients together. Cover and refrigerate overnight before serving.

Per Serving:

calories: 177 | fat: 11g | protein: 5g | carbs: 12g | fiber: 1g | sodium: 319mg

Penne with Roasted Vegetables

Prep time: 20 minutes | Cook time: 25 to 30 minutes | Serves 6

1 large butternut squash, peeled and diced	1 teaspoon paprika
	½ teaspoon garlic powder
1 large zucchini, diced	1 pound (454 g) whole-grain penne
1 large yellow onion, chopped	
2 tablespoons extra-virgin olive oil	½ cup dry white wine or chicken stock
½ teaspoon salt	2 tablespoons grated Parmesan cheese
½ teaspoon freshly ground black pepper	

1. Preheat the oven to 400°F(205°C). Line a baking sheet with aluminum foil. 2. In a large bowl, toss the vegetables with the olive oil, then spread them out on the baking sheet. Sprinkle the vegetables with the salt, pepper, paprika, and garlic powder and bake just until fork-tender, 25 to 30 minutes. 3. Meanwhile, bring a large stockpot of water to a boil over high heat and cook the penne according to the package instructions until al dente (still slightly firm). Drain but do not rinse. 4. Place ½ cup of the roasted vegetables and the wine or stock in a blender or food processor and blend until smooth. 5. Place the purée in a large skillet and heat over medium-high heat. Add the pasta and cook, stirring, just until heated through. 6. Serve the pasta and sauce topped with the roasted vegetables. Sprinkle with Parmesan cheese.

Per Serving:

calories: 456 | fat: 7g | protein: 9g | carbs: 92g | fiber: 14g | sodium: 241mg

Rotini with Spinach, Cherry Tomatoes, and Feta

Prep time: 5 minutes | Cook time: 30 minutes | Serves 2

6 ounces (170 g) uncooked rotini pasta (penne pasta will also work)	9 ounces (255 g) baby leaf spinach, washed and chopped
	1½ ounces (43 g) crumbled feta, divided
1 garlic clove, minced	
3 tablespoons extra virgin olive oil, divided	Kosher salt, to taste
	Freshly ground black pepper, to taste
1½ cups cherry tomatoes, halved and divided	

1. Cook the pasta according to the package instructions, reserving ½ cup of the cooking water. Drain and set aside. 2. While the pasta is cooking, combine the garlic with 2 tablespoons of the olive oil in a small bowl. Set aside. 3. Add the remaining tablespoon of olive oil to a medium pan placed over medium heat and then add 1 cup of the tomatoes. Cook for 2–3 minutes, then use a fork to mash lightly. 4. Add the spinach to the pan and continue cooking, stirring occasionally, until the spinach is wilted and the liquid is absorbed, about 4–5 minutes. 5. Transfer the cooked pasta to the pan with the spinach and tomatoes. Add 3 tablespoons of the pasta water, the garlic and olive oil mixture, and 1 ounce (28 g) of the crumbled feta. Increase the heat to high and cook for 1 minute. 6. Top with the remaining cherry tomatoes and feta, and season to taste with kosher salt and black pepper. Store covered in the refrigerator for up to 2 days.

Per Serving:

calories: 602 | fat: 27g | protein: 19g | carbs: 74g | fiber: 7g | sodium: 307mg

Chapter 13 Staples, Sauces, Dips, and Dressings

Chermoula

Prep time: 10 minutes | Cook time: 0 minutes | Makes about 1½ cups

2¼ cups fresh cilantro leaves
8 garlic cloves, minced
1½ teaspoons ground cumin
1½ teaspoons paprika
½ teaspoon cayenne pepper
½ teaspoon table salt
6 tablespoons lemon juice (2 lemons)
¾ cup extra-virgin olive oil

1. Pulse cilantro, garlic, cumin, paprika, cayenne, and salt in food processor until cilantro is coarsely chopped, about 10 pulses. Add lemon juice and pulse briefly to combine. Transfer mixture to medium bowl and slowly whisk in oil until incorporated and mixture is emulsified. Cover and let sit at room temperature for at least 30 minutes to allow flavors to meld. (Sauce can be refrigerated for up to 2 days; bring to room temperature before serving.)

Per Serving:

¼ cup: calories: 253 | fat: 27g | protein: 1g | carbs: 3g | fiber: 1g | sodium: 199mg

Roasted Harissa

Prep time: 5 minutes | Cook time: 15 minutes | Makes ¾ cup

1 red bell pepper
2 small fresh red chiles, or more to taste
4 garlic cloves, unpeeled
½ teaspoon ground coriander
½ teaspoon ground cumin
½ teaspoon ground caraway
1 tablespoon fresh lemon juice
½ teaspoon salt

1. Preheat the broiler to high. 2. Put the bell pepper, chiles, and garlic on a baking sheet and broil for 6 to 8 minutes. Turn the vegetables over and broil for 5 to 6 minutes more, until the pepper and chiles are softened and blackened. Remove from the broiler and set aside until cool enough to handle. Remove and discard the stems, skin, and seeds from the pepper and chiles. Remove and discard the papery skin from the garlic. 3. Put the flesh of the pepper and chiles with the garlic cloves in a blender or food processor. Add the coriander, cumin, caraway, lemon juice, and salt and blend until smooth. 4. This may be stored refrigerated for up to 3 days. Store in an airtight container, and cover the sauce with a ¼-inch layer of oil.

Per Serving:

calories: 28 | fat: 0g | protein: 1g | carbs: 6g | fiber: 1g | sodium: 393mg

Crunchy Yogurt Dip

Prep time: 5 minutes | Cook time: 0 minutes | Serves 2 to 3

1 cup plain, unsweetened, full-fat Greek yogurt
½ cup cucumber, peeled, seeded, and diced
1 tablespoon freshly squeezed lemon juice
1 tablespoon chopped fresh mint
1 small garlic clove, minced
Salt
Freshly ground black pepper

1. In a food processor, combine the yogurt, cucumber, lemon juice, mint, and garlic. Pulse several times to combine, leaving noticeable cucumber chunks. 2. Taste and season with salt and pepper.

Per Serving:

calories: 128 | fat: 6g | protein: 11g | carbs: 7g | fiber: 0g | sodium: 47mg

Green Olive Tapenade with Harissa

Prep time: 5 minutes | Cook time: 0 minutes | Makes about 1½ cups

1 cup pitted, cured green olives
1 clove garlic, minced
1 tablespoon harissa
1 tablespoon lemon juice
1 tablespoon chopped fresh parsley
¼ cup olive oil, or more to taste

1. Finely chop the olives (or pulse them in a food processor until they resemble a chunky paste). 2. Add the garlic, harissa, lemon juice, parsley, and olive oil and stir or pulse to combine well.

Per Serving:

¼ cup: calories: 215 | fat: 23g | protein: 1g | carbs: 5g | fiber: 2g | sodium: 453mg

Garlic-Rosemary Infused Olive Oil

Prep time: 5 minutes | Cook time: 45 minutes |
Makes 1 cup

1 cup extra-virgin olive oil   4 (4- to 5-inch) sprigs rosemary
4 large garlic cloves, smashed

1. In a medium skillet, heat the olive oil, garlic, and rosemary sprigs over low heat. Cook until fragrant and garlic is very tender, 30 to 45 minutes, stirring occasionally. Don't let the oil get too hot or the garlic will burn and become bitter. 2. Remove from the heat and allow to cool slightly. Remove the garlic and rosemary with a slotted spoon and pour the oil into a glass container. Allow to cool completely before covering. Store covered at room temperature for up to 3 months.

Per Serving:
⅛ cup: calories: 241 | fat: 27g | protein: 0g | carbs: 1g | fiber: 0g | sodium: 1mg

Parsley-Mint Sauce

Prep time: 5 minutes | Cook time: 0 minutes | Serves 6

½ cup fresh flat-leaf parsley   2 tablespoons pomegranate
1 cup fresh mint leaves   molasses
2 garlic cloves, minced   ¼ cup olive oil
2 scallions (green onions),   1 tablespoon fresh lemon juice
chopped

1. Combine all the ingredients in a blender and blend until smooth. Transfer to an airtight container and refrigerate until ready to use. Can be refrigerated for 1 day.

Per Serving:
calories: 90 | fat: 9g | protein: 1g | carbs: 2g | fiber: 0g | sodium: 5mg

Marinated Artichokes

Prep time: 10 minutes | Cook time: 0 minutes |
Makes 2 cups

2 (13¾ ounces / 390 g) cans   leaves
artichoke hearts, drained and   2 teaspoons chopped fresh
quartered   oregano or 1 teaspoon dried
¾ cup extra-virgin olive oil   oregano
4 small garlic cloves, crushed 1 teaspoon red pepper flakes
with the back of a knife   (optional)
1 tablespoon fresh rosemary   1 teaspoon salt

1. In a medium bowl, combine the artichoke hearts, olive oil, garlic, rosemary, oregano, red pepper flakes (if using), and salt. Toss to combine well. 2. Store in an airtight glass container in the refrigerator and marinate for at least 24 hours before using. Store in the refrigerator for up to 2 weeks.

Per Serving:
¼ cup: calories: 228 | fat: 20g | protein: 3g | carbs: 11g | fiber: 5g | sodium: 381mg

Melitzanosalata (Greek Eggplant Dip)

Prep time: 10 minutes | Cook time: 3 minutes |
Serves 8

1 cup water   1 tablespoon red wine vinegar
1 large eggplant, peeled and   ½ cup extra-virgin olive oil
chopped   2 tablespoons minced fresh
1 clove garlic, peeled   parsley
½ teaspoon salt

1. Add water to the Instant Pot®, add the rack to the pot, and place the steamer basket on the rack. 2. Place eggplant in steamer basket. Close lid, set steam release to Sealing, press the Manual button, and set time to 3 minutes. When the timer beeps, quick-release the pressure until the float valve drops. Press the Cancel button and open lid. 3. Transfer eggplant to a food processor and add garlic, salt, and vinegar. Pulse until smooth, about 20 pulses. 4. Slowly add oil to the eggplant mixture while the food processor runs continuously until oil is completely incorporated. Stir in parsley. Serve at room temperature.

Per Serving:
calories: 134 | fat: 14g | protein: 1g | carbs: 3g | fiber: 2g | sodium: 149mg

Artichoke Dip

Prep time: 15 minutes | Cook time: 0 minutes |
Serves 3

1 (14 ounces / 397 g) can   ½ tablespoon chopped basil
artichoke hearts, drained   ½ teaspoon sea salt
1 pound (454 g) goat cheese   ½ teaspoon freshly ground
2 tablespoons extra-virgin olive black pepper
oil   Dash of cayenne pepper
2 teaspoons lemon juice   (optional)
1 garlic clove, minced   ½ cup freshly grated Pecorino
1 tablespoon chopped parsley   Romano
1 tablespoon chopped chives

1. In a food processor, combine all the ingredients, except the Pecorino Romano, and process until well incorporated and creamy. 2. Top with the freshly grated Pecorino Romano. Store in an airtight container in the refrigerator for up to 3 days.

Per Serving:
calories: 588 | fat: 44g | protein: 36g | carbs: 15g | fiber: 7g | sodium: 513mg

Sweet Red Wine Vinaigrette

Prep time: 5 minutes | Cook time: 0 minutes | Serves 2

¼ cup plus 2 tablespoons extra-virgin olive oil

2 tablespoons red wine vinegar

1 tablespoon apple cider vinegar

2 teaspoons honey

2 teaspoons Dijon mustard

½ teaspoon minced garlic

⅛ teaspoon kosher salt

⅛ teaspoon freshly ground black pepper

1. In a jar, combine the olive oil, vinegars, honey, mustard, garlic, salt, and pepper and shake well.

Per Serving:

calories: 386 | fat: 41g | protein: 0g | carbs: 6g | fiber: 0g | sodium: 198mg

Herbed Oil

Prep time: 5 minutes | Cook time: 0 minutes | Serves 2

½ cup extra-virgin olive oil

1 teaspoon dried basil

1 teaspoon dried parsley

1 teaspoon fresh rosemary

leaves

2 teaspoons dried oregano

⅛ teaspoon salt

1. Pour the oil into a small bowl and stir in the basil, parsley, rosemary, oregano, and salt while whisking the oil with a fork.

Per Serving:

calories: 486 | fat: 54g | protein: 1g | carbs: 2g | fiber: 1g | sodium: 78mg

Olive Mint Vinaigrette

Prep time: 5 minutes | Cook time: 0 minutes | Makes ½ cup

¼ cup white wine vinegar

¼ teaspoon honey

¼ teaspoon kosher salt

¼ teaspoon freshly ground black pepper

¼ cup extra-virgin olive oil

¼ cup olives, pitted and minced

2 tablespoons fresh mint, minced

1. In a bowl, whisk together the vinegar, honey, salt, and black pepper. Add the olive oil and whisk well. Add the olives and mint, and mix well. Store any leftovers in the refrigerator in an airtight container for up to 5 days.

Per Serving:

2 tablespoons: calories: 135 | fat: 15g | protein: 0g | carbs: 1g | fiber: 0g | sodium: 135mg

Peanut Sauce

Prep time: 5 minutes | Cook time: 0 minutes | Serves 4

⅓ cup peanut butter

¼ cup hot water

2 tablespoons soy sauce

2 tablespoons rice vinegar

Juice of 1 lime

1 teaspoon minced fresh ginger

1 teaspoon minced garlic

1 teaspoon black pepper

1. In a blender container, combine the peanut butter, hot water, soy sauce, vinegar, lime juice, ginger, garlic, and pepper. Blend until smooth. 2. Use immediately or store in an airtight container in the refrigerator for a week or more.

Per Serving:

calories: 408 | fat: 33g | protein: 16g | carbs: 18g | fiber: 5g | sodium: 2525mg

Apple Cider Dressing

Prep time: 5 minutes | Cook time: 0 minutes | Serves 2

2 tablespoons apple cider vinegar

⅓ lemon, juiced

⅓ lemon, zested

Salt and freshly ground black pepper, to taste

1. In a jar, combine the vinegar, lemon juice, and zest. Season with salt and pepper, cover, and shake well.

Per Serving:

calories: 7 | fat: 0g | protein: 0g | carbs: 1g | fiber: 0g | sodium: 1mg

Maltese Sun-Dried Tomato and Mushroom Dressing

Prep time: 10 minutes | Cook time: 5 minutes | Serves 4

⅓ cup olive oil (use a combination of olive oil and sun-dried tomato oil, if they were packed in oil)

8 ounces (227 g) mushrooms, sliced

3 tablespoons red wine vinegar

Freshly ground black pepper, to taste

½ cup sun-dried tomatoes, drained (if they are packed in oil, reserve the oil) and chopped

1. In a medium skillet, heat 2 tablespoons of the olive oil (or mixed olive oil and sun-dried tomato packing oil) over high heat. Add the mushrooms and cook, stirring, until they have released their liquid. 2. Add vinegar and season with pepper. Remove from the heat and add the remaining oil and the sun-dried tomatoes.

Per Serving:

1 cup: calories: 190 | fat: 18g | protein: 3g | carbs: 6g | fiber: 2g | sodium: 21mg

Italian Dressing

Prep time: 5 minutes | Cook time: 0 minutes | Serves 12

¼ cup red wine vinegar
½ cup extra-virgin olive oil
¼ teaspoon salt
¼ teaspoon freshly ground black pepper

1 teaspoon dried Italian seasoning
1 teaspoon Dijon mustard
1 garlic clove, minced

1. In a small jar, combine the vinegar, olive oil, salt, pepper, Italian seasoning, mustard, and garlic. Close with a tight-fitting lid and shake vigorously for 1 minute. 2. Refrigerate for up to 1 week.

Per Serving:

calories: 82 | fat: 9g | protein: 0g | carbs: 0g | fiber: 0g | sodium: 71mg

Red Pepper and Tomato Chutney

Prep time: 10 minutes | Cook time: 4 hours | Makes 2 to 3 cups

3 tablespoons rapeseed oil
1 teaspoon cumin seeds
4 garlic cloves, roughly chopped
1 large red onion, roughly chopped
2 red bell peppers, seeded and

roughly chopped
1 pound (454 g) fresh tomatoes
1 tablespoon malt vinegar
1 teaspoon salt
1 fresh green chile
¼ cup hot water

1. Heat the slow cooker to high and add the oil. 2. Add the cumin seeds and cook until they are fragrant. Then stir in the garlic and cook 1 to 2 minutes. 3. Add the onion, peppers, tomatoes, vinegar, salt, chile, and water. 4. Cook on low for 4 hours, until the peppers are soft and the tomatoes have burst. 5. Using an immersion or regular blender, purée, and then pour the chutney through a colander. 6. Put the chutney into a sterilized glass jar and leave to cool. When cooled, seal the jar. The chutney will keep for 2 weeks in the refrigerator.

Per Serving:

calories: 99 | fat: 7g | protein: 2g | carbs: 8g | fiber: 2g | sodium: 423mg

White Bean Hummus

Prep time: 10 minutes | Cook time: 30 minutes | Serves 12

⅔ cup dried white beans, rinsed and drained
3 cloves garlic, peeled and crushed

¼ cup olive oil
1 tablespoon lemon juice
½ teaspoon salt

1. Place beans and garlic in the Instant Pot® and stir well. Add enough cold water to cover ingredients. Close lid, set steam release to Sealing, press the Manual button, and set time to 30 minutes. 2. When the timer beeps, let pressure release naturally, about 20 minutes. Press the Cancel button and open lid. Use a fork to check that beans are tender. Drain off excess water and transfer beans to a food processor. 3. Add oil, lemon juice, and salt to the processor and pulse until mixture is smooth with some small chunks. Transfer to a storage container and refrigerate for at least 4 hours. Serve cold or at room temperature. Store in the refrigerator for up to one week.

Per Serving:

calories: 57 | fat: 5g | protein: 1g | carbs: 3g | fiber: 1g | sodium: 99mg

Traditional Caesar Dressing

Prep time: 10 minutes | Cook time: 5 minutes | Makes 1½ cups

2 teaspoons minced garlic
4 large egg yolks
¼ cup wine vinegar
½ teaspoon dry mustard
Dash Worcestershire sauce

1 cup extra-virgin olive oil
¼ cup freshly squeezed lemon juice
Sea salt and freshly ground black pepper, to taste

1. To a small saucepan, add the garlic, egg yolks, vinegar, mustard, and Worcestershire sauce and place over low heat. 2. Whisking constantly, cook the mixture until it thickens and is a little bubbly, about 5 minutes. 3. Remove from saucepan from the heat and let it stand for about 10 minutes to cool. 4. Transfer the egg mixture to a large stainless steel bowl. Whisking constantly, add the olive oil in a thin stream. 5. Whisk in the lemon juice and season the dressing with salt and pepper. 6. Transfer the dressing to an airtight container and keep in the refrigerator for up to 3 days.

Per Serving:

calories: 202 | fat: 21g | protein: 2g | carbs: 2g | fiber: 0g | sodium: 14mg

Appendix 1: Measurement Conversion Chart

MEASUREMENT CONVERSION CHART

VOLUME EQUIVALENTS(DRY)

US STANDARD	METRIC (APPROXIMATE)
1/8 teaspoon	0.5 mL
1/4 teaspoon	1 mL
1/2 teaspoon	2 mL
3/4 teaspoon	4 mL
1 teaspoon	5 mL
1 tablespoon	15 mL
1/4 cup	59 mL
1/2 cup	118 mL
3/4 cup	177 mL
1 cup	235 mL
2 cups	475 mL
3 cups	700 mL
4 cups	1 L

VOLUME EQUIVALENTS(LIQUID)

US STANDARD	US STANDARD (OUNCES)	METRIC (APPROXIMATE)
2 tablespoons	1 fl.oz.	30 mL
1/4 cup	2 fl.oz.	60 mL
1/2 cup	4 fl.oz.	120 mL
1 cup	8 fl.oz.	240 mL
1 1/2 cup	12 fl.oz.	355 mL
2 cups or 1 pint	16 fl.oz.	475 mL
4 cups or 1 quart	32 fl.oz.	1 L
1 gallon	128 fl.oz.	4 L

TEMPERATURES EQUIVALENTS

FAHRENHEIT(F)	CELSIUS(C) (APPROXIMATE)
225 °F	107 °C
250 °F	120 °C
275 °F	135 °C
300 °F	150 °C
325 °F	160 °C
350 °F	180 °C
375 °F	190 °C
400 °F	205 °C
425 °F	220 °C
450 °F	235 °C
475 °F	245 °C
500 °F	260 °C

WEIGHT EQUIVALENTS

US STANDARD	METRIC (APPROXIMATE)
1 ounce	28 g
2 ounces	57 g
5 ounces	142 g
10 ounces	284 g
15 ounces	425 g
16 ounces (1 pound)	455 g
1.5 pounds	680 g
2 pounds	907 g

Appendix 2: The Dirty Dozen and Clean Fifteen

The Dirty Dozen and Clean Fifteen

The Environmental Working Group (EWG) is a nonprofit, nonpartisan organization dedicated to protecting human health and the environment Its mission is to empower people to live healthier lives in a healthier environment. This organization publishes an annual list of the twelve kinds of produce, in sequence, that have the highest amount of pesticide residue-the Dirty Dozen-as well as a list of the fifteen kinds ofproduce that have the least amount of pesticide residue-the Clean Fifteen.

THE DIRTY DOZEN

- The 2016 Dirty Dozen includes the following produce. These are considered among the year's most important produce to buy organic:

Strawberries	Spinach
Apples	Tomatoes
Nectarines	Bell peppers
Peaches	Cherry tomatoes
Celery	Cucumbers
Grapes	Kale/collard greens
Cherries	Hot peppers

- *The Dirty Dozen list contains two additional itemskale/collard greens and hot peppers-because they tend to contain trace levels of highly hazardous pesticides.*

THE CLEAN FIFTEEN

- The least critical to buy organically are the Clean Fifteen list. The following are on the 2016 list:

Avocados	Papayas
Corn	Kiw
Pineapples	Eggplant
Cabbage	Honeydew
Sweet peas	Grapefruit
Onions	Cantaloupe
Asparagus	Cauliflower
Mangos	

- *Some of the sweet corn sold in the United States are made from genetically engineered (GE) seedstock. Buy organic varieties of these crops to avoid GE produce.*

Made in the USA
Las Vegas, NV
12 August 2023

75976533R00063